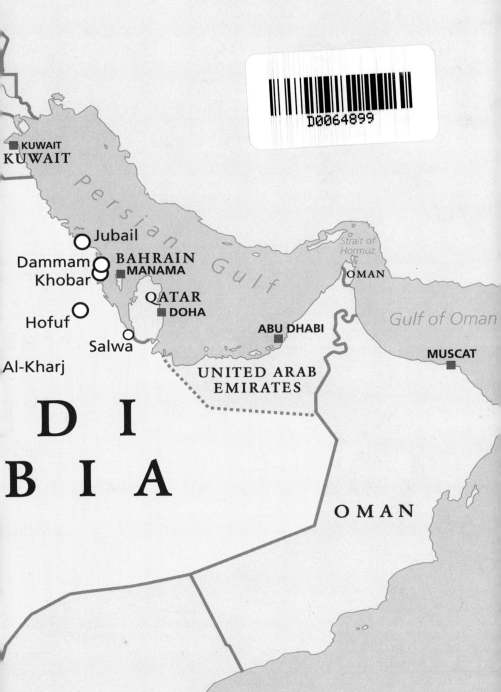

IRAN

KUWAIT
KUWAIT

Persian Gulf

Jubail

Dammam
Khobar

BAHRAIN
MANAMA

QATAR
DOHA

Hofuf

Salwa

Al-Kharj

DI
BIA

UNITED ARAB
EMIRATES

Strait of
Hormuz

OMAN

Gulf of Oman

ABU DHABI

MUSCAT

OMAN

EN

SEA

PRAISE FOR
BEHIND THE KINGDOM'S VEIL

"To be at the cusp of societal change in the midst of conflict and tension is a rare but dangerous privilege. To watch from a ringside seat as an entire society somersaults from extremism to relative moderation is not often easy or permissible.

"Susanne Koelbl, a well-known foreign correspondent for *DER SPIEGEL*, has been at such cusps of change before—in Afghanistan, Iran, and Africa—but never before has she tackled as difficult a subject of change as she faces in Saudi Arabia, a society moving from obscurantist tribalism to modernity.

"Koelbl has written a marvelous book on the recent developments in Saudi Arabia, a book full of analysis, anecdotes, and tension generated by geopolitical changes in the Arabian Gulf. Because Koelbl lived in Saudi Arabia for some time, she has unique access to Saudi officials, princes, shopkeepers, and ordinary women and men struggling with jobs, school, and bringing up children.

"This is not a book of anecdotes and parachute journalism. It is not the result of a few quick visits. Instead, it is built of the insights of someone who has lived in the country and has gotten to know the people. A piercingly powerful book, *Behind the Kingdom's Veil* gives us insight not just into Saudi Arabia, but into how their ongoing experiment could help other Muslim societies change and move forward toward modernity."

—**Ahmed Rashid**, bestselling author of *Taliban* and
Descent into Chaos

"In *Behind the Kingdom's Veil: Inside the New Saudi Arabia under Crown Prince Mohammed bin Salman*, Susanne Koelbl offers very revealing insights into the complex, opaque, and fast-changing society that is Saudi Arabia today. She does this through personal encounters with a wide array of Saudis from different walks of life. This book is an excellent introduction to the kingdom."

> —**Dr. Bernard Haykel**, professor of Near Eastern Studies at Princeton University and director of the Institute for the Transregional Study of the Contemporary Middle East

"A fascinating account of the significant changes underway in Saudi Arabia, based on years of excellent reporting on the ground in the kingdom. The complicated role of the ruthless crown prince who is driving the often-drastic changes is exposed. A brilliant contribution to our understanding of the transformation happening in Saudi Arabia, especially among women."

> —**Bruce Riedel,** former CIA official, Middle East advisor to four US presidents, director of the Intelligence Project at the Brookings Institution and author of *Kings and Presidents: Saudi Arabia and the United States since FDR*

"Koelbl offers a fascinating array of acutely well-observed glimpses into what's changing inside the kingdom—and what isn't. Behind the engaging style and lively scenes lie serious questions that challenge assumptions about where the kingdom is heading. If you want to peek into the kingdom, reading this captivating selection of firsthand snapshots feels like watching a movie, only more informative."

> —**Dr. Elisabeth Kendall**, senior research fellow in Arabic & Islamic Studies, Pembroke College, University of Oxford

"For nearly a century, Saudi Arabia has played a critical role in ensuring global economic stability and promoting regional security. Yet it remains an enigma to the vast majority of Westerners. In *Behind the Kingdom's Veil*, Susanne Koelbl provides an invaluable street-level perspective on the kingdom's rulers and its people, the challenges they face today economically, politically, and socially, and the reforms they need to take tomorrow to prepare their country for the demands of the twenty-first century. There can be no doubt, in reading Koelbl's book, that the success or failure of that transition will affect the security and prosperity of all of us."

—**Gerald Feierstein**, ambassador to Yemen under the Obama administration

"Koelbl's book is an eye-opener. If you want to understand why Saudi Arabia is a key player in all of the conflicts of the region it is essential to understand the inner workings of this country. *Behind the Kingdom's Veil* offers fascinating and often personal insights into everyday life of Saudi society. The kingdom's population has grown, oil prices have sharply declined, money is tight. The young ruler, Crown Prince Mohammad bin Salman races from religious tradition into modernity with the help of authoritarian reforms. He eliminated his opponents among the large royal family, deprived the religious police of its power and appeals to the young generation by opening society to a modern way of life. What is it like to live there? As a woman, as a devout Arab, as guest worker or rebel? Koelbl explains it all and takes the reader along on this most unusual journey through this unprecedented part of the kingdom's history."

—**Tim Guldiman**, advisor to the Geneva-based Conflict Mediation Foundation HD, former Swiss ambassador to Iran, former member of the Swiss Parliament

BEHIND THE KINGDOM'S VEIL

BEHIND THE KINGDOM'S VEIL

INSIDE THE NEW SAUDI ARABIA UNDER CROWN PRINCE MOHAMMED BIN SALMAN

Susanne Koelbl

Coral Gables

Cover Design: Liz Hong
Bottom photo on cover credit: Susanne Koelbl
Layout & Design: Jermaine Lau

Photo credits (unless otherwise noted): by the author, Susanne Koelbl

For permission requests, please contact the publisher at:
Mango Publishing Group
2850 S Douglas Road, 2nd Floor
Coral Gables, FL 33134 USA
info@mango.bz

For special orders, quantity sales, course adoptions and corporate sales,
please email the publisher at sales@mango.bz. For trade and wholesale
sales, please contact Ingram Publisher Services at customer.service@
ingramcontent.com or +1.800.509.4887.

Behind the Kingdom's Veil: Inside the New Saudi Arabia under Crown
Prince Mohammed Bin Salman

Translated from German by Maurice Frank
Original title: Zwölf Wochen in Riad.
Saudi-Arabien zwischen Diktatur und Aufbruch by Susanne Koelbl

Library of Congress Cataloging-in-Publication number: 2020933476

ISBN: (p) 978-1-64250-344-9 (e) 978-1-64250-345-6

BISAC category code: HIS026010, HISTORY / Middle East /
Arabian Peninsula

Printed in the United States of America

To Eman, Fahd, Nora, Tarek, and Abdullah

TABLE OF CONTENTS

PROLOGUE

As a foreign correspondent, I have written about the wars of our time for more than fifteen years, from the Balkans to Afghanistan, Iraq, Libya, and Syria.

In 2011 I started to travel to the kingdom and report about Saudi Arabia. In 2018 I had the opportunity to live in Riyadh as a foreign correspondent for the German magazine *DER SPIEGEL*.

It's a journalist's dream to pierce this closed world of sheikhs, religious zealots, and hidden powers. I wanted to get closer to the people and experience the dizzying social transformation the kingdom was going through. Living in a small apartment as a Western woman among Saudis, I enjoyed unprecedented access. Behind the kingdom's veil I encountered many intelligent minds with unique perspectives on both their own society and the West.

The country is in a race against time to transform itself. The kingdom is in the midst of its most severe crisis since its founding eighty-eight years ago. Oil reserves and their global importance are both waning fast, and Saudi Arabia's neighbors (Iraq, Syria, Libya, and Yemen) are sinking into chaos and war.

Despite the new openness, Crown Prince Mohammed bin Salman—the driving force behind the recent reforms—is also creating an atmosphere of fear. Born in 1985, the young heir has zero tolerance for dissenters and is often ruthless about suppressing opposition. Saudis who voice criticism can expect severe punishment, possibly execution.

While I lived in Saudi Arabia I learned about Salafi society from my landlord, a man with three wives who believed the downfall of humanity to be imminent. He tried everything to win over my soul for Islam and save me from Satan's grip.

I had breakfast with royal highnesses and asked Osama bin Laden's explosives expert how he now looks back on his time as a terrorist. Young Saudi women took me to weddings and on trips to the desert, and shared with me how they cope with the upheaval and how they make the most of these bewildering changes.

I met enigmatic political figures like the long-time Saudi ambassador to Washington and former intelligence chief Prince Bandar bin Sultan, who was critically involved in orchestrating virtually every international crisis of the past thirty years (except perhaps for those involving North Korea). I saw my friends thrown into prison or murdered by the monarchy's secret service, such as the blogger and human rights activist Eman al-Nafjan, or the journalist Jamal Khashoggi, whom I had known for a long time.

Is Mohammed bin Salman an impressive reformer or a power-crazed dictator? Both? The young royal could easily rule for fifty years. Will he learn on the job?

I was lucky to witness these historic changes up close. Every one of my encounters in the kingdom was a small adventure. Together, I hope they can help readers to understand why events in Saudi Arabia have so great an impact on our lives, the economy, and political stability around the world.

The transcription of Arabic names and terminology follows a simple system. In general the phonetic spelling that comes closest to the original pronunciation has been chosen, except in the case of names of persons and locations as well as specific terms already possessing an internationally agreed upon spelling. Inconsistencies cannot be completely avoided.

To protect their identity and privacy, I have changed the names of all private individuals I encountered and wrote about. All public figures are written about under their official names as they appear as part of their official capacity or after they have left those positions.

**This is a time of rapid change in Saudi Arabia. Great efforts have been made to ensure facts and information are up to date at the time of printing.*

FOREWORD

Forty-two years ago, my first visit to Saudi Arabia—as a young diplomatic correspondent for the Wall Street Journal—was remarkably normal. Yes, I was chauffeured, since women weren't permitted to drive. But I wore knee-length skirts and long-sleeve blouses. I didn't own an abaya. I attended dinner parties where Saudi men and women mixed and sipped alcohol. I interviewed a working female pediatrician.

In only a few short years, that normalcy was gone. The Al Saud rulers, determined not to be deposed by religious hardliners as was the shah of Iran, gave their religious scholars carte blanche over every aspect of Saudi social life. The changes were swift and sweeping. No music. No movies. No gender mixing. Women must wear a veil, obey a male guardian, and even shun physical exercise lest they endanger their reproductive abilities. For every one of the scores of trips I made over the past four decades I was given an abaya, a scarf, and a *niqab* by a Saudi official who always declined to let me ride in the front seat of his car unless I was totally obscured from view. Since then, I've worn an abaya to blend in better with the Saudis I meet.

Today the kingdom is in the process of throwing off all these strictures. The new king and crown prince no longer fear religious zealots. They are focused on a new challenge to Al Saud rule: how the royal family can retain power without the elixir of oil revenue to buy their citizens' loyalty (or at least acquiescence). That challenge, already monumental, has been compounded exponentially by COVID-19's crippling impact on global economic growth and by Saudi Arabia's decision to declare an oil price war. The combined impact will be felt for years to come.

The Saudi social contract has long entailed loyalty *to* the ruler in exchange for prosperity *from* the ruler: cradle-to-grave government largesse—free education, free health care, guaranteed jobs—all financed by oil revenue. This contract no longer appears sustainable. The Saudi population continues to grow rapidly, while growth in global energy demand declines due both to greater energy efficiency worldwide and growing efforts to reduce fossil fuel consumption to stem climate change.

To confront this challenge, King Salman (eighty-four) and his son, Crown Prince Mohammed bin Salman (thirty-four), launched "Vision 2030," a futuristic scheme that seeks to wrench their backward kingdom into the high-tech forefront of the twenty-first century. It is no exaggeration to say that their vision, unveiled in 2016, calls for a societal revolution. Out with conservative, anti-modern *Wahhabi* dogma and in with moderation. Out with dependence on government and in with self-reliance. Out with the religious police and in with music, movies, dancing, gender mixing, and women drivers. Out with women's needing a guardian's permission to leave the kingdom and in with women working unveiled alongside unrelated Saudi men. Most surprisingly, perhaps, this long closed kingdom is offering quick e-visas to foreign tourists, whom the government is spending lavishly to lure, in hopes of creating a tourism industry that soon could provide jobs for thousands of young Saudis.

As Saudis—and the world—watch this high-wire transformation act, the question on everyone's minds is: can the Saudis transition successfully from tradition to modernity, or will the changes wind up sparking a backlash like the one that swallowed the shah of Iran's rapid modernization efforts?

Susanne Koelbl, a correspondent for *DER SPIEGEL*, has a ringside seat for this unfolding drama. In this book, she takes readers along as she meets with princes, religious figures, and ordinary Saudi citizens coping daily with the clash between tradition and the changes being pushed by the young crown prince. The successful transformation of Saudi Arabia depends on Saudis themselves. Their active participation, not just their acquiescence, will be needed to transform the economy. Through the close-up look at Saudi people she provides, Koelbl's book will help readers gauge the depth and breadth of the challenge facing the kingdom's attempt to reform.

Her entree to Saudi Arabia was encouraged and assisted by a former Saudi ambassador to Berlin, Osama Shobokshi, who told her, "Just tell the truth."

That's essential advice for any journalist, and I think Ambassador Shobokshi would be proud of Susanne Koelbl's book.

She is exactly what a journalist should be: curious, a careful listener, a perceptive observer, and an eager learner. She clearly loved her time among the Saudi people, and is eager to help foreigners understand the diversity and complexity of this desert kingdom. Her enthusiastic engagement in the everyday aspects of Saudis' lives is infectious. As a result, readers will not only learn, but find themselves joyfully entertained with stories from this book.

She largely avoids imposing Western sensibilities on what she sees, with one exception: she shows her distaste for the jailing and abuse of three female driving activists, whom she knows well. Jailed five weeks before the historic lifting of the ban on women drivers, the three were accused of disloyalty to the government. The author, like many Saudis, believes they were jailed primarily to underscore the crown prince's unchallenged power over his people; women can drive, but the advocates who might be credited for the change can still be locked up. As the Bible notes in the book of Job, "The Lord giveth and the Lord taketh away."

Like most Western citizens, she also takes a dim view of the war in Yemen, the death of Jamal Khashoggi, and the baffling enmity between Saudi Arabia and Qatar. She covers these and other geopolitical issues affecting Saudi Arabia and troubling its relationship with the US and Western Europe.

She is at her best, however, when describing ordinary Saudi life and its changes. Readers will meet numerous Saudis delighted with the crown prince's rapid social changes. Some push for even more—bars, nightclubs, and alcohol. She meets an atheist and his mostly live-in girlfriend whose daring also masks doubt. Either atheism or cohabitation prior to marriage would have been cause for beheading both young people only a few years ago. She attends a wine party where nurses fearlessly serve their home brew to friends. She attends "divorce parties," a novel feature in a kingdom where—thanks to new freedoms to work and travel alone—divorce for women no longer essentially marks the end of their lives. She meets important princes who have managed to retain some influence even as King Salman has ruthlessly sidelined thousands of princes in favor of his own line of descendants. She visits Osama bin Laden's bomb-making expert—now the father of two children—after his time in Guantanamo Bay and a stint in Riyadh's terrorist rehabilitation center. She also visits Salman al-Ouda, a beloved religious sheikh the government imprisoned on charges of disloyalty.

Koelbl also chronicles what isn't changing. Her fundamentalist landlord in Riyadh has three wives, which he explains, "My first wife is getting old. One of them is always on her period. What do you do if you want to sleep with one?" While there is more social freedom these days, even young men still can't do as they please, since the tradition of tending to the diktats of older family members remains still alive and well. Indeed, these days Saudi households are often at war as the mother and father haggle over what government-endorsed freedoms their daughters should be permitted to take.

For some Saudis, accustomed to the religious straitjacket of recent decades, it is too late to change. This is beautifully illustrated by the case of Jamila, twenty-nine years old, who lives in Buraydah, the kingdom's most conservative city. Even though she realizes the rules she follows are the wishes of men, not Allah, she can't bring herself to uncover her face. Her father would be disappointed, her mother saddened, and her reputation in Buraydah destroyed if she did so. Meanwhile, her male cousin is confident it is only a matter of time until Saudi Arabia legalizes alcohol, elects a parliament, and (gasp) institutes a constitutional monarchy. Uttering any of those predictions on social media still could lead to prison.

It is too early to know if the crown prince's reforms will succeed. While social reform is rapid, efforts to transform the economy and create private-sector jobs are stymied. Unemployment hovers around 12 percent and is nearly double that among young Saudis. To buy time, the crown prince is distracting Saudis with social liberties and imposing a near-total muzzle on criticism. Susanne correctly observes that most Saudis aren't seeking democracy, having never experienced it. But young Saudis increasingly say they want a voice in the kingdom's future as they are being asked to accept responsibility for their lives and livelihoods.

Many in the West love to press for more and faster change. Before we presume to impose our views on a society seeking to transition from tradition to modernity at breakneck speed, we ought to pause to understand what's taking place in Saudi Arabia. Susanne Koelbl's book offers readers an engaging—and entertaining—look at Saudi Arabia's entrenched traditions and its efforts to transit to a new and very different future.

Karen Elliott House

Author of On Saudi Arabia: Its People, Past, Religion, Fault Lines— and Future, *Knopf 2012*

WELCOME TO THE SALAFISTS: HOW MY LANDLORD TRIES TO SAVE ME FROM SATAN

Well-intentioned conservative Saudis might try to convert heterodox guests to Islam.

As a woman in Saudi Arabia, it is not as if you can't go places. You can go wherever you like. You just never arrive anywhere.

I wander through the busy streets of Riyadh. Outside of the Bazi Baba Restaurant, known for its delicious food and fresh juices, the tables are packed with men. Women who want to eat or drink have to stand in front of a small window covered by a flap. They order and wait outside until their food is ready. Coffee shops have recently sprouted up on Tahlia Street, the capital's most fashionable boulevard. Here, too, you will see only men. Even the fact that women can sit outside is considered progress.

In the new Saudi Arabia, change is occurring every day, often at a dizzying pace. But a society that has cultivated a certain lifestyle for many decades—actually for centuries—certainly does not shed its traditions and beliefs overnight.

During my first few days in Riyadh, I stay at a hotel, a red building adorned by ornamental arches. In the lobby, guests lounge in blue velvet armchairs with brocade trim, where golden chandeliers hang from the ceiling. Upon my arrival, the receptionist proudly shows me the pool and fitness studio. I inquire about the opening hours: *Sorry, for men only*. Massages are also available, but again, *sorry, men only*.

I retire to my darkened room. Outside, it is scorching hot. I probably won't get used to the curtains being permanently drawn so that no one can look in. I phone Mazen, a realtor I found on the internet. My mood improves considerably when he says he can find me an apartment with windows.

Is a woman even allowed to rent property in Saudi Arabia? In theory, yes. A new law has made it possible. But in practice, it's usually still the family who decide what a woman can and cannot do. Very few families would allow a grown woman to live alone without male protection. Likewise, single men are prohibited from renting an apartment in a building with female residents. However, as a Western woman, the local customs and family rules don't apply to me.

"SIRI TAKE ME HOME": THE LOCATION OF MY APARTMENT IN AL OLAYA IN THE HEART OF RIYADH.

One of the apartments Mazen offers me meets my criteria. It's in the Olaya District and has plenty of light and a balcony with a view of the Al Faisaliyah Center, the second-tallest building in the city, as well as the highest, the thousand-foot Kingdom Center. It's like having a view of the Statue of Liberty and the Empire State Building at the same time.

My landlord, Colonel Hasan, is a former Air Force pilot. He lives with his wives and a lot of children on a large property at the end of the street. Colonel Hasan is without a doubt a shrewd businessman, a man of the world, and deeply religious.

One evening, I join him on his terrace just behind the entrance gate, where he receives his guests. A cook brings soup, lamb with rice, spinach, and coffee. Colonel Hasan recounts his training to become a fighter pilot in the United States. He shows me around the house and introduces me to one of his daughters, a nineteen-year-old studying at university to be a French and English translator.

JESUS WAS A GOOD PROPHET, SAYS MR. HASAN, BUT MOHAMMED IS IN STEP WITH THE TIMES

This family man calls women the "diamonds" of the human race who must be protected from covetous eyes. They are kept safest by remaining at home.

We discuss whether it is important that women should be allowed to drive. "Why should women drive, Susanne? Is this really necessary?" Colonel Hasan asks. "If women leave the house, society falls to pieces."

LANDLORD HASAN IN HIS OFFICE IN CENTRAL RIYADH: PASSIONATE ABOUT SAVING SOULS FROM SATAN.

With sketched drawings Colonel Hasan explains to me how the world came into existence and how God first created Adam and then made Eve from one of his ribs. The world is now barreling toward its end, he says. When houses grow to the sky, when metal can speak, and when weeks become days and days become hours, then the time has come. These prophecies from Islamic scripture have already come true, says Mr. Hasan; I could see the skyscrapers from my balcony. The metal that talks refers to mobile phones. He points to our iPhones on the table and then at his sketch, which shows people roasting in a hellfire that is glowing in sinister yellow and red. People who have strayed from the path of faith.

"Think about it, Susanne! It's only logical," says Mr. Hasan, with urgency in his voice. He would love me to convert to Islam, for my own protection. Of course, Jesus was a good prophet, he says. Mohammed is simply more relevant today. It's like with the former German chancellor, Gerhard Schröder. He was talented, but now it's Angela Merkel who has the power and can wield it.

Colonel Hasan seems to think that a decision to convert requires time. He's stubborn, but also patient. He pours me more coffee, offers me more food. Months after I left the kingdom, he still sends me videos on WhatsApp encouraging me to save my soul from Satan.

I've hit the jackpot with my new home on Ibn Ammar Street. It has two big corner windows that open up onto a small terrace, an American-style kitchenette, and a bedroom. It looks out across an expanse of palms to the glittering skyline of skyscrapers and palaces, the sprawling residential neighborhoods behind them, and the eight-lane freeways that cut through the desert at a ninety-degree angle. A mere one hundred years ago, this land was home to a few shepherds living alongside the Bedouins. Today, the heart of the kingdom has swollen into a pulsating metropolis of over seven million people. For the next three months, this third-floor apartment will be my retreat.

My patio—my refuge.

SYRIA

DAMASCUS

IRAQ

BAGHDAD

Tigris

AMMAN

Kaf

ORDAN

Arar

Euphrates

Sakakah

Tabuk

Hafar
Al-Batin

KUWAIT
KUWAIT

Ha'il

Persian

Al Wajh

Buraidah

Al Majma'ah

Jubail

Dammam

BAHRAIN
MANAMA

Khobar

Umm Lajj

QATA
DO

Medina

RIYADH

Hofuf

Yanbu

'igh

Al-Kharj

Salwa

Jeddah

Mecca

SAUDI

Ta'if

ARABIA

Al Bahah

As Sulayyil

Al Qunfudhah

Khamis Mushait

Abha

Najran

Jizan

Farasan

ERITREA

ASMARA

YEMEN

SANAA

RED SEA

Gulf of Aden

DJIBOUTI

HIOPIA

DJIBOUTI

Nil

CROWN PRINCE MOHAMMED BIN SALMAN: TIME OF THE BULLDOZER

THE AMBITIOUS YOUNG HEIR APPARENT IS THE KINGDOM'S GREAT HOPE. A RELENTLESS MODERNIZER, HE WANTS TO SHIELD THE COUNTRY FROM BANKRUPTCY BY DECREASING ITS DEPENDENCE ON OIL. BESIDES HIS MANY TALENTS, THE PRINCE ALSO HAS A DEEPER, DARKER SIDE.

Prince Mohammed is twelve years old when he begins to attend meetings with his father, then the governor of Riyadh. His father is a capable, tough manager, and in a few decades, he has successfully transformed what was once only a patch of desert into a vibrant, modern capital city. Even then, it was already rumored that Governor Salman possessed a secret file on everyone of any importance in the state—and with his archives he supposedly kept the entire kingdom under his thumb.

Governor Salman is especially fond of Mohammed, the firstborn son of his third wife. Prince Mohammed is a boy with full lips and an endearing smile. His chestnut eyes are framed by thick black lashes. As a kid, the little prince enjoys goofing around with the palace guards instead of attending his lessons. He winds his private English teacher up so much that the instructor professes himself unable to continue the class, which consists solely of Mohammed and his siblings. Yet his father lets him get away with far more than his twelve other children.

By nineteen, Prince Mohammed is accompanying his father everywhere. He takes notes like a personal assistant, and whispers ideas into his father's ear. He learns how the kingdom is run and how to behave with foreign politicians, princes, and international businesspeople. What he doesn't learn is the art of compromise and the kind of diplomacy and poise that princes are usually trained in when they attend Ivy League or elite British schools. Mohammed has never lived outside Saudi Arabia.

The prince grasps things quickly, but has a reputation for being emotional, passionate and dynamic, and having a volatile temper.

During his college years, Mohammed—also known as MBS— prefers to stay close to his father, Crown Prince Salman, who is on course to succeed King Abdullah. Thus, MBS attains a BA in law at King Saud University in Riyadh.

In January 2015, his father, Salman bin Abdulaziz bin Saud, becomes king at age seventy-nine. He appoints his favorite son defense minister. At twenty-nine, Prince Mohammed is the youngest defense minister in the world.

NEW FREEDOMS, ZERO TOLERANCE FOR DISSENT

There are rumors that the king's health is becoming fragile and that signs of dementia are beginning to show; the royal court, however, denies it. The king remains in the driver's seat, but hands responsibility for day-to-day government affairs to his son and does not travel a lot. Young Prince Mohammed has now reached the locus of power, representing the country almost as if he was already its ruler.

MBS is put in charge of the "Vision 2030" transformation program, which he developed together with his father. It's the centerpiece of a package of reforms intended to move the Saudi economy beyond its dependence on oil. It vigorously promotes the expansion of the private sector. "Vision 2030" has already turned the kingdom on its head.

Some say that Prince Mohammed is building the fourth Saudi kingdom. What they mean is that, after two earlier Saudi kingdoms collapsed in the eighteenth and nineteenth centuries, the succeeding third one is currently being transformed into a fourth—and a totally different country at that. They call Mohammed "Mr. Everything," half mockingly, half reverently.

There's not a single area of life in which the prince hasn't managed to have an impact.

THE CROWN PRINCE (LEFT), HIS FATHER, THE KING (RIGHT), AND IBN SAUD, THE FOUNDER OF THE NATION: THE RULERS ARE OMNIPRESENT ON BILLBOARDS, COFFEE MUGS, AND CELL PHONE CASES.

One day in 2016, the prince gathers the country's most influential media professionals for a meeting in Riyadh. He informs them of his plans and introduces them to "Vision 2030." The young ruler explains that in order to kick-start the economy, social structures need to undergo a radical change. The current doctrine, a puritanical, ultra-conservative interpretation of Islam, should have less influence on daily life, and women must play a more visible role. According to one attendee, the prince intimidates the journalists. "I'm a bulldozer and I will clear everyone out of the way who doesn't play along."

Where exactly does this strongman want to take his country? MBS grants new liberties but has zero tolerance for dissent. And why exactly is this economic and cultural tsunami occurring now?

Shortly after joining the government, MBS goes for a trip around the world, visiting China, Russia, and the United States. In front of astonished audiences, he paints a brutally honest picture of his country. Speaking to influential investors at the Fairmont Hotel in San Francisco, he explains, "In twenty years the importance of oil will be exactly zero. Renewable energy will take over. I have twenty years to change the course of my country and to lead it into the future."

The perplexed investors quickly begin to feel upbeat about the young maverick Saudi pitching his country as a once-in-a-lifetime opportunity. MBS promises vast profits to those who invest in the metamorphosis of the kingdom now: a five-hundred-billion-dollar future city on the Red Sea shore with solar parks, extensive infrastructure, top-notch educational institutes, enticing leisure spaces, a thriving entertainment industry, and exclusive vacation resorts.

In short, Saudi Arabia put off preparing for the future for too long. But now a historic effort is being made to revolutionize the kingdom from the top down. New industries. New jobs. Everything as fast as possible.

Three months after King Salman's coronation, something unusual happens. In April 2015, the monarch replaces the designated crown prince—the next man in line to become king. He first moves his nephew, the very successful interior minister Mohammed bin Nayef, into the position. But then King Salman, in another surprise reshuffle, names his son, MBS, deputy crown prince, making it abundantly clear he wants to pave the way for his own progeny to take the throne.

The aggressive move triggers uneasiness in the royal family. Despite constant internal competition, there has always been an agreement that the different branches of the family are to be fairly represented throughout the country's influential positions. Now, for the first time, it looks like all power could be consolidated in a single branch of the family if Mohammed becomes crown prince. This might effectively marginalize all other lines.

Just two years later, in June 2017, King Salman indeed strips Crown Prince Mohammed bin Nayef of his position in a cunning overnight maneuver. Immediately, his favorite son, MBS, is named the new heir to the throne. Experienced observers say that Prince Mohammed and the king spent months working on the plan.

Within a short time, MBS gains a frightening amount of influence. He is crown prince, defense minister, and deputy prime minister, while also heading the royal court, the real center of power, which controls access to the king. Mohammed now oversees the "Vision 2030" economic program, the country's sovereign wealth fund, as well as Saudi Aramco, the state's huge oil company.

BRAZEN MODERNIZER

Prince Mohammed bin Salman is already a hero to many. Nearly half of Saudis are under the age of twenty-five. They feel that the country has been ruled by a clique of geriatric monarchs for decades. Finally, someone their own age holds the power.

Placing his hand on his heart, a young musician swears his loyalty to MBS "till the end." The twenty-three-year-old is happy to finally be able to openly pursue his passion—playing the trumpet in front of live audiences. For religious fundamentalists, music is the Devil's work. Now the musician is performing with his band at a jazz festival near the port city of Jeddah, part of the kingdom's new cultural agenda, recently launched by Prince Mohammed.

The greatest obstacle to implementing "Vision 2030" might be fundamentalist religious doctrine. As a result, King Salman strips the religious police of their power at the very beginning of his reign. MBS confuses a lot of people when, in an interview, he says, "We are simply reverting to what we once followed—a moderate Islam open to the world and all religions."

Another time, as an afterthought, MBS abruptly annuls the laws obliging women to cover their entire bodies. From now on women must be sensibly and appropriately dressed, explains the prince. They no longer have to wear the black, floor-length abaya. For decades, the abaya has been a symbol of Saudi Arabia as much as the camel or the holy sites in Mecca and Medina. Now, in Mohammed bin Salman's new kingdom, more and more young women are wearing fashionable designer variations of this traditional robe, which adorn more than they cover.

COMIC CON FESTIVAL IN SAUDI ARABIA: NEW FORMS OF ENTERTAINMENT CREATE EXCITEMENT AND A SENSE OF FREEDOM.

MBS authorizes women's marathons, cinemas, monster truck shows, and street festivals. Women can drive, and in some cities, girls can go to cafes with their male friends—all *haram*, forbidden, a short while ago. I ask myself, why don't the ultra-conservative *Wahhabis* protest the changes?

The religious establishment knows all too well that it can't survive without its old pact with the monarchy and the order that the government provides. If the country's transition to an economy that is no longer dependent on oil fails, their project could falter. A Western observer who has lived in Riyadh for more than a decade is certain that if the state goes bankrupt—which is likely to happen in ten to fifteen years if nothing is done—the royals can pack their bags and flee to their properties in Switzerland, France, or the US, places where the political situation is stable and the climate pleasant. Meanwhile, the *Wahhabis*—the men with the long beards and the trousers with short hems—would stay behind amidst economic depression and political chaos.

WISHFUL THINKING IN THE WEST

Things continue going well for the crown prince. During a trip to the US in spring 2018, MBS is courted by the liberal American elite. He's the talk of the town at Harvard and dines with media mogul Rupert Murdoch. Mohammed bin Salman is seen wearing jeans, a casual shirt, and an open blazer. He speaks English, and laughs—a lot. Billionaire Richard Branson meets him in the California desert to discuss space tourism and other ventures. He hobnobs with Bill Gates and Jeff Bezos, the world's richest men. He pays President Trump a visit and they talk arms deals. He even meets Oprah.

Those who encounter MBS like this are convinced the young prince is serious about stopping the export of radical Islam around the world. As evidence, the prince presents the newly appointed leader of the controversial Muslim World League, an Islamic NGO operating worldwide. For decades, the Mecca-based organization has systematically spread *Wahhabi* doctrine around the world. It has financed mosque-building projects, distributed copies of the Qur'an, organized Islamic courses and conferences, and forged links between the global Muslim community and the kingdom. Salafist movements sympathetic to the Saudi regime could always count on generous support. Then, out of nowhere, the new general secretary, the cleric Mohammed bin Abdul Karim Issa, calls for peace between the three largest Abrahamic religions, Christianity, Islam, and Judaism. He encourages imams to visit Jerusalem to overcome animosities. Hallelujah!

The prince's two-week cross-country trip is reminiscent of a journey taken by King Faisal bin Abdulaziz to the United States in 1971. At the time, Faisal forged a strong relationship between America and the fledgling desert state founded in 1932. Now, Prince Mohammed bin Salman aims to breathe new life into the relationship and make himself the central actor in the Saudi-US alliance.

The crown prince's visit to the US is a huge success. The US and other Western countries are more than happy to have found a modern partner with moderate religious views in Riyadh.

ARRESTS AND EXECUTIONS BOOMING UNDER MBS

At this point, the West is still in denial about the fact that the kingdom has been waging a destructive war in Yemen since 2015. A Saudi-led military alliance is fighting the Houthi rebels who have seized power in Yemen, filling a power vacuum in the unstable nation.

Barely three months into his tenure as defense minister, MBS orders an attack. He promises victory will be swift. The deposed—but internationally recognized—government of Yemen had asked the Saudis and their allies for help. International law is on their side. But the military offensive is devastating. The Arab coalition is bombing the country back to the Stone Age. The US and Britain provide intelligence and logistical support. Yemen is turning into the greatest humanitarian catastrophe of our time. The death toll reaches one hundred thousand. Approximately the same number of children have starved to death due to famine according to estimates by NGOs on the ground.

Prince Mohammed is obsessed with defeating the Houthis. For the Saudis, the Shi'ite rebels are Iran's subversives. By no means will they tolerate them controlling a neighboring country. Yet the operation in Yemen is going badly. Victory is nowhere in sight. Though Saudi Arabia and Iran-backed Houthis have started talks to contain the level of violence, a peace agreement is still far off. It seems that the young defense minister has gotten bogged down in the conflict.

The West continues to turn a blind eye, especially since the Saudis virtually sealed off the country from observers. What's more, many simply don't want to believe that this charismatic prince has a sinister side.

Some numbers: In Mohammed bin Salman's first eight months as crown prince, 133 people were executed, either decapitated by sword or stoned to death. That's twice as many as in the same period before he took office. Countless activists have disappeared. Security services silence critics or detain them immediately, commando squads in black uniforms simply showing up on their doorstep.

On November 4, 2017, the king and his son Mohammed break all the unwritten laws of Arab society. More than three hundred influential people are detained in a meticulously planned operation. The detainees are kept under arrest in the glamorous Riyadh Ritz-Carlton Hotel. Among them are a dozen of Prince Mohammed's cousins and uncles. The detained even include billionaire real-estate tycoons; Saad Hariri, then prime minister of Lebanon, is just one example, held at a different location from the other prisoners. Of course, Hariri is also a Saudi citizen, and previously ran one of the biggest construction firms in the kingdom, Saudi Oger.

NEUTRALIZING COMPETITORS

To secure their release, the accused must hand over a portion of their wealth. They're shown secret files containing the reasons for their arrest—probably files that King Salman had already compiled during his stint as governor of Riyadh. Out of the blue, witnesses with embarrassing things to tell are flown in. Trained interrogation experts apply pressure until agreements are reached. The royal court calls the operation an "anti-corruption crackdown" and, in many cases, this is true. Endemic corruption has gnawed away at the country for decades. But as the weeks go by and the world remains puzzled by the events, one thing becomes more and more certain: the motivation behind the wave of arrests goes far beyond the mere desire to collect money from the corrupt elites. Old scores are being settled, competitors neutralized.

The crown prince continues to strengthen his grip on society. He now controls all four pillars of power: the military, the secret service, business, and the media. Among the involuntary guests at the Ritz is even the head of the National Guard, a son of former King Abdullah who has now been removed from his post. The National Guard is the one-hundred-thousand-strong force responsible for protecting the royal family. In March 2020 he removed the two remaining legitimate candidates to the throne by arresting the king's nephew, Mohammed bin Nayef, as well as the king's full brother, Ahmed bin Adbulaziz, for treason.

CRACKING DOWN ON THE ENEMY WITHIN

Crown Prince Mohammed bin Salman governs with the help of a small, informal group of five or six ambitious men between thirty and fifty who are well aware that this is a unique moment in Saudi history. Their access to MBS makes them extremely powerful. One name crops up again and again: Saud al-Qahtani, director of the Center for Studies and Media Affairs.

Al-Qahtani is an ambitious, talented lawyer and former Air Force officer. He is seven years older than the crown prince. For more than ten years, he has served the royal court. To prove his loyalty, al-Qahtani builds up a network of social media surveillance and manipulation. His job is to extol the virtues of the crown prince while suppressing his enemies. Experts estimate that half of all Saudi Twitter profiles are bots or fake accounts deployed to deceive and influence public opinion. The electronic army trashes dissidents and opponents of the regime. They slander and destroy reputations. To do the job, al-Qahtani purchases surveillance technology from Italy and Israel normally deployed by intelligence services.

Al-Qahtani soon comes to be seen as the crown prince's right hand, giving him access to extraordinary inside knowledge. He belongs to the inner circle who knew about the planned crackdown at the Ritz from the beginning.

The anti-corruption operation is seen by many as an attack on the old order. To the outside, the royal family puts on a display of unity, as they always do in times of crisis, despite the deep wounds that have been inflicted. It's about damage control and ensuring the ongoing rule of the House of Saud. As is commonly said, the family comes before any individual members. Yet behind the gates of the palaces of Riyadh and Jeddah, things are simmering. Many dignitaries are no longer permitted to leave the country, and their communications are monitored.

The crown prince has made plenty of new enemies. People who know him say that his greatest strength is his ability to turn every success into an even greater one. His weakness is that he doesn't learn from failure. This impression is confirmed when, just weeks before the first Saudi women are set to receive their driver's licenses in June 2018, Mohammed bin Salman decides to arrest the very women who had fought for decades for the right to drive. Overnight, the activists are seen as heroines amongst the vanguard in Saudi Arabia and around the world.

THE CROWN PRINCE THREATENS THE FRENCH PRESIDENT

MBS doesn't want the women to emerge as the winners of the struggle. He wants to keep the glory for himself alone and so denounces the activists as traitors. In prison, the women are tortured and sexually harassed. One of the crown prince's closest confidants oversees the torture: Saud al-Qahtani.

There is no legitimate reason to arrest the activists. The women pose no threat, but are charged with the most serious of crimes, including treason. Western media are unanimously outraged by the crown prince, who they had celebrated as a champion of women's rights the day before. The decision to lock up the women's rights activists marks the beginning of the end of MBS's shining ascent as an enlightened modernizer. His erratic nature and tendency to overreach become painfully clear.

In June 2017, Riyadh abruptly ends relations with its smaller Gulf neighbor Qatar after Mohammed bin Salman is annoyed by a speech the emir had reportedly delivered, one which, it turns out, was probably manufactured by the Russian intelligence service. Observers say MBS's reaction is far too extreme. In November 2017, the crown prince threatens the French president, Emmanuel Macron, saying he will break off trade with France if Paris continues to do business with Iran. Macron responds with serene self-confidence and states that France can do business with whomever it wants, somehow preventing further escalation of the situation.

Something similar occurs with the former German foreign minister Sigmar Gabriel, but this time things end badly. When the Lebanese prime minister is detained in Riyadh, Gabriel warns of "adventuring" in the Gulf. In retaliation, MBS temporarily cancels all new German-Saudi trade contracts and withdraws the Saudi ambassador from Berlin.

In summer 2018, Mohammed bin Salman punishes the Canadian government because of a tweet by Foreign Minister Chrystia Freeland, who had criticized the arrest of an activist. Thousands of Saudi students are forced to interrupt their studies in Canada and return home. All Saudi flights to Canada are canceled.

UNPREDICTABLE, CRUEL, NEFARIOUS

The next and truly shocking incident soon follows. On October 2, 2018, a prominent journalist with broad international connections, Jamal Khashoggi, is brutally murdered. The horror seems beyond description: the execution, professional butchering, and disposal of the remains inside the Saudi consulate in Istanbul of one of MBS's fiercest critics changes everything.

Although the murder was likely commissioned at the highest level, it takes more than two weeks for the royal court in Riyadh to even admit that they knew about the crime. American intelligence agencies believe that the crown prince himself ordered the execution. According to intelligence reports, the media consultant in the royal court and the crown prince's right-hand man, Saud al-Qahtani, kept in personal contact with the executioners in Istanbul.

While Khashoggi is being killed, his body cut to pieces and dissolved in acid or else taken out of the embassy, the head of the execution team, Maher Mutreb, alludes directly to the Saudi royal court during a Skype call to al-Qahtani: "Tell your boss," he says. Investigators understand these words to refer to the crown prince. The young prince, who has only just recently strolled through the hallowed halls of Harvard and discussed how to make the world a better place with Bill Gates, suddenly looks like a monster. Unpredictable, cruel, nefarious.

In Riyadh, eerie scenes play out, carefully choreographed to limit the damage. In reality, they make everything look even more bizarre. For example, the crown prince takes to the stage at an international investors' conference. Various Western business leaders stay away in protest. Richard Branson cancels all joint ventures with Saudi Arabia. Before the world's cameras, the crown prince calls the Khashoggi killing a "heinous crime." He personally guarantees that "all of those involved will be held accountable."

THE SMOKING BONE SAW

On the Saudi evening news, the king and the crown prince are seen consoling the victim's oldest son, Salah Khashoggi, at their palace in the capital. There are close-ups of the crown prince shaking the thirty-five-year-old banker's hand and of both of their faces: one sad and exhausted, the other strong and determined. The next day, the photo makes it to the front page of newspapers around the world.

At the time, Salah Khashoggi, the son, is barred from leaving the country and was stuck in Saudi Arabia for months. While his father was alive and living in exile in the United States, the regime had prevented Salah from visiting him. Only after Salah accepts the condolences in the palace is he allowed to leave the country with his family.

The Republican senator Lindsey Graham says there's no "smoking gun" in the Khashoggi case, no evidence that points to a particular perpetrator. Instead, Graham continues, there's a "smoking saw." In fact, one of the members of the execution squad from Riyadh is a coroner who carried a bone saw in his luggage, which he most likely used to cut Khashoggi to pieces. Detractors murmur that MBS actually stands for "Mister Bone Saw."

Many Saudis are sad, shaken, and outraged. They had placed great hope in the young leader. But they aren't necessarily angry that MBS is most likely responsible for the crime. Murdering political opponents is not unusual in this part of the world. What embitters people is that their young leader has damaged the reputation of their country. If the West turns away from Saudi Arabia and the country is isolated politically, this could bring about harmful consequences. As this book goes to print, eleven suspects were tried in Riyadh for the murder of Jamal Khashoggi. All of them have been found guilty and sentenced. Five of them were sentenced to death, but all were pardoned.

It's unclear, though, who is being charged and who isn't. The court refuses to release names. The hit squad that traveled to Istanbul was composed of fifteen men. One thing is for sure: the name of the crown prince's confidant, al-Qahtani, is not among them. While all international investigations into the Khashoggi murder seemed to lead to the crown prince's most influential aide, the Saudi prosecutors said they found no evidence linking al-Qahtani to the crime.

Obviously, MBS has no intention of sacrificing his friend.

The royal court is largely silent on the subject. Strategists are working to contain the international damage. "Did you order the murder of Jamal Khashoggi?" a CBS presenter asks MBS one year later, in early October 2019. Crown Prince Mohammed bin Salman is a tall, strong guy sitting in a room at the royal court in Jeddah. He shakes his head as if the idea that he murdered a journalist is so absurd that the question answers itself.

"No way," the crown prince replies. He says he knew nothing about a scheme to kill Khashoggi in the Saudi consulate in Istanbul. "But I take full responsibility as one of the leaders in Saudi Arabia, especially because it was committed by members of the Saudi government." It sounds as if lawyers spent nights working on a statement that simultaneously admits his liability but disavows any personal culpability.

Surprisingly, even Jamal Khashoggi's son Salah demonstrates his satisfaction with the verdict. The *Washington Post* reports that Khashoggi's sons have received multimillion-dollar homes and monthly five-figure payments as compensation for the killing of their father, which Salah denies. Of course, to accept "blood money" would be in line with Islam and Saudi cultural customs. "Fairness of the judiciary is based on two principles, justice and swift litigation," Salah Khashoggi tweets. He declares "full confidence" in the Saudi justice system. Astonishingly, neither al-Qahtani nor the crown prince himself seems to play a role anymore.

INTO THE ABYSS

Al-Qahtani is officially suspended from his position in the royal court, allegedly by order of the king. Nonetheless, writes David Ignatius of the *Washington Post*, al-Qahtani continues to be active online, where he lashes out at critics of the government with aggressive media campaigns. To date, Western diplomats in Riyadh report that al-Qahtani continues to been seen occasionally at functions and meetings in Riyadh. According to insiders, al-Qahtani never stopped advising the crown prince. If Ignatius is right, Khashoggi was murdered because the prominent journalist may have had enough influence to trigger a hashtag protest in Saudi Arabia. In other words, he could have sparked an uprising against the monarchy over social media.

Ignatius cites an American insider who visited the crown prince. He laid out Prince Mohammed bin Salman's options for him. According to the source, the US intelligence community was in the process of determining whether or not to categorize MBS as a dictator—meaning he would either be classified as unreliable, just as Saddam Hussein once was, or continue to be seen as a modernizer and therefore a reliable ally of the United States. "As long as you keep al-Qahtani, people will say you're more like Saddam," the American guest warned.

Those words encapsulate Saudi Arabia's current dilemma. The kingdom is in urgent need of renewal. It needs to push back against extremism, create a more open society, and strengthen private enterprise. Mohammed bin Salman has certainly initiated all of this, which was brave. He deserves praise for that. But the same courage—in combination with the prince's temper and hubris—has brought the country back to the edge of the abyss.

In foreign policy, MBS's impulsiveness gets him involved in unnecessary conflicts and wars. The Qatar story is an example of this. Domestically, his mania for control results in severe human rights violations, among them the murder of Jamal Khashoggi.

It is in the West's interest that Saudi Arabia succeed in its transformation into a modern society. Many diplomats and people in intelligence services believe that this is only possible if the crown prince is replaced. Yet King Salman shows no intention of switching out his heir. His support for his favorite son is unshakable.

Prince Mohammed bin Salman once outlined his plans for Saudi Arabia in an early interview on CBS *60 Minutes*. When asked if there was anything that could prevent him from governing the kingdom over the next fifty years, he said "only death."

LIFE UNDER THE ABAYA: BLACK OR BLACK?

LIKE HALF OF THE SAUDI POPULATION, I MUST CONCEAL MY BODY BENEATH A PIECE OF SHAPELESS BLACK FABRIC—BUT SOCIAL RULES ARE CHANGING FAST THESE DAYS.

Fifteen minutes before landing at King Khaled International Airport in Riyadh, the young woman with the long curls in seat 43A transforms herself into a faceless, bodiless being. She throws a black baggy gown—an abaya—over her jeans and top, and wraps a dark scarf around her neck and hair. She ties a second scarf, the *niqab*, so tightly around the back of her head that it covers her face. All that's left is a slit for her eyes.

If we hadn't just been having a lively conversation, I wouldn't have known that it was Anood, a twenty-three-year-old marketing professional at a chocolate manufacturer in Riyadh. She's returning from a visit to relatives in Istanbul. Her brother Alaa sits three rows ahead. He's only seventeen, but without a male guardian, a *wali*, her father wouldn't have approved of the trip, Anood tells me as the plane is landing.

I ask her whether what I've read is still true: Do men still control women's movements in Saudi Arabia? Anood nods. Even though it is no longer required by law, most women follow the old family traditions, she says. Men decide where their daughters and wives are allowed to go, as well as how much of themselves they should cover.

In a high-profile TV interview in America in 2018, Crown Prince Mohammed bin Salman said that men and women are equal in Saudi Arabia. Women are free to choose whether or not they wear the abaya and the face veil, as long as their clothing is decent and respectful, that's all. My encounter with Anood on the plane tells another story. The day-to-day reality for women in Saudi Arabia is a far cry from what Prince Mohammed claims it is.

One morning in March 2018, after living in Riyadh for several months, I'm walking along the street to throw out the trash in the dumpster. It's Friday, the day of prayer and the most important day of the week. I'm wearing jeans and a long-sleeve T-shirt; I've forgotten to throw on my abaya. A neighbor who's getting into his car freezes for a second and shouts "Cover up!" with the same urgency as if a fire had broken out. Only now do I realize that something's wrong with me. For a fraction of a second, I feel as if I've left the house naked. I tell the man to calm down and head back inside.

The neighbor's reaction might not quite be so harsh today, at least not in the center of the capital city. But what's considered indecent or immoral still varies radically between Saudi Arabia and Germany—where I grew up—or any other Western country. This makes it hard sometimes to deal with the pressure of having to follow different cultural norms.

Before my first Riyadh trip, I visited an Islamic boutique in Neukölln, an immigrant neighborhood of Berlin. As I squeezed between the racks of black gowns, I told myself that my abaya would be work clothing, the way you need safety glasses in a chemistry lab. Alongside a lot of inconspicuous models were colorful, sequined ones as well as fancy party abayas with batwing sleeves. I would have to disappear in one of these gowns, with or without batwings. It annoyed me that women were advising other women on how to best hide their figures in these frumpy sheaths. In the end, I chose the cheapest model, a simple black abaya for forty-nine euros (about fifty-four dollars).

I wondered if it would change me to have most of my body covered up. Whether in a cafe or at the grocery store, at a dinner or on the beach, I would be just one black smock among other black smocks. Since moving to Riyadh, I've been trying to find out: What does it do to women when both their bodies and

AUTHOR AT RIYADH'S DEERA SQUARE—ALSO REFERRED TO AS CHOP-CHOP SQUARE SINCE CONVICTS TRADITIONALLY ARE PUBLICLY BEHEADED THERE BY THE STATE EXECUTIONER: USING THE ABAYA AS PROTECTIVE GEAR LIKE SAFETY GLASSES IN A CHEMISTRY LAB.

their faces are invisible? I won't cover my face. No written law requires it, and as a foreigner I don't have a *wali* who decides what I can wear. All the same, the abaya is my uniform over the coming months.

NORA ENJOYS HER NEW FREEDOM

Change is in the air and the old social order is being challenged. When the first woman joined the Saudi cabinet in 2009 as deputy minister for education and upbringing, it caused a stir. Now there's also a female deputy minister for social affairs. Not phenomenal, but a start. A sexual harassment law has been passed. The HR policies at a lot of companies now require men and women to work in mixed offices. For many Saudis, this is still unimaginable.

Since 2017, women have been able to rent an apartment without their guardian's signature. And since June 2018, women have been allowed to drive, a right that activists have been fighting for since the 1970s. The right to drive has always been about more than just being allowed behind the wheel. It's about freedom of movement and autonomy. The road to equality is long, but there are signs of change.

Women now work in public. You see them at the supermarket checkout, in banks, in boutiques. In the future, they may even be allowed to choose how they live their lives. At least in theory.

Nora works part-time at an international trading company. She comes from Diriyah, a suburb northwest of the capital, and is thirty-three. She has two kids, a six-year-old girl and an eleven-year-old boy. She's been married for almost twelve years. Her husband went to college, saw the world. He's a good-natured guy, and yet Nora isn't permitted to leave the city without him at her side. Nora is no rebel, but she makes the best of her new freedoms.

In the 1980s, her grandmother and mother were forced to cover themselves and obey the new religious rules. That's the way things have been for four generations, if you add her and her daughter Sara. "I don't want to struggle," Nora says. "I don't want to fight. I want to live a good life."

"ARE YOU NOW WEARING A CURTAIN?"

In Saudi Arabia, Nora is what you call "open-minded." That means I can talk to her about anything without worrying about saying something inappropriate. As a result, we become friendly with one another. Here, you can often see little signs of rebellion in the details. Today, for the first time, I see Nora wearing an open coat made of light-colored fabric with saffron-colored silk slits in the sleeves. She bought it at Happy Hijab at the Royal Mall on King Fahd Road; an insider's tip for flamboyant abaya fashion. Previously, I've seen Nora wear only black, high-necked abayas.

Two years ago, a prominent Saudi cleric appealed to the "sisters" in his country to show more modesty in their clothing. Women should avoid wearing elaborate abayas. No ornamentation, no slits. Conservative imams and citizens alike worry that religious rules on clothing are being ignored since the religious police were stripped of their enforcement powers. They accuse women who wear colorful abayas of vanity and, even worse, of trying to attract male attention.

Nora is a delicate woman, not particularly tall, with an oval face and brown eyes. She wears a loose scarf over her hair. Her mother-in-law is Egyptian, and Nora's husband Saleh grew up with slightly less radical religious views than most Saudis. Saleh's mother never wears the *niqab*, so Saleh explicitly wants Nora to keep her face uncovered. "Are you now wearing a curtain?" Nora's mother expresses disapproval when Nora proudly shows her the latest fashion from the Royal Mall, an abaya with fringed sleeves, red lace on the collar and pockets. We all laugh.

FEAR OF THE RELIGIOUS POLICE HAS EVAPORATED

Nora and I wander through a food festival in central Riyadh. Burgers and hot dogs are on sale, and sofas made of pallets, the kind that are trendy in the West, have been set up on Astroturf. The event is organized by the so-called General Entertainment Authority, a state body tasked with making the boring everyday lives of young Saudis more fun and colorful. Here, men and women mingle without the curtains or walls that usually separate the sexes. The religious police sometimes send their moral guardians around, but currently, in the new Saudi Arabia, no one fears them anymore since their influence has evaporated. This is tangible progress. Up until recently, there was not a single public space where men and women could socialize together.

The food festival is taking place outside the new Riyadh Park Mall, a futuristic complex with a round structure that resembles a giant turbine. A couple of weeks ago, the country's first movie theater opened up here. Cinemas had been illegal in Saudi Arabia for forty years. The theater is as big as a palace, and opened with *Black Panther*, a movie chock-full of powerful women and featuring a black superhero, a white villain, and female bodyguards.

"Are we finally normal?" Nora asks. She's proud of the progress being made, but dislikes the fact that her country is portrayed as a stereotypical cradle of extremism and backwardness in the Western media. Difficult question, I think. After all, what's normal?

Nations differ based on the circumstances of their histories. For decades, the monarchy felt threatened by the string of revolutions taking place in the region—in Iran and, before that, in Egypt. It decided to immunize its society with extreme puritan religiosity. The reinforced *Wahhabi* ideology was intended to unite the country and to protect it from the outside world. For decades, the plan worked, and one of the main pillars of the ideology was to grant men dominion over women. But now the country is rapidly changing course.

WHAT'S NORMAL?

It's not easy to get rid of decades-old ideas. Today in Saudi Arabia, it is still normal to separate girls from their male relatives and exclude them from public life at the age of ten or eleven. Family homes usually have separate entrances for men and women, and the sexes still live in separate quarters. In general, girls attend different schools and universities than boys. At twenty or twenty-one, or even earlier, their parents select a husband for their daughters. In many families it continues to be the case that, after marriage, only the husband will see his wife's face.

When we talk about societal norms, we usually mean a cultural consensus reached through a public discussion about opportunity and equality. In a conservative, absolute monarchy like Saudi Arabia, such a process is non-existent.

YOUNG WOMEN AT THE JANADRIYAH FESTIVAL IN RIYADH: MEN STILL DECIDE WOMEN'S DRESS CODE.

Nora's question about whether Saudi Arabia is a normal country hangs in the air. I tell her about how, during my childhood, German women fought to be able to drive streetcars, to become mayors and professors, and that, even in Germany, men had the right to cancel their wives' employment contracts against their will until 1976. And then in 2005 came the first female chancellor,

Angela Merkel, a sensation. She showed the world that women can do anything that men can, sometimes better.

I tell Nora that it is normal for me that Germany has a female face. So, has Saudi Arabia become normal? "No, I don't think so."

THE FIRST POP CONCERT FOR MEN AND WOMEN

Recently, public pop concerts have been held not far from the coastal city of Jeddah. These shows are also open to women—again, sensational news. As with movies, live music had been prohibited in Saudi Arabia since the 1980s. Saudi religious scholars say that everything that estranges people from God has been sent by Satan. For the ultra-religious, music is such a vice.

Jeddah lies on the Red Sea in Hejaz Province. Here, society has always been a little freer, more open and more cosmopolitan than in Riyadh. People say *"Jeddah ghair"*—Jeddah is different.

Indeed, history is being made here. The Egyptian pop star Tamer Hosny is giving his first performance in Saudi Arabia, and for the first time, men and women can attend an open-air concert together. They have to sit on separate bleachers, but they're under the same sky.

Tonight, Tamer Hosny, a superstar in the Arab world, wears a suit and bowtie and a closely trimmed beard. His big hits, like "180 Degrees," are about love, loyalty, betrayal, and being dumped. The six thousand tickets sold out within two hours.

Hosny's appearance in Jeddah is more than just a concert. It's the promise of a better future.

Fans begin to arrive hours early. The girls and women wear their hair loose, and many put on elaborate makeup. The inconspicuous abayas have been replaced with coats of bright-green or shiny turquoise silk, or are made of linen and chiffon. Some are cut like kimonos, with colorful embroidery. In the spacious area in front of the stage, men and women wait together, laughing, drinking alcohol-free beer and fresh juice.

When Tamer Hosny finally shows up shortly after ten o'clock, the crowd erupts. The fans know every word of his songs by heart and sing along, especially the women. "Dancing prohibited" is printed on the ticket, so when several young women get carried away and jump up, the ushers warn them to take it easy. Although transformation is sweeping the country, there are still taboos; dancing is one of them. But at least in some places, even this ban is now being relaxed.

JAMILA WANTS TO BE AN ARTIST AND SEE THE WORLD—MOM'S ALREADY LOOKING FOR A HUSBAND

Sitting on the bleachers are two sisters: Hala, twenty-three, and Jamila, twenty-one. They're wearing giant glow-in-the-dark joke glasses. The sisters, almost glowing with joy themselves, are having a truly special evening.

TWO YOUNG WOMEN AT A CONCERT: A WOMAN'S FREEDOM MUST BE CONSTANTLY NEGOTIATED WITH HER MALE GUARDIAN.

Apart from their oversized glasses, both are dressed simply, unlike most in the audience. Hala wears a baggy, dark-gray abaya, Jamila, a loose taupe coat—colors that make them blend in with the background. The sisters' hair is hidden behind their hijabs, and their faces are free of makeup.

Jamila sings well. She loves to dance and wants to study art and see the world. She is unmarried and lives with her parents. To leave the house, she requires her father's permission. "He means well," says Jamila, "but he's really conservative." Her father wants her to study economics or Islamic Studies. Her mother is trying to find her a husband.

Women here are treated as if they have to be protected from their own childish naiveté. Here, women have always been considered immature, regardless of age. Important decisions were always made by male guardians: who they marry, whether to apply for a passport, where to travel. When women married, the guardianship was transferred from their father to their husband. When women went out for long periods of time or traveled, they had to be accompanied by a close male relative.

Recently, many laws have changed. But a lot of men have not. This is why, for women, a potential life partner's looks, his age, or the compatibility of his character are often secondary. "The most important question is how much breathing room, how much freedom, this man gives you," says Jamila.

That Hala and Jamila are attending a concert tonight is the result of days of negotiation with their father and Hala's husband. The latter finally said he was willing to drive the sisters to the concert in the King Abdullah Economic City. That's the glamorous new venue for shows, an hour outside of Jeddah. It's a leisure city with restaurants, a golf course, vacation apartments, and water sports. Hala's husband waits in the parking lot until the show ends. Then the two young women will immediately return to the meeting point, as agreed.

Jamila and Hala both say they want to make something of their lives. They ask themselves how they can take advantage of the new opportunities for women. Jamila dreams of running her own taxi company—by women for women—together with her sister. "Right now, we're trying to convince our father of the idea," says Hala. The older sister already has a foreign driver's license. She lived in Canada with her husband for a few years during an international fellowship. Jamila applied for her license a week ago.

YOUR HUSBAND IS YOUR LIFE

If a man grants his daughter or his wife new freedoms, he is quickly labeled as weak by other men—as someone who doesn't fulfill his duty as a male protector.

That's why Saleh forbade Nora from traveling to Mecca last year. She planned to visit the holy sites with female friends and her two children. "If Sara or Karim get lost in the crowd, could you live with that?" he asked his wife. Nora suddenly felt unsure. She told him that no one could guarantee 100 percent that nothing would happen, but that it was very unlikely. It didn't help. She had to stay in Riyadh. Nora's freedom ends at the city limits. Saleh says it's too dangerous for an unaccompanied woman to leave Riyadh.

Nora complains that Saleh sometimes treats her like one of his kids, yet she doesn't want to anger him. "Your husband is your life," her father told her at her wedding eleven years ago. She wants to be a good wife, and preserving tradition is part of that.

Ever since her son Karim turned ten, Nora has woken him up at five thirty in the morning for prayer. Afterward, he's allowed to go back to bed. Nora's daughter Sara visits the Qur'an center in her neighborhood three afternoons a week. Sara is learning the Qur'an by heart, all 114 surahs. The youngest "students" are three years old.

Once a year, the country's Qur'anic schools—including Sara's—celebrate the "Day of the Abaya." The festivities kick off tomorrow at four in the afternoon.

Sara lies on the sofa in tights with an iPad in front of her. An Islamic learning app is running on the screen. A voice reads out part of a surah and Sara is supposed to repeat what she hears. Every pupil has been assigned a different segment, and she is expected to recite the verse at the celebration. Sara says she doesn't want to go, so Nora scolds her: "Because you're lazy!"

The next day, the three of us are on our way. The entrance hall to the Qur'anic school is packed with women and girls in black abayas. Little Sara also wears a floor-length coat with buttons down the front. She was given her first abaya—complete with *niqab*—at age three. It was Sara's greatest wish.

Girls copy their mothers and aunts and begin wearing the veil early. Normally, girls start wearing abayas at eleven, twelve, or thirteen, making it all the more desirable for the younger ones to show that they belong with the big kids.

HANDHELD SIGNS CRAFTED FOR THE ABAYA DAY: THE BLACK GOWN IS CONSIDERED THE ULTIMATE PROTECTION AGAINST SIN AND SEDUCTION.

In the Qur'anic school, qahwah—light Arabic coffee—is already being served with cake and sweets. The kids have made cardboard abayas as decoration, and little paper women on sticks have been stuck into the cakes. Each female figure is adorned with a different verse of the Qur'an.

"WOMEN ARE SEDUCTIVE, SEDUCIBLE, ALWAYS AT RISK"

The competition begins: Who can recite the Qur'an the longest without making a mistake? It's Sara's turn. Her verse deals with the amazing creation of earth—and paradise, which is even more fantastic. Suddenly, she becomes insecure and hesitates. She looks at Nora, who whispers a hint. Sara remembers the rest of the verse. We all clap, and Nora beams with pride.

The walls are decorated with exemplary abaya-wearing women from Saudi history. The pictures show women during the so-called "War of Unification" in the early twentieth century. Next to them hangs a picture of Al-Jawhara, one of the four wives of King Faisal who ruled the country until his nephew assassinated him in 1975. Faisal is highly respected to this day.

The photo shows Princess Al-Jawhara on a state visit to the West with her husband in the 1960s. Not only is she wearing an abaya and *niqab*, but she's also draped a chiffon veil over her head as if she were attending a funeral. You can't even make out the contours of her face.

"We must protect beauty from men," says Amira, a woman in her early forties who speaks perfect English and wears elegant makeup with bright red lipstick. She's an English teacher and the wife of a diplomat. Every day she comes to the Qur'anic school once her kids have been picked up from classes and taken care of at home. With women from the neighborhood, she reads from the holy book. Sometimes, forty or fifty like-minded women of every age group attend.

For Amira, women are seductive and seducible: "Always at risk." The idea that men should show restraint or be punished when they sexually harass women or become violent doesn't seem to cross her mind.

Amira is also learning the Qur'an by heart. "When I get to the last page, I go back to the beginning," she says. At the end of our conversation, Amira gives me three paper abaya women on sticks as a souvenir and invites me back. Islam could give me more peace. "Tomorrow?" she asks.

FANTASY COSTUMES AT THE COMIC CON FESTIVAL (JEDDAH 2018).

"AM I PRETTY ENOUGH?"

Currently, Saudis are debating what will happen now that the abaya is no longer obligatory. The crown prince triggered the discussion in a *60 Minutes* interview in America. High-ranking Saudi clerics rushed to support the prince, even though they had been saying exactly the opposite for forty years: that wearing the abaya is obligatory and non-negotiable. "More than 90 percent of pious Muslim women in the world don't wear the abayas," Sheikh Abdullah al-Mutlaq, a member of the Council of Senior Scholars, the highest religious institution in the country, explained in a radio message. "We should not force people to wear abayas."

Reading the comments on social media, it sounds as if a lot of women's *niqab*s slid off their faces in shock. Not all Saudi women would be happy if the abaya and face veil were abolished tomorrow. Quite a few of them see the full-body cloak and the *niqab* as protection that allows them to move around anonymously. Others wonder what would happen if their husbands could suddenly see the face of a female neighbor or coworker. The same question keeps coming up: "Will I be pretty enough?"

Apparently, the veil prevents the beauty contest that Western women have to contend with every day.

Then there are those like my acquaintance Uli, an international businessman. He's been selling natural house paint all over the world and in the kingdom for nearly twenty years. He says that Western women have to constantly present themselves in seductive clothing to please men, which he finds undignified—a view that corresponds with the position of most Saudi men and many pious women.

Robert, a thirty-six-year-old nurse from Bavaria who works in a hospital in Riyadh, tells me about the victim of an accident who was from the governorate of Al-Kharj, southeast of the capital: the woman died but couldn't be identified by her husband because he'd never seen her face. According to a regional custom in Al-Kharj, it's not permitted for women to lift their veil even in the most intimate moments.

After a few weeks in Riyadh, I've almost gotten used to the abaya. I don't want to detract from its practical benefits. You're always well dressed and can go to the supermarket to buy toothpaste and milk in your pajamas. And I do a lot less shopping for new clothes.

Still, we'll never become good friends. I'll always associate the abaya with something I can't bear: the absence of choice, at least for most women. The abaya nonetheless occupies a place of honor in my life. The three paper abaya ladies on wooden sticks from Sara's Qur'anic school now hang, framed, on my kitchen wall.

COMPLEX FAMILY AFFAIRS

UNDER ISLAMIC LAW, A MAN CAN BE MARRIED TO UP TO FOUR
WOMEN AT THE SAME TIME—IF HE HAS ENOUGH MONEY. IN SAUDI
ARABIA, ONE IN TWENTY MEN PARTAKE OF THIS CUSTOM. BUT
HOW DO THE WIVES FEEL ABOUT POLYGAMY?

My landlord, Colonel Hasan, invites me for dinner with his family. His mother has arrived from Jeddah with her entourage. Everyone's coming, Hasan's brother, his brother's wife, the kids— all want to celebrate. Hasan has slaughtered a lamb. "We're waiting for you, Miss Susanne," says the colonel.

At 9:00 p.m. on the dot, I head over. The host greets me under the high walls of his house. Beyond the front yard lie lavish, carpeted chambers. Long tables are decked out with crystal and golden porcelain. We move from one living quarter to the next. Finally, we arrive in the women's salon.

Some of the women—those not directly related to the man of the house, such as Colonel Hasan's sister-in-law, a doctor—hastily pull their veils over their faces. When she greets me, she raises the woolen flap that covers her eyes a tiny bit. Her husband's brother cannot see her face, she explains. False desires must be nipped in the bud!

It promises to be an interesting evening with a very normal Salafist family. Salafists are Muslim puritans who honor the traditions of the Salaf, as the first three generations of Muslims and earliest followers of Mohammed are referred to in the Qur'an. In Saudi Arabia, the Salafists adhere to the teachings of Abd al-Wahhab, an ultra-conservative cleric who sealed a political-religious pact with the House of Saud in the eighteenth century. The *Wahhabis* are loyal monarchists, and theirs is probably the strictest school of Sunni Islam. Wahhabism has been Saudi Arabia's state religion since the founding of the modern kingdom in 1932.

Colonel Hasan has five daughters, all of them pretty young women. In the parlor, they stand beside the blue velvet sofa. Their hair is perfectly coiffed, as if they all just came from the salon.

The conversation screeches to a halt when we come in, as if a teacher was entering a classroom. Colonel Hasan's wife Jawhara is also present, unveiled like her daughters—but of course only here in the women's parlor and as long as her husband's brothers or male staff don't set eyes on her. Jawhara is in her late forties, with high cheekbones and big dark eyes. She wears a cornflower-blue chiffon pantsuit. According to my Lebanese realtor who found the apartment for me, she is the first of Colonel Hasan's three wives.

Up to this point, Colonel Hasan hasn't mentioned his complicated family situation. He probably thinks that a Western woman wouldn't understand the arrangement. He brings up his little harem for the first time when a British friend of mine decides to rent an apartment from Colonel Hasan and I accompany him to the office. Once the formalities are completed, Mr. Hasan tells his new tenant about his latest marriage—the third one—which took place a few months ago. The bride was twenty-three.

WOMEN'S RIGHT TO THEIR NIGHT

It's not unheard of for Western men to brag to their buddies about having an extramarital affair with an attractive woman. But polygamy is legal in Saudi Arabia. Apart from the pride of conquest, there is also a certain social prestige: having multiple wives implies that you have considerable wealth. Saudi husbands are required by law to pay for the upkeep of their wives and all resulting children, even if the women earn their own money. Not something everyone can afford.

"Why three wives?" my British friend asks.

It appears Colonel Hasan has forgotten there's a woman in the room. The conversation veers toward locker-room talk: "My first wife is getting old. One of them is always on her period. What do you do if you want to sleep with one?"

The conversation is getting difficult for me. The Brit is also irritated that Colonel Hasan classifies his three life partners in terms of their sexual availability.

I ask the husband-of-three how he manages to distribute his affection fairly, as Islam requires. And I ask how well the three wives get along. Colonel Hasan becomes monosyllabic. He sucks air through his teeth as if afflicted by a sudden pain. "Not so well," he says. Quite the understatement, one can assume. "They dislike each other," Mr. Hasan explains. "They're jealous."

He assures me that he's doing all he can to make all three of them happy. Pointing roughly between the Kingdom Center and Al Faisaliyah Tower, he says that in that direction live wives number two and three. Each of them gets what they are entitled to and, of course, there is a schedule for when he spends the night with which wife. He says it works best if the ladies have zero contact with each other. And when talking to one of his wives, he never mentions the others.

BOOSTING WOMEN'S RIGHTS WITH THE FOUR-WIFE LIMIT

If one wife isn't enough for a man, he usually has to marry a second time. Even nowadays, sex outside of wedlock is virtually impossible. Women seldom enter casual relationships. If such a relationship becomes known, the woman's honor is tarnished forever, and her chances of marrying "well" are ruined for good. Adulterous men, in contrast, do not suffer such repercussions and are always free to look for a new partner.

The four-wives-per-man limit was supposedly one of Islam's more progressive tenets. Allegedly, the rule was originally intended to strengthen the rights of women. Back in the eighth century, a man could marry as many women as he wanted without giving a thought to how he would provide for the resulting families. And so, the upper limit of four wives was a step forward, a minor revolution. Women, who had few rights at the time, gained privileges through marriage. For example, if her husband died, a woman and her children could be taken up by her husband's brother. This made it possible for women to have a family even when few men were available, after a war for example. For the well-educated women of today the polygamous model makes very little sense, according to Syrian-German scholar of Islamic Studies Lamya Kaddor. She believes it's time to move on.

At the family get-together, Colonel Hasan leaves the women behind in their salon and walks into the garden, past the pool. He lights a fire and hands out sheepskin-lined Bedouin coats adorned with brocade. Winter nights are chilly in Riyadh.

The colonel's mother reclines comfortably on a bench beside the fire. She must have had Hasan, her first son, very young, because she doesn't look much older than him. She has jet-black hair and wears a leopard-print sweater, tight black leggings—and no abaya. Apart from me, she's the only woman here who can have contact with everyone in the household without putting on a veil. Colonel Hasan drapes a blanket over her shoulders. His younger brother from Jeddah rubs her feet. "Paradise lies at the feet of the mother," says Colonel Hasan, quoting a passage in the Qur'an describing the special intimacy between Arab mothers and their sons.

He helps his mother up and accompanies her to the table. The mother presides at the head and Mr. Hasan serves her himself: boiled lamb with plums, cinnamon, and cardamom. The sauce simmers in a glowing hot tajine. Also on the menu are

DINNER PARTY WITH THE LANDLORD: "I DO EVERYTHING TO MAKE THEM HAPPY."

vegetables, salad, and cola. Only when the mother of the man of the house has been served are the other women allowed to serve themselves: the daughter-in-law, the wives, the daughters—all of them veiled—line up with their plates. Each of them quickly takes a piece of meat from the tajine. Without saying a word, they return to the house.

WORSHIP YOUR MOM, OPPRESS YOUR WIVES

I ask Colonel Hasan if we can eat together to make it easier for us to talk. The table has been set for four: him, his mother, his brother, and me. The really small kids—boys and girls— are jumping around outside. Colonel Hasan's response isn't unfriendly, but it's resolute: The Creator made people different and He made the rules. One of them was that women should be treated as "queens" that require the protection of men. For me, his treatment of women doesn't come across as particularly royal. But I'm a guest in Colonel Hasan's house, so for the rest of the evening, we politely talk past each other whenever gender-issues come up.

One of the contradictions of life in the kingdom is that Saudi men worship their mothers, but seldom give their wives any space in which to grow and develop.

Here young boys are greeted by their mothers as "God's greatest gift" when they get up in the morning. It is the mothers who instill a sense of superiority and omnipotence in their sons— even over their sisters, and later their wives.

By contrast, girls are isolated from society at eleven or twelve. Until their wedding day, they spend most of their time at home. A driver brings them to school (and later college), which is, of course, strictly segregated by gender, and then picks them up again. After the wedding, the husband will make sure no other man ever sees his wife's face. Only when women are older—their strength depleted, and their youth expired—are they rewarded for their sacrifice. Then the world opens up for them.

Colonel Hasan is in his late fifties, maybe early sixties. He wears a white *thawb*, the traditional ankle-length robe, and leather sandals. He has a gray-blond beard. His English is excellent, thanks to his pilot training in the US. When the young Air Force officer returned to Saudi Arabia in the early 1980s, the dark times had only just begun. Radical imams took control of the mosques. The clerics stoked up fear of Satan and the afterlife. To this day, many Saudis are terrified of burning in hell for eternity because they haven't followed the rules of "true Islam" to the letter.

For Mr. Hasan, this new, even greater devotion to faith made absolute sense at the time. To this day, he is a zealous believer in "true Islam." When the religious police arrested sinners and brought them to the correctional services, who would then publicly beat them with rods, this was simply the right way of putting society on the correct path.

The 1980s were the height of the oil boom. Many Saudis amassed substantial wealth, built houses, hired servants, and took expensive trips abroad. More and more oil fields were discovered. Settlements and streets rose out of the vast desert. The country developed rapidly. Ministry and administrative buildings were erected. To oversee the process, the government hired tens of thousands of international consultants and engineers who needed to be housed. Colonel Hasan entered the construction business. Today, he owns several apartment complexes right behind Tahlia Street, one of the best neighborhoods of Riyadh. Thanks to his wealth, he was able to marry multiple times.

"A GOOD HUSBAND IS A STROKE OF LUCK"

My friend Nora gets me access to the secret world of women. Nora lives with her husband and their two kids in a neighborhood near the foreign ministry. Their home is a modern stone house with a small garden. Naturally, they have a driver and a maid.

Nora knows second and third wives who nobody talks about. She knows women who divorced their husbands because they married a second time. She knows women who were forced to divorce when their husbands took on new wives. In Saudi Arabia, men have the right to divorce at any time without providing a reason. Until recently, they didn't even have to inform their wives, but a new law has ended the practice of "secret divorces." Now women must be informed of the intention to end a marriage and have access to all official documents.

I want to find out from Nora how women cope when their competitors become legitimate members of the family. Do the wives sit together at breakfast? Do the new half-siblings get along, or are there rivalries and conflicts? And who inherits the husband's wealth?

A good husband is an absolute stroke of luck, says Nora. A second wife is "an imposition," just like anywhere else in the world. She tells me that richer, older men in the countryside are more likely to marry several wives than young urbanites. The older ones make an effort to adhere to the rules that come with polygamy. One such rule is that wives have an alternating right to "their night." And when it comes to gifts, all women must be equally considered—in terms of both the number and the value of the presents.

Nora tells me about a male coworker at her office who married a younger second wife. He is in his mid-thirties and is now being harassed by the first wife who is his age. "Our generation doesn't accept this anymore," she says.

Why do women accept becoming second or third wives? Don't you always feel less valued if you're not number one? Doesn't polygamy turn women into rivals?

It turns out that a woman will accept being a second wife if the relationship ensures that she will rise to a higher social class. Everything is put into a written contract: the value of the dowry, the size of the house she will live in, what kind of car will be available, whether she'll have servants, and if she will, how many.

MORE WOMEN THAN EVER ARE FILING FOR DIVORCE

The children of the second or third wife have a lesser standing in the social hierarchy than those of the first wife, but they receive more attention from the father, says Nora. That must have been the case with the thirty-four-year-old heir to the throne, Mohammed bin Salman. His father, King Salman, is now eighty-four. He has sons from his first marriage in the 1950s. According to tradition, one of them should succeed him. But Salman designated his favorite son Mohammed, the first child of his third wife, to become crown prince.

Compared to Catholicism, in which divorce isn't seen as an option, Islam is very pragmatic when it comes to marital separation. The fact that the number of divorces has almost reached half of the number of marriages celebrated in the same year has shocked the land of the pious. In 2017, each day 149 marriages were terminated in Saudi Arabia, according to Saudi statisticians. Many marriages fall apart in the first year and the divorce rate is rising steadily. Women who work, in particular, are filing for divorce more frequently.

To find out why women get divorced, I visit a psychotherapist who has been practicing in Saudi Arabia for ten years. She asserts that most married women in the country are deeply unhappy with their life partner and are simply glad if he doesn't lock them up or beat them. Of course, the people who come to her office are those who are experiencing problems. It's hard to say how many couples are actually happily married in Saudi Arabia.

For decades, women and children have been dependent on their *wali* or guardian in almost every respect, whether he's sweet-tempered or a tyrant. The male guardian had to consent when a woman applied for a passport or wanted to travel. If a married woman left the country, her husband was sent a text message by the authorities. A woman required her guardian's signature to give birth in a hospital or to be released from prison. If he didn't sign, she would simply remain incarcerated.

Most of these laws were recently repealed or replaced by less restrictive versions. But the traditional rules observed by families show no signs of changing anytime soon. The struggle to stand up to possessive men and claim their new freedoms still lies ahead for women in the kingdom.

I ask the psychotherapist what happens to women after they get divorced. I assume poverty, depression, social ostracism. The answer surprises me: "They throw a party and eat cake!"

A few days later, I read about it in the newspaper. Divorce parties, writes *Arab News*, are the hottest thing. There are bakeries that specialize in divorce cakes. In the paper there is a photoshopped image of a cake with pink icing. On one side of the cake is a fighting couple. On the other side, you see the woman who is happy because she's shoved the man over the edge of the cake. Beneath, written in sugar frosting, is the message, "Problem solved—enjoy!"

CAKE FOR THE DIVORCE PARTY: WOMEN HAVE BEGUN TO GIVE THEIR HUSBANDS HELL

So, things are clearly improving for women, right? Their lives must be better today than they were ten or twenty years ago. Astonishingly enough, Nora is not so sure. Since women have begun giving their husbands hell if they take a second wife, more and more men have been resorting to *misyar* or "secret marriage." *Misyar* wives don't appear in public. They are discreet lovers that nobody knows about. *Misyar* marriages are arranged by agencies and performed in secret. The matchmaking service can cost between five and ten thousand dollars.

Both spouses forfeit the right to live together. The husband comes and goes at arranged times. She has no claim upon his time or his financial support. He can't expect her to do any housework. But he gets custody of any children resulting from the relationship. A sheikh certifies the contract.

SECRET SECOND MARRIAGES

For divorcees or women over thirty-five—who often have a hard time finding a husband—*misyar* can be an emergency solution. "A divorcee is like a used car that has lost a lot of value," an acquaintance of mine explains. It doesn't help to point out that all of Prophet Mohammed's wives, except one, were either divorced or widowed. In the past, single women could use *misyar* marriage to acquire a male guardian. Although women have no financial security under such an arrangement, they are free to do more or less whatever they want.

Nora says that *misyar* marriages destroy families. They are growing in popularity, but are, according to her, a form of legalized prostitution. The first wives sometimes find out about the second family, at the very latest once the husband has died. The social position of the secret wife is problematic. In a conservative society, a woman must rely on her officially married status. Her social standing is based on her background and her unspoiled beauty, and of course how many sons she bears for her husband. A *misyar* wife has no standing. She is invisible.

Nora has lived in Spain, Romania, and Venezuela. She travels to Europe every year. "Men are the same everywhere," she claims. She remembers witnessing a fight over a husband's infidelity in Caracas. The husband of a European diplomat had an affair with her closest coworker of all people. The relationship lasted for years. Is that any better?

Polygamy is seen more positively in Saudi Arabia than just about anywhere else, thanks to the nation's founding myth. The first ruler, Ibn Saud, united the many rival tribes first by defeating and killing their leaders and then by marrying their wives, uniting the nation in the flesh, so to speak. With his seventeen wives (never more than four at a time), Ibn Saud sired forty-five sons. The current monarch, King Salman, is one of them.

CAR COWBOYS

WHEN YOUNG SAUDI MEN MEET FOR DAREDEVIL ILLEGAL CAR RACES, DEATHS ARE DISTURBINGLY FREQUENT. BUT "DRIFTING" IS ABOUT MORE THAN JUST BEING RECKLESS.

Sa'id is the little brother of Abdullah, a software engineer. Abdullah sends photos over WhatsApp. The images catch me unprepared: a young man in jeans and a faded blue T-shirt, lying in the back seat of a car that has slammed into another vehicle.

In 2016, some nine thousand people died in car accidents in Saudi Arabia, more than one fatality an hour—a quarter of the annual auto-related deaths in the United States, a country with a population more than ten times the size.

I had met the victim, Sa'id, by chance at a family dinner three weeks before. We sat on the floor together and ate Sa'id's favorite meal—chicken with rice, fresh tomatoes, and peppers—and washed it down with cola. He was in a great mood. Sa'id was basically just a kid, a guy who liked to play catch with his little nieces from next door. And who loved racing cars.

Now his mother cries every night. Aged nineteen when he died, Sa'id was her youngest son. During the day, she suppresses her tears. "Sa'id's life had only just begun," she wails when I see her again and try to console her. Her bright clothing stands out against her dark hair. She is fifty-six.

The cars sped toward each other at stomach-churning speeds. Neither driver wanted to chicken out. Skid marks on the asphalt speak of the drag races and car stunts that are the obsession of young Saudi men. You see them everywhere, in the city and on remote desert roads. Favorite stunts include spinning your car as fast as possible or standing on the roof while the car goes up on two wheels.

Joyriding Saudis seem to be mimicking what they imagine is the unbridled lifestyle of California youth. But it's about more than

reckless driving and a testosterone-fueled addiction to danger.
Young Saudis get drunk, steal cars, get chased by the police.
Usually, they steal small, common Hyundai sedans from their
own neighborhoods.

GUTS AND GLORY

Search online for "drifting in Saudi Arabia" or "crazy drifting"
and you'll find videos of races ending in near misses or tragedy,
like when a driver is thrown out of his car, rolls over, and ends up
motionless on the ground.

SIDEWALL SKIING: A KINGDOM OF OUTCASTS.

How can one explain mass-scale illegal car racing? Why do
so many young Saudi men get sucked into this madness? The
French anthropologist Pascal Ménoret submerged himself in the
scene for four years. In his book *Joyriding in Riyadh: Oil, Urbanism*

and Road Revolt, he argues that this is how young men rebel against police repression and state and religious surveillance. They're rebelling against a world that is too small for so much testosterone. It's their way of expressing their need for more agency and more autonomy.

Joyriders have created a parallel kingdom, a kingdom of outcasts with its own rules, in which misfits become celebrities. The drifting kingdom's currencies are guts and glory. The country seems to have too little of either on offer for the average lower-middle-class Saudi.

Abdullah and Fahd, a twenty-six-year-old photographer, aren't drifters, but they're huge fans. They go to the races, which are announced on social media like the hottest secret parties. The drifting scene brings together the desire to escape and a space where young men can create something together.

I meet the young men at an art gallery in the north of Riyadh to talk to them about their country. The gallery lies in a concrete wasteland on the fringe of the city, not unlike the post-industrial creative locations you find across the Western world. There are studios, a lounge, a coffee bar. This sort of thing is new for Riyadh. The guys here aren't different from young men in the West. Some wear traditional Arab robes, some just jeans and T-shirts. They work as journalists, graphic designers, and lawyers. And they yearn for the same things that young adults want in the West.

"GIVE US ROOM TO BREATHE"

"I don't want to be stopped by anyone when I'm out with my girlfriend, neither by the police nor by my mother," says Masen, a twenty-six-year-old software engineer. "I don't believe in the separation of the sexes. If someone behaves badly, there's another way of dealing with it." He's proud to be a part of the change that's now occurring. It's just happening too slowly.

"We want bars and night clubs," says a thirty-one-year-old lawyer. He enjoys his trips to Morocco and Thailand. Once a month, he drives with friends to Bahrain, the small kingdom three hundred miles northeast of Riyadh. There, they can find everything that's still forbidden here.

To the lawyer's side sits Abd al-Malik, a marketing professional. "Before, we didn't have a normal life here," al-Malik, twenty-nine, says. "At least now they let us breathe."

Although their lives are far less restricted than those of women, young men in Saudi Arabia aren't free to do as they please. It is also expected that they conform to the demands of the older generation and follow the life plans their families have made for them. They too find it frustrating to be separated from the opposite sex.

Their grandfathers and fathers had their glory. They witnessed the rapid growth of their country into a modern state within a few decades, thanks to billions of petrodollars. Today, nearly two-thirds of the workforce is in some way employed by the state. The jobs are cushy. Working times are manageable and bonuses are paid regularly. But there won't be much left for the next generation. The oil boom is a thing of the past. Today, one in four men between fifteen and twenty-four is unemployed.

If possible, they escape. Young men often study abroad and remain there for as long as possible. Others, like Iskander, create their own fantasy world. The medical student from Medina has founded a secret Michael Jackson fan club. He and his friends imitate the King of Pop's dance moves, including the moonwalk, and know every one of his songs by heart.

MICHAEL JACKSON IN JEDDAH

I meet Iskander at ComicCon in Jeddah. Visitors are dressed as Superman or the Joker, Jack Sparrow or Star Wars clone troopers. Girls go as Wonder Woman doppelgangers or Disney's evil fairy, Maleficent. Iskander shows up as Michael Jackson, of course, sporting a black wig, makeup, leggings, and a short red tailcoat.

Comic fairs like this originated in the US nearly half a century ago and now take place around the world, even in Saudi Arabia. It's one way the government hopes to disperse young people's frustration. Events like these are a pressure valve, releasing tension, preventing an explosion.

Here, men and women eat burgers and fries together, chill out on bean bags under the clear blue sky, and listen to music—just like young people all over the world. "For one day I can be someone I'm never allowed to be," says Iskander. ComicCon lasts for three crazy days. Then the dream goes up in smoke.

Saudi millennials are living in a state of transition. The old Saudi Arabia is long gone. A new one is still in the making. Recently, the government started effectively sending low-wage workers from Bangladesh and Pakistan back to their home countries by imposing penalty fees on employers who hire them. They call this "Saudization." The government wants young Saudis to become plumbers and to work in construction—for low wages if need be.

FREEDOM, RISK, UNCERTAINTY

For decades, the government provided handsomely for Saudi citizens. People were kept passive with good state jobs, bonuses, and gifts. Young Saudis won't see any of this. The kingdom can't afford it. In recent years, the once fantastically rich country has lost hundreds of billions of dollars of its former wealth.

AFTERMATH OF A DEADLY CAR ACCIDENT: LOOKING FOR A WAY TO LET OFF STEAM.

Nevertheless, the young heir to the throne, Mohammed bin Salman, promises the younger generation a glowing future. Under his plan, "Vision 2030," Saudi Arabia is supposed to morph into a diverse, modern, and moderate place. The strict laws of the *Wahhabis* present an obstacle to this ambitious restructuring, so many rules are now being loosened. If MBS gets his way, the religions of the future will be nationalism, entertainment, tourism, and sports. It's a future of amusement parks, innovative industries, five-star hotels, and modern mega-cities—all powered by renewable energy. And, if you believe the crown prince, this glittering future will offer fantastic opportunities for entrepreneurs and investors.

Yet in the eyes of many young Saudis, the future is riddled with risk and uncertainty. Of course, they see the pop concerts, the monster truck shows, and the spectacular Formula E electric car races. But they also see little happening at large construction sites and investors pulling out of projects. They know that the state has had trouble paying its bills on time. In short, they feel things are headed in the wrong direction.

Sometimes, conversations here remind me of the end of communist East Germany after 1989, where citizens were exposed to the brutality of the free market overnight. They could finally enjoy the freedoms of capitalism that they had longed for, but no longer had secure jobs or a guaranteed apartment. Old certainties crumbled—as did the security that the old system had provided.

SPEEDING TOWARD A PRECARIOUS FUTURE

What will life be like for a young Saudi from As-Suwaidi or Al-Masha'il in Riyadh's poorer south, once the state's resources have been exhausted? Will he work construction during the day and moonlight as an Uber driver at night, as his wife staffs the supermarket checkout? While people believe that the royals continue to hold decadent whiskey parties in their palace basements?

The drifters probably can't put a name on what or whom they're rebelling against, and yet they are hitting their opponents where it hurts. Clerics, police, and the elites feel threatened by the daredevil drivers. They represent a serious danger to the established order. These are marginalized kids from poor neighborhoods, and their spectacular, gruesome deaths are a brutal kind of performance art.

Car-drifters have been around since the start of the oil boom in the 1970s. They were emblematic of the country's transition to the modern era, a time when oil was the motor of growth and progress. Joyriding has since become a mass phenomenon, and the drifters' raw creativity is the language of the street.

While these young men speed toward an uncertain future, most older men have long since landed on secure ground. They spend their time fretting over fluctuating share prices or battling diabetes and obesity. But they are relics of a bygone era.

One such older man, a surgeon, invites me to his friends' *istiraha* in the desert, thirty minutes outside of the city. *Istiraha*s are traditional men's retreats. The word means "where you seek relaxation." In Russia, it's the dacha. In the US, it's the weekend house. Here, it's a mud hut in the country or a Bedouin tent. In the east of Saudi Arabia, they're called nakhla—a plot of land with palm trees. Men gather there, the way a group of friends in the US might meet up for poker night.

The *istiraha* I'm visiting is an expansive tent with several small extensions. It's decked out with thick carpets, plush sofas, a stove, and a fireplace. A dozen men are chilling out, playing baloot, a popular card game immigrants brought to the Arabian Peninsula a hundred years ago, similar to the French game belote.

The men are fifty, sixty, seventy years old. They work in government ministries, embassies, or offices. Some are retired. They've been coming here to be together three times a week for decades. They've built up careers, started families. And they help each other out. Here, life's problems get solved quickly.

Egyptian romance movies with famous actresses like Shadia or Soad Hosny are playing on a flat screen. A cook roasts chicken in a wood-fired oven. Chicken or lamb with rice is a favorite dish among men in this part of the world, perhaps one of the few things that nearly all men of all generations and classes have in common. For dessert, there is milk pudding with pistachios.

Shishas are smoked. A servant brings tea and the glowing coals that keep the steaming glasses hot.

Outside, the stars shine bright over the desert. There's no other way of putting it: these gentlemen have a nice set-up out here in their Bedouin tent—as nice as it can get without women.

THE MEN'S RUNNING GROUP, OR HOW MR. ZAYD LOST HIS GROOVE

IN 1979, THE VIOLENT SEIZURE OF THE GRAND MOSQUE OF MECCA BY ISLAMISTS FUNDAMENTALLY CHANGED SAUDI ARABIA. A CIVIL ENGINEER RECALLS THE PAINFUL TRANSITION TO ULTRA-CONSERVATIVE ISLAM—WHEN HE WAS A YOUNG MAN IN LOVE.

On Ibn Ammar Street in central Riyadh, it's nearly as quiet as an alpine meadow. The guttural calls of the muezzin occasionally fill the alleyways, but there is otherwise not much noise. There are no children playing, no cars, no pedestrians. Here, people conduct their lives behind walls.

The stationary, couch-potato lifestyle has become a national epidemic. 13 percent of Saudis move their bodies for less than one hour per week. They never walk and always drive. Only the poor, foreigners, or weirdos ride bikes. Occasionally, young men ride through the city on fashionable racing bikes, because that too is now possible in the new Saudi Arabia. But it goes without saying that women don't cycle. That would be indecent. Seven out of ten Saudis are obese. Stomach reduction surgery is the new big thing.

Since I arrived here, I've also become a homebody and only leave the apartment when I have an appointment. But after nearly three weeks, I've had enough. I want to get outside and move my body. But where do I go?

NO CHILDREN PLAYING, NO PEDESTRIANS IN SIGHT.

I phone a German friend who has a solution to every problem. He tells me he jogs with a men's group three times a week. As luck would have it, his group is meeting today!

We drive to a house in the north of Riyadh. Half a dozen Saudi gentlemen sit together in a guest room. There are benches along the walls. Anyone introduced by a friend is welcome. Not much happens at these get-togethers. The men hang out, they either talk or don't say a word. Sometimes the news is discussed. Problems, large and small, get solved.

RITUAL FROM A BYGONE ERA

The room belongs to a larger house where several brothers live with their families. The host, Abdulaziz, presides over an empire of construction companies. He comes across as self-confident yet reserved.

He's not bothered by the fact that I'm a woman. As long as I'm not a Saudi woman; naturally, they're not permitted to participate in this kind of men's night. Only Western women have the privilege of access to both female and male worlds— which, by the way, is the same in Afghanistan, Pakistan, and Iraq.

Qahwah, coffee made from lightly roasted beans, is served in a bulbous silver pot. The refills keep coming automatically until you swing your little cup back and forth. The ritual harks back to former times when bigwigs hired deaf servants to ensure they wouldn't overhear confidential information.

Finally, the athletes muster up enough energy for the run: a Brit, a Saudi, my German friend, and me. The men's running group.

One of the few jogging paths in Riyadh runs along the walls of the newly built Ministry of Education. Mr. Zayd, a civil engineer and a long-time colleague of the contractor-king, leads the group at a frighteningly rapid pace. Next month, he turns sixty. The fact that I'm running around a government ministry with three men I barely know, with uncovered hair, without a veil, with just an abaya over my sweatpants, is still a minor sensation.

For some reason, as we run, Mr. Zayd begins to recall his young days when he had no worries. A youth that was robbed from him when the new strict religious rules were introduced. He was nineteen years old at the time, says Mr. Zayd, a student. Back then, you could listen to music in public. Most women did not wear a veil. Their coats reached down to their thighs, not to the floor. He had already met his future wife, Amira, a friend of his sister.

MODERN JIHADISM IS BORN

The country has always been very conservative and the devoutly religious always present, "but they didn't dominate our society," Mr. Zayd says, puffing along, as we circle the ministry. The lives of men and women weren't completely segregated the way they are today. It was the height of the oil boom and the country was developing into a more modern nation, thanks to the countless expatriate specialists from the US and Britain.

A cataclysmic event changed everything—an event that, in hindsight, is seen by many as the birth of modern Jihadism. On the morning of November 20, 1979, a Tuesday—the first day of the year 1400 of the Islamic calendar—hundreds of heavily armed Islamists stormed the Grand Mosque of Mecca, in the middle of which is situated the Kaaba ("the House of God"), making it the holiest site for Muslims.

RADICAL ISLAMIST JUHAYMAN AL-OTABI: PHONES, TV, AND CARS ALIENATE MAN FROM GOD.

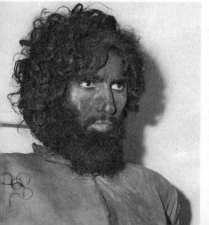

The leader of the terrorist squad was Juhayman al-Otaybi, forty-two years old, with broad cheekbones, thick black hair, and a shaggy beard. He was the son of a Bedouin family from Al-Qassim Province in the center of the country. Al-Otaybi was educated at the Sharia Faculty of the Islamic University of Medina. There he was a student of Abdulaziz bin Baz, one of the most reactionary Saudi theologians of the twentieth century, who eventually became the Grand Mufti of Saudi Arabia in 1993. At university, al-Otaybi wrote angry essays condemning modernity and the corrupt Saudi state. He believed that the telephone, television, and cars separated man from God. He detested the House of Saud, to him it consisted of nothing more than corrupt lackeys of the West. His dream was to provoke a religious uprising against the king.

That morning in the mosque, the rebel leader snatched the microphone from the imam. To the worshippers' astonishment, he introduced a young man as the "Mahdi," the redeemer announced in holy scripture who would appear to the people before the Day of Judgment. The royal guards opened fire, and a gunfight broke out. Minutes later, the first victims lay dead on the mosque's white marble floor. It took two weeks to end the occupation of the Kaaba. Hundreds were killed.

HANDCUFFED IN 115-DEGREE HEAT

For the Saudi monarchy, the incident was a disaster. "The Protector of the Two Holy Cities" of Mecca and Medina, as the Saudi king is officially titled, had to call in French Special Forces to end the occupation. The fact that "infidels" liberated the Kaaba was, in the eyes of the devout, an inexcusable disgrace.

Mr. Zayd is circling the flowerbed at the end of the Ministry of Education. Halftime. We've jogged three kilometers. The civil engineer bends down to stretch, agilely touching the ground with his fingertips. "You could say the trail of blood began back then in Mecca," he says, breathing deeply and standing upright once more. By "trail of blood" he means the death cult of al-Qaeda. The seeds of Bin Laden's infamous terror cell were sown by Juhayman al-Otaybi on that November day in Mecca. It was the beginning of the "Holy War" against the House of Saud. A war that continued when al-Otaybi's spiritual brothers flew airplanes into the World Trade Center in 2001 and then continued with brutal terrorist attacks in London, Madrid, Paris, and Berlin.

The Mecca crisis tested the legitimacy of the king. The monarchy had a long-standing pact with Wahhabi clerics. The attack forced King Khaled to shore up his power while at the same time appeasing the ultra-conservative religious establishment. He hoped to kill two birds with one stone by giving the clerics a free hand to impose harsh rules on the population as a way of keeping them under control.

Before long, the religious police of the Committee for the Promotion of Virtue and the Prevention of Vice were patrolling the streets. From then on, women were only permitted to leave the house accompanied by their father, brother, or husband— their *wali*, or guardian. Any other contact between men and women became haram—forbidden.

WOMEN IN PUBLIC: FUNDAMENTALISM BECAME A TOOL TO CONTROL ALL ASPECTS OF SOCIETY.

To show their devotion to God, women had to cover their faces, and preferably their feet and hands as well, even in 115-degree heat. To this day, many Saudi women place an additional dark gauze veil over the *niqab*, so that even their eyes are concealed from the desirous looks of men.

Until King Salman weakened the enforcement powers of the "virtue-protectors" some thirty-five years later, the religious police would even raid market sellers who sold women's gowns to check if they were offering abayas with decorative details or in colors other than black.

Seen from a historical perspective, this was an effective strategy to appease the country's elites and suppress the potential for unrest among the people.

THE DEVIL'S MUSIC, WICKED DRINKS

The royal family's power is based on a pact made between the ultra-conservative cleric Abd al-Wahhab and Ibn Saud in 1744. It was agreed that Abd al-Wahhab and his descendants would control religious and social affairs, while Ibn Saud would see to military and political matters. Both leaders wanted to establish a state. Neither of them could do it alone, so they swore their allegiance to one another and promised to share power in a future kingdom. The Faustian pact between the Al Saud and the Al Sheikh—as the descendants of al-Wahhab are called because the scholar was reverently called ash-Sheikh at the time—still holds today.

The puritanical *Wahhabi*s banned tobacco, alcohol, and music. Playing the oud, a traditional string instrument, could get you branded a wicked person who seduces women with intoxicating sounds and leads them to give up their chastity.

Mr. Zayd has always loved the movies, even as a teenager. He's especially passionate about films from the heyday of Egyptian cinema in the 1970s and 1980s, when films critical of society were common, not unlike those in the West. But while Western society continued to progress, Saudis' freedoms were radically cut. "Finished!" says Zayd the civil engineer, mimicking the hand gestures of a strict dad telling his kids they're grounded. Naturally, movies were added to the long list of forbidden pleasures. We—the men's group and I—are moved by Mr. Zayd's story and stop jogging. We stroll the last few yards to the ministry's exit.

ONLY ONE STEP AWAY FROM HELLFIRE

The life of young Mr. Zayd took a drastic turn in 1979. No more picnics with his girlfriend while listening to music on the tape player. Mr. Zayd had to marry Amira so that he could keep seeing her. Only when he had earned enough money as an engineer and could afford to travel was he able to watch movies while abroad. His kids—two daughters and three sons—grew up in a totally different world. The sexes were segregated, and young girls were forced to wear the veil. Clerics taught them they would burn in hell for eternity if they made one wrong move.

Fundamentalism became the instrument of absolute social control. The strict rules formed a bulwark against the revolutionary ideas that had infected neighboring countries, first Egypt and then Iran. The people of both nations had expelled their monarchs and proclaimed republics. The Persian shah, Reza Pahlavi, was overthrown in Tehran just months before al-Otaybi's attack in Mecca. The Sauds hoped to ward off a similar fate—by any means.

We've burned 540 calories and run 6,205 meters according to the tracker on the British friend's wrist. All of us are happy about that, even Mr. Zayd. As always, the men will hang out in the guest room for the rest of the evening. Abdulaziz, the construction mogul, has a surprise for us: a movie starring the "Cinderella of Egyptian cinema," Soad Hosny, made in 1981, shortly after films were banned in Saudi Arabia. The film has a promising title, *People on the Top*.

BRIEF ESCAPES: THE MALLS

TRAVEL GUIDES LIST RIYADH'S GLITTERING MALLS AS MUST-SEE
SIGHTS. IN SAUDI ARABIA, THE GAUDY TEMPLES OF CONSUMPTION
ARE WHERE REAL LIFE HAPPENS.

In the burning hot desert, air-conditioned malls are the oases of
our era. The mall is a magical space, an artificial land of milk and
honey—although these days you're more likely to find Häagen-
Dazs and Coca-Cola. The most important thing about the mall
is that you get to see other people. After being holed up in my
apartment for days, I have an urgent need to people-watch. I'm
getting that gotta-get-to-the-mall itch myself. I've finished my
work for the day, and I've done the dishes. There must be more
to life.

The streets in Saudi Arabia are virtually devoid of people. Even
the capital's central squares are dead. Not surprising when
summer temperatures average 102 degrees. But society is also to
blame. Saudis believe public spaces are uncontrollable, sinful,
and should be avoided whenever possible. Seduction and crime
are lurking everywhere! That's why women and children usually
get into the family car through the garage, only to get out again
once safely behind walls.

A MALL IN RIYADH: SLEAZY MEN MIGHT FILM OUR WOMEN.

Travel guides name Riyadh's best-known malls as must-see sights, right behind the National Museum and Masmak Fort: Al Nakheel Mall, Centria, Granada Center, Riyadh Park Mall, the Kingdom Center. These indoor oases are some of the very few public meeting places in the country. For ultra-conservatives, these temples to consumption are an unholy bridge that leads directly from shopping heaven to actual hell.

SORRY, NO FITTING ROOMS

Rules about clothing are usually posted at mall entrances, as they are outside churches in Southern Europe: "No shorts, no bare arms, no unusual hairstyles." Sometimes when you're shopping, the lights go out and the shutters go down, meaning it's prayer time. Five times a day, all of the stores close for thirty minutes. Shoppers know to give themselves plenty of time.

To fit in with the fashions of my new home, I head to the elegant Centria Mall, where I find a women's boutique. With a heap of tunics and floor-length dresses over my arm, I look for the fitting room, in vain. The concept of trying on clothes before buying them is alien to the Saudis. The reason is obvious: sleazy men could hide cameras in the changing rooms in order to film women. Here, women buy all of the clothes they're interested in, try them on at home, and bring back everything that doesn't fit. Somewhat confused, I hand the clothes back. Later I will decide to shop like the locals.

Men don't have it easy here either. Up until King Salman's ascension to the throne in January 2015, unmarried men weren't allowed to enter a mall without their mother or sister. It was believed young men would frequent the mall solely for the purpose of hitting on young women. They weren't so far off the mark. Until recently, the religious police kept guard and made sure that unaccompanied single men stayed outside.

These guardians of virtue are known as *mutawween*. They have long shaggy beards and wear high-water robes. Supposedly, this is the way the Prophet Mohammed's supporters dressed back in the seventh century. Back then, the rich and the vain wore extra-long robes, so a too-short robe was seen as a sign of modesty.

If the mutawwa spotted a sinner at the mall, they would throw him out, insulting and shaming him, or maybe take him down to the local station. There they would decide whether the sinner should be taken back to his family home for punishment by his own father, transferred to the justice system, or—in case he was uncooperative—dealt a few blows to the head.

SAUDI WOMAN SHOPPING: PUBLIC PLACES OFFER TEMPTATION AND LEAD TO RISKY BEHAVIOR.

If I spend more than an hour at my local mall in my hometown of Berlin, with its more than one hundred shops and all its excesses, I get depressed and start asking myself whether shopping is a way of compensating for my neglect of real life. Have I lost contact with nature and the things that matter? In Saudi Arabia, though, I am so starved for contact and consumption after being cooped up in my apartment for three weeks, that I delay the drive back to my place with a visit to the mall's very own spa—and then a visit to Bateel, the kingdom's finest chocolate maker. I try the latest praline creations made with nougat, date mousse, and brittle.

In the end, I sit, happy with my purchases, on the roof terrace of the Centria Mall. Men and women have been permitted to sit here together at the same table for some time now. Allegedly, women are permitted to smoke—a real insider's tip. The long-bearded mutawween still exist, but they were stripped of their power to arrest people in April 2016, surely a milestone on the long road to an open society. As a result, women have a good deal more freedom of movement.

The surprising thing about the religious police's loss of power is that it met with very little resistance among clerics. To this day, there have been no protests in mosques, no critical tweets. Not a single imam in Saudi Arabia has publicly criticized the king's decree. An explanation could be that most imams' salaries are paid by the state and the security apparatus listens to the orders of the government. Apparently, Saudi religious leaders have very worldly fears about their income and their freedom. These days, a few critical remarks can quickly land the defiant in prison.

I manage to find a member of the religious police who is willing to talk. Sulayman surprises me. He's forty-eight years old, has the obligatory beard and shining eyes, and wears a black bisht, a linen robe with gold trim. His *ghutra* rests loosely on his head. I meet him in a mall in Riyadh. He invites me for an Arabic coffee in his office down the street. "Is this loss of power a problem for you?" I ask. "Do you fear that young people will be morally ruined?"

The mutawwa seems pretty pragmatic. He says that God guides the king and, therefore, he follows the king. "Whether it's right that the mutawween no longer support and guide the Muslims so that they do not stray from the path, that is beyond my wisdom," he says cautiously. He tells me that he has a personal relationship to God, according to which he raises his children. One of his three daughters is studying abroad, in France, and her brothers went along to watch over her.

In everyday life, the new liberalization often clashes with state-sanctioned religious rigor. A few days after the meeting with Sulayman, while in Riyadh's best-known mall, the Kingdom Center, I observe a mutawwa chastising two women at a marble perfume counter because their heads are uncovered. The mutawwa shouts that the women are neglecting their religious duties, that they're sullying the Holy Land and will soon be roasting in hell for eternity. Half of the shoppers on the floor witness the spectacle. The two women briefly turn toward the fuming moral policeman, then shrug their shoulders and direct their attention back to the perfumes.

Five minutes pass, until the frustrated guardian of virtue gives up and withdraws from the scene.

WE'LL GET YOU:
DEATH OF A DISSIDENT

Jamal Khashoggi was an influential insider with exclusive access to the Saudi ruling elite. When he went into exile in the US and publicly criticized the policies of the crown prince, the leadership in Riyadh pegged him as a traitor. For that, he had to die.

On October 2, 2018, the day that Jamal Khashoggi disappeared, I was visiting Dammam, a city in eastern Saudi Arabia. I had met Jamal for the first time seven years before, and we'd kept in contact since then. Every now and then we'd catch up, meeting in Riyadh or Jeddah. After he went into exile in the US. in 2017 we Skyped occasionally. Jamal was an invaluable contact for me and many other journalists.

Over the ensuing days, I followed the news of his disappearance—and the subsequent revelation of his murder—with utter disbelief. The word "dismembered" kept appearing in Turkish police reports. Sound recordings proved that Khashoggi was tortured, killed, and hacked to pieces.

BREAKING NEWS
LIVE
CNN: SAUDIS PREPARING TO ADMIT KHASHOGGI WAS KILLED
Sources: Will say death was result of interrogation that went wrong
9:18 PM CET
STAY WITH CNN FOR MORE ON THIS & THE LATEST INTERNATIONAL NEWS

CNN LIVE IN MY HOTEL ROOM IN DAMMAM.

There was talk of a bone saw, brought by a team of hitmen from Riyadh. Disguised as tourists, the death squad flew to Istanbul and stayed just long enough to kill and dismember Khashoggi inside the Saudi consulate. It turned out that one of the agents belonged to Crown Prince Mohammed bin Salman's personal security team. There was also mention of a forensics officer who knew a thing or two about cutting up bodies.

The packages containing the remains were brought to the consul's residence a few hundred feet away in a van with darkened windows. In Saudi Arabia, it is rumored that the remains are probably still there, possibly buried in the garden. Or did the Saudi men take Jamal's body parts back home in their suitcases? Later, some speculated that his remains might have been dissolved in acid. As of writing, the remains have not turned up.

Before Khashoggi decided to go into exile in the US, he was one of the kingdom's leading journalists, or at least one of its best connected. The first time we met was in 2011 and it was a thousand feet off the ground in an office with floor-to-ceiling windows at the Kingdom Center, Riyadh's tallest building. It was the time of the Arab Spring.

Change was in the air. The political mood was shifting. Back then, Jamal voiced incredibly risky thoughts: "The era of the absolute monarchy is over," and "Democracy is the only solution." Any other Saudi journalist uttering these words publicly would have been thrown into prison.

JAMAL AND OSAMA WERE OLD PALS

At the time, Khashoggi was working for one of the richest men in the Arab world, Prince Al-Waleed bin Talal, a nephew of King Abdullah. From his office in the Kingdom Center, Khashoggi was launching a TV channel for the prince. It was a classic move for a billionaire who wanted to expand his power and influence. The plan to launch a private TV station in order to shape the political debate was considered a special provocation by the Saudi leadership. The monarchy smelled rebellion and revolution. Khashoggi's sponsor, Prince Al-Waleed, was considered progressive, non-conformist, a reformer.

Khashoggi felt comfortable moving in these high circles. He knew the royals better than anyone, he was well-informed about internal rivalries over politics and business within the House of Saud, and he worked under the protection of various powerful sponsors.

The country was in a state of upheaval. Those who had expressed independent political ideas under King Salman's predecessor, King Abdullah, quickly got their wings clipped.

KHASHOGGI'S OFFICE AT AL-WALEED BIN TALAL'S KINGDOM HOLDING (2011):
"I'M REALLY ANGRY, BUT I'M STAYING CALM FOR NOW."

KINGDOM CENTER: THE TALLEST BUILDING IN THE COUNTRY.

After four years and millions of dollars invested, the TV station set up by Khashoggi went on air in Bahrain. When I congratulated him, instead of the expected enthusiastic response, I received a short and rather dry reply: "Thanks, but they shut us down after ten hours. I'm really angry, but I'm staying calm for now."

Before this, Khashoggi had worked as a media consultant for Prince Turki bin Faisal, the former head of Saudi intelligence, who served as ambassador in London and Washington.

Through this connection Khashoggi enjoyed unfettered access to inside information that even leading Saudi politicians could only dream of. He knew the future leader of al-Qaeda, Osama bin Laden—son of a Yemeni, the wealthiest construction contractor in Saudi Arabia—before he became radicalized and formed his terror network. Back in the 1970s, Bin Laden and Khashoggi, almost the same age, sympathized with the ideology of the Muslim Brotherhood.

The two of them met again in the 1980s, when Khashoggi worked as a reporter in Afghanistan. He interviewed Bin Laden in a Tora Bora cave—a hideout for the *mujahideen*—and several more times later in his life. He showed me a photo taken there of himself with Bin Laden and his fighters, all of whom were armed with AK-47s. He emailed me the shot, which is printed in the photo section of this book.

In the 1980s, Bin Laden was still considered a hero in the struggle against the Soviet invaders in Afghanistan, even by Western intelligence services. At the time, Bin Laden and the West shared the common goal of driving the Red Army out of the country.

AUTHOR (RIGHT) INTERVIEWING FREEDOM FIGHTERS IN ONE OF THE TORA BORA CAVES, WHERE OSAMA BIN LADEN PREACHED TO HIS FOLLOWERS (2001, NOVEMBER).

In the early 1990s, Bin Laden fled to Sudan and declared war against his own country. Osama bin Laden and Jamal Khashoggi remained in touch. The Saudi leadership hoped to use the connection between the two men and hired Khashoggi as an envoy to negotiate a peace agreement between Bin Laden and the regime. In 1995, Khashoggi traveled to the Sudanese capital Khartoum to convince the terrorist leader to return home, but he failed.

THE KING IS THE LAW

Much of what goes on in the kingdom can only be understood if you have access to information from the innermost circle of power. Why the royal family supports particular religious leaders inside the country and certain militant groups outside the country, while persecuting others, for example.

PRINCE TURKI BIN FAISAL, FORMER HEAD OF SAUDI SECRET SERVICE AND AUTHOR (2015): JAMAL KHASHOGGI, WHO WORKED FOR TURKI BIN FAISAL FOR QUITE SOME TIME, HAD A DEEP UNDERSTANDING OF THE ROYAL FAMILY'S SECRETS. LONG CONSIDERED A TRUSTED INSIDER, HE WAS CLOSE TO MANY INFLUENTIAL PEOPLE.

The fact that Khashoggi had access to such insights made him a valuable contact for analysts, diplomats, and journalists. He acted as an intermediary and served the kingdom well in that role. Yet the very moment he left the sphere of loyal insiders, he became a dangerous player for exactly that same reason.

When I returned to Riyadh in the fall of 2017, I reached out to Jamal as usual, suggesting we meet over coffee. "I've moved to the US," he wrote back. "It became suffocating. I was banned from writing and was afraid it would get worse, so I've decided to go into exile."

What he didn't mention was that his wife had remained in Saudi Arabia. When she tried to join him in the US, she was told at the airport that she was barred from leaving the country. Since Jamal couldn't return to the kingdom for security reasons, the regime forced the couple to divorce.

I experienced the news of his death very differently in Saudi Arabia than I would have had I been in Europe. The situation felt horrifying. For weeks, the state denied any responsibility for the hideous murder. I became painfully aware of the despotism under which people lived. I asked myself what was next for Saudi dissidents and nonconformists. The CIA was certain that the crown prince had ordered the killing personally. If that was true, what would it mean when this young man assumes the throne?

What happened sent a clear message to anyone who might wish harm to the king and his powerful son. In essence, it read: Nobody is safe from us. All the power is with us. No matter where you are in the world, we'll get you.

In the days after Jamal's murder, my Saudi friends remained silent, lowering their gaze when I brought the story up. They changed the subject. "It's too dangerous. Here, everyone knows someone in prison. The West is getting worked up about Khashoggi's execution," a friend of mine commented. "Yet there are so many Khashoggis."

If you haven't grown up in an absolute monarchy, it's hard for you to imagine what crime Khashoggi could have committed to deserve such punishment. For most Saudis, the incident makes perfect sense. Jamal Khashoggi was once at the top, he was one of them, as it was explained to me in Riyadh. "He betrayed them. That's why he was executed."

Khashoggi's case demands we accept that no reliable legal standards apply in this country beyond the facade offered by impressive institutions and government officials. There is no possibility of an impartial investigation, no independent public prosecutor, or judge. In short, the king is the law.

"IMMEDIATE RETALIATION"

"I am envious that you can spend time in Saudi Arabia," said Jamal, when we talked on the phone in the fall of 2017. He was homesick. It was painful for him to leave his old life, his family, and his work behind. Friends had warned him he would be in danger if he stayed. Countless activists and acquaintances had already been imprisoned.

He was banned not only from writing his weekly column in the *al-Watan* newspaper, but also from publishing in *al-Hayat*, which is widely read in nearly every Arab country. Khashoggi was even banned from using social media.

Of course he knew he was in danger. Critics are usually warned once or twice. Those who ignore the warnings are banned from traveling and quickly end up in prison. After Khashoggi went into exile, one of his friends, a wealthy Riyadh businessman, confirmed that "Jamal would have gone to prison if he had stayed here."

According to Khashoggi himself, he ended up on the crown prince's blacklist because he criticized the way King Salman's regime had sucked up to the Trump administration. There's no space for public discussion anymore, Jamal once said. "Since MBS became crown prince, they retaliate immediately."

After Khashoggi's disappearance, the Saudi stock exchange, the Tadawul, crashed. There was a massive sell-off by foreign investors wanting to pull out of the country. This was a direct result of the horrifying news about Khashoggi, and it infuriated the Saudis. An acquaintance told me he lost 30,000 riyals (about $8,000) in a single day. Like many middle-class Saudis, the forty-three-year-old family man had invested in big state companies, particularly in Sabic, the huge petrochemical corporation.

A MAFIA-STYLE ORGANIZATION?

In late October 2018, hundreds of international investors had planned to travel to Riyadh for a big conference—after being personally invited by the crown prince. The event was nicknamed "Desert Davos," yet, in the aftermath of the Khashoggi killing, many business leaders canceled. The CEO of JPMorgan Chase, Jamie Dimon, called off his attendance, as did Ford chief executive William Clay Ford and Siemens boss Joe Kaeser, who came under tremendous public pressure to withdraw from the event. CNN said that it could no longer be a media partner under such circumstances. *New York Times* writers fell in line and canceled their flights to Riyadh.

Appearing on *60 Minutes*, President Trump vowed "severe punishment" if it was confirmed that Saudi agents were involved in Khashoggi's murder. He didn't specify what such a punishment would entail, but one could imagine sanctions or an arms embargo. Trump's threats didn't last long. Two hours later, the president explained that he had phoned the Saudi king and crown prince. He claimed that both had vehemently denied having any knowledge of the operation. This is when freestyling Trump hatched a theory that lets everyone off the hook: "rogue killers," assassins from within the security apparatus, might have acted independently.

Trump didn't want to endanger trade with Saudi Arabia, especially their flourishing arms deals. The weapons trade secures jobs for Americans. He said out loud what a lot of other people are thinking: his predecessor, Barack Obama, acted no differently, but he used a more diplomatic choice of words. Obama distanced himself politically from Saudi Arabia but sold the kingdom weapons all the same—to the tune of $115 billion, more than any previous US president.

A short while later, the US Senate passed a resolution naming Crown Prince Mohammed bin Salman responsible for the murder. The US imposed sanctions upon seventeen Saudis, with Saud al-Qahtani at the top of the list. The crown prince remained unscathed.

British writer John Bradley worked with Jamal Khashoggi at various Saudi newspapers. Bradley has deep insights into the mechanisms of state power. In his view, the House of Saud operates "like the mafia." The ruling clan follows its own laws exclusively, and has no scruples. According to Bradley, Khashoggi agreed to join the club. Unfortunately for him, "it's well known that the mafia only makes lifetime contracts," Bradley said following the death of his colleague. Jamal tried to leave the organization and paid the ultimate price.

KHASHOGGI OPPOSED THE ABSOLUTE MONARCHY

The crown prince's lack of self-control is now well documented beyond the Saudi royal court. It's not hard to imagine how MBS reacted when Khashoggi wrote about his political failures in columns and essays in respected international newspapers: the war in Yemen, the Qatar crisis, the alleged kidnapping of Lebanese Prime Minister Saad Hariri.

Khashoggi and MBS had diverging visions on how Saudi Arabia should be governed. The crown prince defended his absolute power. Khashoggi hoped for democratic transformation. When Jamal spoke with Western colleagues, though, they probably didn't exactly share his same vision of democracy. Khashoggi's coworker Bradley claims that the journalist never dreamt of a pluralistic democracy modeled after the West. For him, "secularism was the enemy," Bradley writes. Khashoggi's ideology was close to that of the Muslim Brotherhood, which strives for a republic based on Sharia law. He believed that such a form of government should replace the absolute monarchy in Riyadh.

In exile, Khashoggi founded a political movement called Democracy for the Arab World Now, with the optimistic acronym DAWN. The group was supposed to grow into a formidable political movement by banding together moderate Islamists.

His ideas were popular. He had 1.7 million Twitter followers. Through his various channels of influence, he had grown into a political force in his own right. For many, his ideas provided a viable alternative to those of Crown Prince MBS.

The House of Saud fears nothing more than having to share its power with the people. From their point of view, there were plenty of reasons to make Khashoggi disappear.

IN THE NORTH:
WITH THE PROUD SHAMMAR,
WHERE MEN CAN STILL BE MEN

THE MEN OF NORTH CENTRAL SAUDI ARABIA ENJOY ALL THE
COMFORTS OF MODERN LIFE. BUT IN THEIR TIME OFF, THEY DREAM
OF LIVING AS FREELY AS THEIR BEDOUIN ANCESTORS.

It's six in the morning when the plane lands in Ha'il, three thousand feet above sea level in the north of the country. Abd ar-Rahman picks me up from the airport. He's going to introduce me to the world of the Shammar, a Bedouin tribe with an extraordinary and storied past.

On the phone, Abd ar-Rahman told me that the spirit of the Bedouins lives on to this day on the long "sand ridge" of the Nefud Desert—meaning their pride, their sense of honor, and their famous generosity. Naturally, my guide is also referring to himself.

Abd ar-Rahman, fifty, is a land surveyor. He has a head of thick black hair and an artfully sculpted goatee. He wears a woolen tank top, a tweed jacket, and a gray *thawb*. It's pretty cold up here this morning, no more than forty degrees.

In his Jeep's passenger seat sits his friend Ali, a heavyset man with dark skin wearing a dark robe. Ali laughs a lot, showing his big yellow teeth. His eyes twinkle as we speed through the pale morning fog into the land of the Shammar. The broad plain of the Ha'il Province is how I imagine the moon: dusty, dotted with craters and mountains. A shimmering light-blue sky.

In reality, the kind of Bedouin who tends sheep and drives camels through the dunes chasing the rain has become a rarity. Only a few hundred thousand of the kingdom's thirty-four million inhabitants live like the nomads of old. Since the early twentieth century, the monarchy has systematically resettled

BEHIND THE KINGDOM'S VEIL

Bedouin tribes in oases and ports, to have better control over them. This is how the large cities of Saudi Arabia arose. Yet the myth of the Bedouins as a people who feared nothing but the sky, who have crisscrossed the endless deserts since ancient times, is alive and well today. The people of the Arabian Peninsula see their roots in the Bedouins.

THE SAUDS' OLD RIVALS

Abd ar-Rahman slams on the brakes and points to the left, toward a dark rock formation that rises for hundreds of feet. Light desert sand has accumulated at its center. "The hand of God!" he says, beaming with reverence.

I squint to get a better look. Ali explains that the boundaries of the Kingdom of Saudi Arabia are clearly recognizable here. Everyone understands "the sign."

"We have to show her the village," says Abd ar-Rahman.

This place feels very different from Riyadh. There is something almost spiritual about the absence of urban development and the vast landscape with its spectacular rock formations.

Here in Ha'il, the Shammar are the dominant tribe. The House of Rashid is a clan within the tribe. Famously, the Rashids were long-time rivals of the royal family in Riyadh, the House of Saud. In their heyday, the Rashids' influence reached well beyond the borders of today's kingdom, into Jordan and Iraq. They were known as the rulers of Jabal Shammar (the Shammar Mountains). Between the two clans, the fight for dominance of the Arabian Peninsula lasted for two centuries.

With help from their Ottoman allies, the Rashids drove the Sauds into exile. However, in April 1906, the Rashids were defeated decisively by the founder of the modern Saudi state, Abdulaziz bin Saud, in a fierce battle with hundreds of casualties. By 1921, the Jabal Shammar region was fully under Saudi control. Although both sides took heavy losses, these wars of subjugation are celebrated today as the "unification" of Saudi Arabia.

A GRAVE FROM ARABIAN NIGHTS

The village Abd ar-Rahman and Ali want to show me is a series of ruins dating back to the sixth century. Still visible are crumbled mud-and-straw walls, storage rooms, sleeping chambers, and terraces, all spaciously laid out and long abandoned. A watchtower overlooks the settlement—from up here, visitors and enemies could be spotted at a distance. Next to the tower lays a cemetery where unadorned graves are marked by ovals of stone.

Abd ar-Rahman explains that the famous Shammar leader, Hatim at-Tai, is buried here. His story became one of the folk tales in *Arabian Nights*. Hatim at-Tai appears in the book as a kind of "Hans in Luck," an extremely generous man—the more he gives, the more he receives.

Hatim's proverbial generosity is the root of a common expression in the Arab world. To pamper guests, to share with friends, to show generosity "like Hatim at-Tai," even if it costs you the last lamb in the house, is considered one of the most honorable Bedouin virtues. "That's how we are," says Abd ar-Rahman. Ali stands beside him at Tai's grave, nodding.

Hatim at-Tai was a Shammar ruler and poet who lived in the late sixth century. An orphan, he was raised by his grandfather. According to legend, little Hatim bartered away everything his grandfather owned, including his best camels. He exchanged them for moving poems and stories, which he then embellished and retold himself.

Naturally, as a Shammari, my host Abd ar-Rahman is also "like Hatim." To belong to such a proud Bedouin tribe creates a strong identity that has little to do with citizenship. It means having a profound connection to the place where your ancestors stuck it out in the face of hardship and adversity.

Like most people in the northern provinces, Abd ar-Rahman doesn't live in a tent. He owns a house in a pleasant neighborhood. Water comes out of the faucet at the right temperature, and the AC keeps the house cool in the summer and warm in the winter. The four-lane road is well-lit. Everywhere you look are telephone wires and satellite dishes. Nonetheless, Abd ar-Rahman feels connected to the world of the past.

The stories of the early desert dwellers are told in huge petroglyphs preserved for all to see in an open-air museum. The scenes were chiseled into the hard rocks, yellow on copper-colored stone. Some of the depictions are seven thousand years old. They tell of hunts, battles, births, and deaths.

The presence of strong female figures is notable. In one rock drawing, a woman stands in the center of the action. She has long hair and wide hips—a symbol of her fertility. She is surrounded by warriors and animals. Her hands are stretched out as if she ruled over the world like a goddess. Saudi photographer Madeha al-Ajroush documented this fascinating testimony to Saudi Arabia's prehistoric era in her 2016 photography book *reSURFACE*.

MUSEUM PIECES SAUDI-STYLE: A PROUD COLLECTION OF EARLY TVS, RADIOS, AND TELEPHONES DEMONSTRATE THE DIZZYING SPEED OF HISTORY.

Part of the romanticism surrounding the Bedouins comes from the fact that Abd ar-Rahman's desert ancestors tended to show their generous side just after they had ambushed a caravan and shared their spoils with others in a big feast around the fire. The hardships of life were shouldered primarily by women. They did most of the hard work: milking, skinning animals, preparing furs, making clothing and tools.

The nomads divided their tents into two halves with colorful swathes of fabric or *gata*. One half was reserved for women and children, as well as for storing food and possessions. In the other half was a firepit. This was the male area, where tribesmen would foster their friendships and devise plans for the clan.

CAMELS AT A WELL IN A SHAMMAR VILLAGE: PRESERVING THE OLD WAY OF LIFE.

FOURTEEN-YEAR-OLD MOHAMMED: "IT'S LEGAL NOW, BUT I WILL NOT ALLOW MY MOM TO DRIVE."

MEN'S COUNTRY

Abd ar-Rahman went to college. He's an engineer, a respected professional who worked his way up the formal hierarchy of a state ruled by the Saud dynasty, who his ancestors once fought with swords. Abd ar-Rahman doesn't have many positive things to say about his ancestors. Today, he's a loyal subject of the king.

Like most Saudis, Ali also works for the state, but in a lower position than Abd ar-Rahman. Ali is the son of an unskilled worker who had nineteen children with four wives but never provided for his offspring. Ali buys water at the gas station. He's always ready to help when Abd ar-Rahman asks for small favors, and he keeps quiet while his friend is talking.

We arrive in Jubbah, a town near the provincial capital Ha'il. We enter a small house, a kind of windowless cave. They call it a *sheba*, which translates as "campfire." The walls are blackened by a layer of soot. This is the domain of men.

SHAMMAR TRADITIONALISTS CELEBRATE THEIR BEDOUIN ROOTS: TEA AND TALK IN A MUD-BRICK "SHEBA."

The *sheba* is a Bedouin hut built by Abd ar-Rahman's friends for their private get-togethers. *Shebas* have been around for about eighty years, ever since the nomads began to settle down. Their day-to-day life has become easier, but their yearning for the simple life in the desert remains strong.

The men meet here after the first dawn prayer and again after the *isha* or nighttime prayer, once the last red shimmer of dusk has disappeared. Food is served on brightly colored Bedouin plates. The carpets are thick and made of dyed wool. The men get comfy on the colorful cushions. It feels a little like a lodge where men hang out with their hunting buddies.

BRINGING HOME WIFE NUMBER TWO—
AN "UNAVOIDABLE EARTHQUAKE"

Abd ar-Rahman has to take several hectic phone calls. A lot of different people seem to be calling. He answers with consoling noises: "Yes," "No," "Soon." He rolls his eyes, looks to Ali for help.

A young man hands Abd ar-Rahman some fresh coffee, heated over the open fire.

A year ago, Abd ar-Rahman married a younger woman—his second wife. When he brought her home to meet the family, there was an "explosion," he says. He's been married to the mother of his five children for twenty-four years, but she simply refuses to accept the new domestic reality, i.e. having wife number two around. "What should I do?" laments Abd ar-Rahman.

Ali consoles his friend: "Such an earthquake is unavoidable." He can't afford a second wife, so he only has one. But as the son of a man with four wives and nineteen children, he is very familiar with constant fighting in the home—quarrels about which of the wives was his dad's favorite. The kids also competed for their father's affection, over the insufficient amount of food, or to see who should get a new shirt or shoes.

Abd ar-Rahman says he owns a splendid 21,000-square-foot plot of land on the edge of Jubbah where his house stands. He's now built a second house at the other end of the land. A small one, for the new wife. He feels his wives should have as little contact as possible.

In Jubbah, there are a good dozen *shebas*. They are more than just retreats for grown men. They are also a kind of school of life for boys where they can see how their fathers solve problems. Today, males of almost every age are here, the youngest are aged ten and fourteen.

"As a husband, you must have the patience of a camel," says an elderly gentleman sitting on a large square cushion, the host of the evening. The seventy-year-old wears a white *ghutra*, the traditional headdress. "If you have just one wife, you have to tame your hunger like a pack animal in the desert. And later, when you have new wives, you must learn from the camel and become desensitized to external changes in the weather."

"You shouldn't talk back!" advises Ali. "In one ear and out the other." Ali points to one ear and then to the other.

Statistically, every twentieth Saudi man has more than one wife. In some regions, like Ha'il, they have more than in others.

"We're not liberal here," clarifies a young man with a hostile expression and a long beard. His pants are extra-short. No doubt a mutawwa, one who believes in the radical doctrine of Abd al-Wahhab. "We don't want anything to change here," he says. Obviously, he's bothered by the presence of a Western woman.

He despises any deviation from social traditions, and hates open societies like those in the West. Women's rights and liberalism, as they are understood in Europe, are dirty words in his language.

ULTRA-CONSERVATIVE MEN IN HA'IL: "WORKING WOMEN ARE LESS COMMITTED TO THEIR HUSBANDS."

Over the past few weeks, Crown Prince Mohammed bin Salman has introduced some far-reaching social reforms, turning old certainties on their heads. Women are now allowed to drive, work, and participate in sports. And pop musicians are being flown in from America. All of this is also supposed to come to Ha'il, after religious leaders have spent forty years telling people that Satan mercilessly punishes exactly those activities and that anyone who promotes such sinful behavior will roast in hell. The men I'm with are having a hard time acting as if they approve of these latest developments.

A man in his forties with a neatly trimmed beard and a brown Bedouin coat with red check lining tries to explain. Women, he says, are less committed to their husbands if they work. Another man nods and tells the story of his cousin who married a nurse. He wanted to go on the *Hajj*—the pilgrimage to Mecca—with her, but she had to work on holidays. That's how the couple's troubles began. "She doesn't pay him enough attention."

The door flies open. A boy steps into the smoke-filled hut. It's Abd ar-Rahman's fourteen-year-old son, Mohammed. He holds a set of car keys and says he's just driven his mother to the women's *sheba*, as ordered by his father. Abd ar-Rahman's first wife, Muna, is now waiting for me there.

I ask Mohammed if his mother will drive him to school now that women are allowed behind the wheel. "She won't drive," Mohammed replies. "I won't allow it."

Muna is forty, ten years younger than Abd ar-Rahman, a stocky woman with shoulder-length hair which she wears loose. She greets me with three kisses on the cheek. The women's *sheba* is a robust tent permanently erected in a field. Four other women, all close relatives, have joined us. Here, women seldom make new acquaintances. All of them have taken off their veils. They sit comfortably in skirts and blouses. We eat grape leaves stuffed with rice and pomegranate seeds.

When I bring up the subject of driving, there is little agreement among the five women. Most of them feel such reforms are unnecessary. The discussion reminds me of the Swiss canton Appenzell-Innerrhoden, where female lobby groups boycotted the women's right to vote until 1990. In the West, this was considered exotic. Here, however, women are so isolated that they can hardly imagine playing a visible role in society.

MUNA IS SILENT IN HER PAIN

One woman stands out. She is younger and comes across as self-confident and a little snarky. She wears blue eye shadow and discreet lipstick. Aziza teaches Islamic Studies at a girl's school. "I would like to drive," she tells the group, "but somebody would have to teach me." Aziza's words don't sound like an accusation, but it's clear to all that her husband doesn't support her wish. There's not much a royal decree can do to change that. At the end of the day, women are still dependent on the consent of their male guardians. Later, I find out that Aziza married only recently. Her husband is a relative of Abd ar-Rahman. She is his third wife.

Aziza is thirty-six, an age at which some Saudi women have already become grandmothers. She received no previous marriage proposals. People say that she was considered too demanding, too brash. When an offer finally came, she went for it.

Abd ar-Rahman's first wife, Muna, does not utter a single word about the existence of her husband's new partner. The feeling of rejection is the same in all cultures. It's painful when your man finds a new lover. And yet the Qur'an grants men the right to marry four women at the same time, as long as he treats them as equals. In practical terms, it means that he spends one night with one wife and then the next night with another. Not all women accept this rule, and many are consumed by envy and jealousy. And yet everyone involved makes an effort to keep up the appearance of an intact family. Muna remains silent about her pain.

After the evening prayer, the men's *sheba* fills up again. The host with the white *ghutra* offers us fresh fruit. The mood is relaxed, but Abd ar-Rahman is still conflicted about which of his two houses he will return to tonight.

The host looks at him with his old man's eyes and reveals how he found peace as the husband of two women: He always keeps four weeks of supplies and camping gear in his SUV. "Just disappear if it gets too much. After ten days at the most, the trouble will have blown over."

IN THE EAST:
WITH THE SHI'ITES, WHERE OIL
AND TROUBLE CAN BE FOUND

THE REBELLIOUS SHI'ITE SHEIKH NIMR BAQIR AN-NIMR WAS
LOVED BY YOUNG BELIEVERS AND DETESTED BY THE SAUDI
REGIME. HIS EXECUTION IN 2016 UNLEASHED A STORM OF VIOLENT
PROTESTS. THE SHEIKH'S BROTHER TELLS ME THE STORY OF THE
STRUGGLE AND HOW IT ALL ENDED.

The Sheraton Hotel is probably the most public place in the
city of Dammam. In the swanky foyer, Mohammed an-Nimr sits
across from me in a leather armchair. He orders fresh pineapple
juice. An-Nimr is the brother of the Shi'ite sheikh Nimr Baqir an-
Nimr, who was decapitated by a Saudi executioner on January 2,
2016.

The Saudi security forces—always worried about the country's
international reputation—are never pleased when critics of the
regime or their relatives meet foreign journalists. I am concerned
that our conversation could spell trouble for an-Nimr. But
an-Nimr insists on this public meeting place. He doesn't have
to hide his views, he tells me. Besides, the secret services know
everything about him anyway.

We meet in 2018. Mohammed an-Nimr is fifty-four and the
younger of the two brothers. He has gray hair and a goatee.
His white *thawb* is freshly laundered and ironed. He gives off
a reserved, polite impression. Mohammed an-Nimr's life is an
endless purgatory. His twenty-four-year-old son Ali has also been
sentenced to death by beheading. After the decapitation, Ali's
head is supposed to be sewn back onto his body, which will then
be crucified. The sentence could be carried out at any time, and
Ali's father is "95 percent sure" that the execution will take place.
He visited Ali three days ago, an-Nimr says. He is only permitted
to see his son for one hour per month.

Mohammed an-Nimr imports Chinese construction materials to Saudi Arabia. Trade is slow. The businessman has been banned from traveling for the past three years. His phone calls are monitored. His email is read and archived by Saudi intelligence.

Until a few years ago, the an-Nimr family lived under a single roof in Al-Awamiya, a small town inhabited by Shi'ites with a population of 25,000, twelve miles north of Dammam. Most of the Shi'ites in Saudi Arabia live in the Eastern Province. Between one-in-ten and one-in-eight of the approximately twenty-two million native Saudis adhere to the Shi'ite confession, but no one knows the exact number.

TODAY THE CITY OF DAMMAM IS THE CENTER OF THE OIL-RICH EASTERN PROVINCE, MAINLY POPULATED BY SHI'ITES. IN 1802, SAUDI SOLDIERS CONQUERED THE CITY OF KARBALA AND DESTROYED THE MOST REVERED SHI'ITE SHRINES—THE WOUNDS REMAIN UNHEALED EVEN TODAY.

Relations between the Shi'ites and the Sunnis have always been tumultuous. The two main Islamic creeds fundamentally disagree about who was the Prophet Mohammed's rightful successor. The Prophet never conclusively appointed an heir. The Shi'ites believe Mohammed's son-in-law Ali to be the legitimate heir. Following the death of the Prophet, however, a group of early Muslims who would become known as Sunnis selected Mohammed's father-in-law and closest confidante, Abu Bakr, to be the first caliph, the spiritual leader of Islam.

Centuries later, the Shi'ites' distrust of the Sunnis was reinforced when, in 1802, Saudi soldiers conquered the city of Karbala—under the control of the Ottomans at the time—and destroyed the most revered Shi'ite shrines, including the mosque housing the tomb of the Prophet's grandson Husayn, the third Shi'ite imam. For the Shi'ites, the pilgrimage sites in Karbala and Najaf are nearly as important as Mecca and Medina. And the wounds remain unhealed until today.

In Saudi Arabia, the Shi'ites have been dominated by radical Sunnis for 275 years. In 1913, some years before the foundation of the modern Saudi state, King Abdulaziz sent *Wahhabi* militias to take control of the Al-Ahsa region. Just as they did a century before in Karbala, the Saudi soldiers destroyed Shi'ite tombs and mosques. They murdered and tortured people simply for following a different branch of Islam. Many Shi'ites fled to Bahrain or Iraq. But many remain to this day. The trauma still lies deep.

The struggle for dominance of the Gulf region between Shi'ite Iran and predominantly Sunni Saudi Arabia is currently fueling the mutual mistrust. The conflict in Yemen is just the latest in a series of proxy wars.

THE AUTHOR IN A NEWLY BUILT SHI'I MOSQUE WITH TRADITIONAL FEATURES (IN AL-AHSA): THE NEW CROWN PRINCE MOHAMMED BIN SALMAN MADE IT VERY CLEAR TO THE MINORITY SHI'I POPULATION THAT HE VALUES LOYALTY OVER RELIGION.

AGENT OF IRANIAN TERROR?

Nowadays, Saudi Arabia believes it is being deliberately targeted by a hostile Iran. Riyadh fears that Tehran is constantly trying to expand its sphere of influence as much as it can get away with. In the eyes of the Saudi monarchy, Iran supports every imaginable anti-Saudi militia on the perimeters of the kingdom. To the south, in Yemen, it's the Shi'i Houthi rebels. In the east, militant groups in Bahrain. To the north and west, Iran backs Hezbollah in Lebanon and Syria.

The Iranians, on the other hand, say that a religious minority needs allies wherever it can find them. After decades of isolation and the 2015 nuclear deal, Tehran is hoping to finally regain its old standing in the Middle East. But in May 2018 Iran experienced a major setback when US President Trump withdrew from the nuclear treaty. Another blow followed in 2020 when the COVID-19 epidemic hit and the oil-price war caused a dramatic drop to historic lows.

Riyadh is convinced that Nimr Baqir an-Nimr was an agent of Iranian terror. An-Nimr received his religious training in Iran in the 1980s. Following his return in the mid-1990s, he tried to stir up the Saudi Shi'ite against the government in Riyadh—with Iranian backing, according to the Saudi intelligence services. The alleged goal was to destabilize the kingdom from within.

It didn't help the sheikh much that he constantly denied being the extended arm of Iran. It is true, though, that many Shi'ites in the kingdom felt harassed and found a leader in the outspoken cleric. The sheikh expressed what they had long felt, and they would hang on his every word when he voiced things they wouldn't even dare think, like "We don't accept the House of Saud as our rulers. We want to get rid of them."

"WHY DO THEY HATE US?"

Because they are distrusted by the regime, members of the Shi'ite community occupy very few influential posts in the Saudi government, military, or police. To this day, the Eastern Province is one of the country's poorest regions, even though the oil that has made the country rich lies here. Officially, Shi'ites have long been banned from building mosques. They usually worship in their own homes.

In Saudi schools, children learn that those who do not follow "true Islam," or who don't "profess the oneness of God," are infidels. Consequently, everyone apart from the *Wahhabis* must be infidels, meaning Jews, Sufis, Christians—as well as the Shi'ites, of course. Students are advised not to greet infidels. They shouldn't befriend them or show them any respect at all.

After 9/11, Riyadh combed through the school curriculum for extremist teachings and anything inciting hatred toward people of other faiths. Some changes were made. For example, passages in which the *Wahhabis* openly justify the killing of non-believers were removed. Still, decades of intolerant teachings are buried deep in the consciousness of the Sunni majority and are still passed on to the next generation.

One day in Riyadh, I witness a conversation between a thirteen-year-old boy and his father, an IT worker. He's updating a program on my laptop when his son arrives home from school in a state of anxiety. Although he's just a kid with a good deal of baby fat, he's already been bullied because of his religion. Ahmad is a passionate soccer player. Sports are his life.

"Why do they hate us simply for being Shi'ites?" Ahmad asks. The father explains to his son: "They hate us because they have false information about us." At the same time, I can see the anger simmering under the surface. "My children and I live in two worlds," the forty-three-year-old tells me. "If the teachers knew my kids were Shi'ite, they would exclude them. Ahmad couldn't play on the soccer team. In the Kingdom of Al Saud, we are what African Americans are in the US."

Since the family moved to the capital, they have deliberately concealed their faith from neighbors, teachers, and classmates. They celebrate religious holidays such as Ashura—the Shi'ite commemoration of the suffering of the Prophet's grandson Husayn, killed in the battle of Karbala in 680—secretly and behind locked doors.

For Sunnis, the event has little significance. They also consider other details of Shi'ite practice nonsense—such as the belief that the Prophet's daughter, Fatima, could heal wounds by laying her hand on them.

HATE KILLINGS

The hate goes so deep it sometimes leads to acts of horrific violence. In February 2019, a taxi driver in Medina asked a passenger and her son Zakariya whether they were Shi'ites. They originated from Ash-Shoba near Al-Ahsa, a few villages away from where soccer fanatic Ahmad and his father come from.

They were on their way to the mosque housing the tomb of the Prophet Mohammed.

When the woman answered yes, they were Shi'tes, the man stopped the taxi and dragged the boy out of the car and into a cafe, where he broke a bottle and slit the boy's throat with a shard of glass. It was the spontaneous execution of an innocent child. The mother tried to save her son and subsequently collapsed in tears. A policeman couldn't do anything to stop the man, and eventually little Zakariya died from his wounds. The incident made headlines, but only outside the country.

"THEY STEAL MY MONEY, SHED MY BLOOD"

It's an extreme case, but it reminds me of something Sheikh an-Nimr said at a demonstration in 2011: "Since the day that I was born, I have never felt safe in this country."

During the Arab Spring of 2011, many Shi'ites in the Eastern Province hoped that the wave of upheaval would improve their situation. They yearned to be treated as equals, and huge numbers took to the streets to demonstrate. In central Al-Qatif, the masses filled the main thoroughfare, Al-Quds.

At that time, Sheikh an-Nimr was a key leader of the rebellion. The cleric was a wiry man with pronounced cheekbones. His graying beard made him look older than his years. He wore the white turban of Shi'ite scholars, and his eyes gleamed with defiance.

An-Nimr publicly called the Saudi king a tyrant and condemned the discrimination against the Shia. "What kind of country is this? This regime that oppresses me? The regime that takes my money, that sheds my blood and wounds my honor?"

An-Nimr was close to his then sixteen-year-old nephew, Ali. The teenager was a witty young man with a lock of dark hair that hung over the left side of his forehead. Ali handled social media for his uncle. He called for more demonstrations with the help of his Blackberry, in the words of the official indictment. Street fighting broke out between protesters and the police.

"THE WORMS WILL EAT HIM"

In February 2012, the secret services arrested young Ali an-Nimr. They picked him up one evening on his way to the pharmacy, where he wanted to get medicine for his mother. He never made it back home.

Ali's arrest was supposed to tame his uncle Sheikh an-Nimr, but it had the opposite effect. An-Nimr continued to publicly insult the powerful. When Nayef bin Abdulaziz, then crown prince and interior minister, died in June 2012, the sheikh shouted, "The worms will eat him, and he will suffer infernal torments in his grave. Because of this man, we lived in fear and terror. Shouldn't we rejoice at his death?"

Sheikh an-Nimr was finally arrested in July 2012, unleashing the rage of the Shi'ites in Al-Awamiya. Thousands took to the streets to demand the release of the religious leader loved by so many.

Residents of Al-Awamiya said that their city was home to a mafia who smuggled arms, drugs, and people. The mafia—in contrast to the demonstrators—were uninterested in finding solutions to improve people's lives. They managed to use the permanent state of tension between the government and the Shi'ite group around Sheikh an-Nimr as cover for their shady dealings.

The criminals were infiltrating the protests, said a demonstrator who was involved in the movement in Al-Qatif since the beginning. She said the mafia was interested in maintaining the status quo—a permanent small-scale war. "They deliberately became violent, causing the demonstrations to escalate." Everything went wrong from the start.

At least twenty-five Shi'ites were killed, countless were injured. The security forces also suffered casualties. The police struck back hard. There were interrogations. Prison sentences were handed down. Some were sentenced to death. The government offered the occasional olive branch, but the crisis of Al-Awamiya seemed to know no end.

Then the unthinkable occurred. On January 2, 2016, the regime executed Sheikh an-Nimr along with forty-six other protesters. It was the biggest mass execution in the kingdom in more than three decades. According to the verdict, the men were either guilty of adopting the ideology of the infidels or of joining terrorist organizations and committing criminal acts. The execution sent a clear signal to the people of Al-Qatif, but first and foremost to Iran, which the monarchy suspected of masterminding the protests.

STRONGHOLD OF THE RESISTANCE OF THE SHI'ITES, THE CITY OF AL-QATIF: THE RELATIONSHIP WITH THE SUNNI LEADERSHIP HAS ALWAYS BEEN TUMULTUOUS.

On the night after Sheikh an-Nimr's execution, an enraged mob gathered outside the Saudi embassy in Tehran. Demonstrators stormed the premises, hurled Molotov cocktails, and smashed windows. The offices were plundered and the building set on fire. The Iranian government did nothing to stop the destruction. It's as if the government tolerated, or even orchestrated, the attack. Relations between the two regional powers have since gone from chilly to ice-cold.

The fighting in Al-Awamiya developed into small-scale civil war. The security forces no longer distinguished between violent mafia provocateurs and political activists. About two hundred armed rebel fighters were entrenched in the town.

The military laid siege. More than 20,000 people fled their homes. Access points and central junctions in the city were occupied by the military, and those inhabitants who stayed behind risked being shot if they ventured outside. The facades of buildings were riddled with bullet holes.

ONLY THE LOYAL ARE SAFE

The armed rebels were finally defeated by government forces. The last pockets of resistance were suppressed. Calm returned to the city.

The conflict had become a nightmare for both sides. "People are exhausted by the fighting," said an Al-Awamiya resident in February 2018. "Everyone has experienced a death in the family or has a relative in prison."

The government began to rebuild the city. At the same time, the monarchy sent a clear message to its inhabitants: If you rise against us, we'll cut off your leaders' heads and we'll smoke out their spawn. But the new crown prince, Mohammed bin Salman, also made it clear to the Shi'ites that a better future awaited them if they showed loyalty.

The case of Al-Awamiya shows how hardened the fronts have become over the past few years. Of course, defamatory speeches like those of Sheikh an-Nimr always have explosive power in an absolute monarchy. Yet Riyadh's furious response was over the top.

Until then, the security forces would usually pressure protesters into backing down from their positions. Dissidents would be detained and interrogated. A deal would be made. Most of them would walk out of jail alive if they renounced their convictions and promised to never act against the regime again. Those who refused would remain behind bars, often until death.

However, Crown Prince Mohammed bin Salman made very clear that he values loyalty over religion, and made some positive changes. Shi'i ceremonies are now officially recognized, and some mosques where Shi'ites pray are under the protection of police officers.

Mohammed admits that his brother, Sheikh an-Nimr, said some very bad things. "But he didn't kill anyone. He fired words, not bullets. Why did they have to cut off his head?"

One possible explanation is that the Arab Spring was the beginning of a new era in the Middle East. When people began to rise against autocrats across the region, the royals felt the fragility of their grip on power for the first time.

A Western intelligence agent explains the developments thus: "The rulers in Riyadh have adapted to the new policy of the West, which wants to retreat from the troublesome Middle East, especially the US. In the old days, Saudi Arabia would do checkbook politics. Today, they're displaying robust self-defense." The monarchy sees that Washington is abandoning old allies one after the other, even close friends of the US like former Egyptian leader Husni Mubarak. When the Tunisian people overthrew the dictator Ben Ali, President Barack Obama left him to his own devices. Meanwhile, the Libyan dictator Muammar Gaddafi was chased to his death by a mob.

ON DEATH ROW

In Riyadh, the leadership is asking itself whether Washington is still a trusted partner. What are America's old security guarantees worth now? And what does it all mean for the future of Saudi Arabia?

When the Arab Spring reached Syria, the kingdom did exactly what its enemies accuse it of doing: it armed the Syrian opposition—together with Qatar—to destabilize the regime of Bashar al-Assad. Riyadh hoped to replace its former ally with a friendly Sunni ruler. Al-Assad became Riyadh's enemy when he strengthened ties to Iran and Tehran's allies, the Hezbollah in Lebanon.

Riyadh firmly believed that its American friends would send in Air Force bombers the next time the Syrian regime deployed chemical weapons against civilians. That was how the Saudis understood their agreement with President Obama. But the US President was reluctant to wage another war in the Middle East. Obama didn't even react when al-Assad stepped over his "red line" and again targeted civilians with chemical weapons. In turn, President al-Assad was able to count on the support of Iran and Russia. Now, Saudi Arabia and Qatar are the losers of this particular battle.

Riyadh became disillusioned for good when the US and five other nations signed a nuclear deal with Iran. With the election of Donald Trump, the Saudis briefly hoped everything would be as before. But even Trump did not send a single bomber to punish the alleged Iranian aggressors when Saudi Arabia's oil production was attacked in September 2019. Therefore the Saudis decided to take their defense into their own hands. Seen this way, Sheikh an-Nimr was one of the first victims of their new, robust foreign policy.

Sheikh an-Nimr's nephew Ali has been sitting on death row in Riyadh for the last eight years. Ali's father, Mohammed an-Nimr, says that Ali has always been a very angry young man, but he's become calmer now. He's even doing a correspondence course in business—as if he still had a future. But every time they come to get him—for a formality or another interrogation—the young man fears his time is up.

Mohammed an-Nimr sips his pineapple juice. During our conversation, he has barely touched his glass. "I feel I am in Allah's hands," he says, and attempts a smile.

SYRIA
DAMASCUS
AMMAN
BAGHDAD
IRAQ
Tigris
Euphrates
Kaf
Arar
Sakakah
Tabuk
KUWAIT
KUWAIT
Persian
Hafar Al-Batin
Ha'il
Jubail
Al Wajh
Buraidah
Al Majmaah
Dammam
Khobar
BAHRAIN
MANAMA
Umm Lajj
Hofuf
Yanbu
Medina
RIYADH
Salwa
Al-Kharj
RED SEA
SAUDI ARABIA
Mecca
Jeddah
Ta'if
As Sulayyil
Al Bahah
Al Qunfudhah
Khamis Mushait
Abha
Najran
Jizan
Farasan
ERITREA
ASMARA
YEMEN
SANAA
Gulf of Aden
DJIBOUTI
DJIBOUTI

ALCOHOL: HOW THE BUZZ GETS INTO THE BOTTLE

ALCOHOL IS STRICTLY PROHIBITED IN HOLIER-THAN-THOU SAUDI ARABIA. YET THE THREAT OF SEVERE PUNISHMENT DOES LITTLE TO STOP THE FLOW OF SMUGGLED OR HOMEMADE WINE AND LIQUOR.

Everything is ritualized in this country: how you're born, how you live your life, how you spend your youth, how you marry, and how you have children. Your life is strictly regulated, even after it's over. Whether beggar or king, everyone is buried in the same type of small, austere, unmarked grave. Such are the rules of the puritanical *Wahhabis*. Islam governs every detail of existence. Everyone knows the rules. Everyone sticks to them—at least on the surface, which means that life goes on without any major surprises.

To tolerate the monotony, people must summon supreme patience. Or else live a duplicitous life, like Abdulaziz. The thirty-four-year-old owns three supermarkets and a cafe. He spent three years in the US, where he attended art school in Miami. Abdulaziz's mother is an acquaintance of mine, an artist who I met at a reception. She invites me for dinner at her place. Afterward, she calls her son and asks him to drive me home because it's late.

Ten minutes later Abdulaziz is at the door, a man with cropped hair, jeans, a white T-shirt, and a blazer. He greets his mom with a bow. On the way out, he kisses her hand and takes me to his car, a silver C-Class Mercedes convertible. The drive home should take about fifteen minutes. Little do I know that I'm on a ride through Riyadh's shadow side.

The driver's-side door slams shut. Abdulaziz turns on the car stereo, reaches into the center console and hands me a steel beaker full to the brim with whiskey. Lady Gaga screams "Is that alright?" so loud, I bite back asking the same question and take a swig instead.

We speed down King Saud Road, pass the education ministry and swerve into the six-lane Al Takhassusi Street with its fancy furniture shops and swanky restaurants. I ask myself how many times Abdulaziz dipped into the console before picking me up. "No matter what you want, Susanne, whether it's an AK-47 or a bottle of champagne, I can help you," he promises. Now he's driving with two fingers on the wheel and a cup of liquor in his other hand. At the same time, he manages to show me a video on his iPhone X. A party last Friday, in Olaya, somewhere around the corner from me.

In the video, Saudis are dancing at someone's house: the men in *thawbs*, with and without *ghutras*, the women in expensive dresses, high heels, their hair hanging loose over their shoulders—young women of the Saudi upper class in other words. The music could just as well be playing in a club in London, Beirut, or Berlin. Nearly everyone is holding drinks, and they don't look like glasses of Coke.

"What if the police bust us?" I ask. As long as we don't slam into the next concrete pylon, this is a fascinating encounter. I'm getting a peek behind the scenes of an extremely closed society.

BASEMENT BARS, BOOTLEG LIQUOR, CALL GIRLS

The kingdom is one big village, Abdulaziz says. You just have to know someone who knows the mayor. The mayor of Saudi Arabia is, of course, the powerful Crown Prince Mohammed bin Salman. And the people you need to know when you have a run-in with the law are the people in his entourage at the royal court: ministers, governors, and other influential royals. Anyone without such a contact who is found drunk or caught with alcohol will be thrown in jail and lashed with a stick. Foreigners must pack their bags and leave the country.

I recall the case of an engineer whose European employee was busted for DUI in Riyadh. It required the concerted effort and the reputation of a befriended high-up government official to get the worker out of jail. He was sent back to Europe for a cooling-off period of a few months before he could return to Saudi Arabia.

In August 2014, the British oil executive Karl Andree was caught with homemade wine in his car in Jeddah. A court sentenced the seventy-two-year-old to 350 blows with the cane. Only through the intervention of British Prime Minister David Cameron was Andree set free—after fourteen months behind bars.

Meanwhile, Abdulaziz and I have arrived on Tahlia Street, one of Riyadh's grand boulevards. From here it's just a couple of blocks to my apartment. "You only see the surface," he says. "Saudi Arabia is much more diverse, much more colorful than the country you know."

Abdulaziz is right, of course. Diplomats talk about the wild parties among the ruling elite, like at a certain prince's palace in Jeddah. In 2009, US consular staff were guests at a royal party with 150 young, dancing Saudis, all of them in costumes. Working girls—a.k.a. call girls—had been hired to brighten the mood. Lurid details were released over WikiLeaks.

The strict *wahhabi* ideology never completely shut down the wild parties, one of the guests present told the US consul in Jeddah. It just forced the fun into the privacy of people's homes. Hence, many of the most opulent houses have basement bars, discotheques, and clubs.

Former Shell manager Paddy Briggs reports that no place in the world imports as much Johnnie Walker Black Label as the kingdom. Briggs lived in Saudi Arabia for decades and gets his information from a trustworthy Saudi insider who says that the distribution of liquor is organized by a high-ranking member of the royal family. No names mentioned, of course, but the high-proof evidence is not hard to find.

I can't remember the last time I had a drink. In my apartment, I imbibe tea and lemon water. When I'm feeling adventurous, I pick up a Holsten at the Indian store around the corner—alcohol free, naturally. The beer from Hamburg is sold in pomegranate and grape flavor.

Not only is alcohol prohibited in Saudi Arabia, in most Saudi families drinking is severely frowned upon. Believers consider even a connoisseur of fine wine to be an out-of-control person who has succumbed to Satan's seduction.

Whether the consumption of alcohol is actually sinful from a religious point of view is hard to pin down by reading the relevant Islamic texts. The trade and consumption of wine were apparently rather common in Mohammed's time. His Muslim contemporaries, the Salaf—the role models of the modern Salafists—were known to drink wine. The renowned Qur'an expert Hartmut Bobzin points out, for example, that alcohol isn't explicitly banned in the holy book. In Sura 16:67, intoxicating drinks are even endorsed: "And from the fruits of the palm trees and grapevines you take intoxicant and good provision. Indeed in that is a sign for a people who reason."

Passages in the Hadiths, however, are rigorously anti-booze: "Whoever drinks wine, whip him; then if he drinks again, whip him; then if he drinks again, whip him; then if he drinks again, kill him." The Hadiths are a collection of quotations and actions attributed to Mohammed and his disciples and, after the Qur'an, are considered to be the second most important source of Islamic teachings.

A WHOLE LOTTA FERMENTATION GOIN' ON

All the same, I'm happy when, two weeks after my encounter with Abdulaziz, I receive an invitation to a wine tasting. The vintners are Sophia from Romania and Janusch from Poland.

140

Both work as nurses in King Saud Medical City. Today, we'll be sampling their Cuvée 2018 with some snacks on their terrace.

Like most foreigners in Saudi Arabia, Sophia and Janusch live in a compound in the southwest of Riyadh. The compound is a collection of apartment buildings enclosed by a wall. Men armed with automatic weapons guard the gates. The underside of my taxi is inspected with a mirror on a stick, and I have to show my passport. In May 2003, two suicide attacks on compounds like this killed fifty-six people, an attempt by al-Qaeda to blast the infidels out of the country.

Behind the walls, life is a lot like in the West: no abayas, no separation of the sexes, bikinis at the pool. Alcohol, though, is strictly taboo. That doesn't stop people across Saudi Arabia from making moonshine like there was no tomorrow. Illegal brewing and winemaking are everywhere. When the Americans came to develop the oil fields, the oil firms banned their staff from bringing alcohol into the country. To make up for it, a very valuable recipe book circulated among expats, *The Blue Flame*. The book describes in great detail how to produce high-proof liquor, from simple vodka to orange liqueur. The book is now available online and is as popular as ever.

```
APPLE SHERRY

2 lbs. apricots (dried)
6 lbs. apples (windfalls will do)
1 gallon water
1 lb. raisins
1 cake shredded wheat
3 ½ lbs. sugar (less for drier wine)

1) Boil the apricots in the water until very tender, then strain the liquid off
   and use the apricots as food.
2) Cut up the apples (leaving skin and brown patches on) and pour the apricot
   liquid over. Squeeze and mash every day for 14 days, then strain all pulp out.
3) Add the shredded wheat, chopped raisins and sugar and leave to ferment 21 days.
4) Then skim, strain and bottle. Keep 12 months.

               ***********************
```

THE ORIGINAL EXPAT'S RECIPE BOOKLET: *THE BLUE FLAME* IS STILL AVAILABLE ON EBAY FOR THIRTY-FIVE DOLLARS.

Sophia, thirty-nine, is tall and skinny. She opens the door wearing a red strap dress, barefoot. Her black hair is loosely clipped to the back of her head with a colorful barrette. She lives in a small three-room house with a garden. As a nurse in Riyadh, she earns around $3,500 per month after taxes, ten times what she would earn back home in Bucharest. The house is free of charge. Janusch's apartment is two streets away.

Sophia takes me to a closet. We move a wall of water bottles and cans to one side. A precaution, in case there's a raid. Behind the barrier are three mid-sized glass demijohns, glass vessels like those that hold cider that I remember from my childhood in Germany. Each one contains about five liters of liquid. Two are red. One is white.

A few years ago, I visited a Swiss landscape architect on his farm outside of Riyadh. In the washroom, I heard bubbling and fizzing. Startled, I pulled back the shower curtain. Before my eyes was a full distillery with glass cylinders and transparent hoses. Through the ingenious glass contraption flowed a dark red liquid.

"RIYADH RED LANTERN 2018"

Sophia's production process is, by contrast, comparatively simple. The nurse mixes grape juice from the supermarket with yeast and seals the bottle's neck with a latex glove from the hospital. The yeast transforms the sugar into alcohol. Sophia can monitor the fermentation progress through the rising gases: as long as the glove's five fingers point upward, things are going well. Every few days, she rolls the bottles back and forth. After two or three weeks, the wine is ready for tasting.

In the end, it's all about trial and error, Sophia says. The right amounts of sugar, yeast, and movement result in a magical finish, the taste that is left on your palate after you swallow a sip of wine. The three of us relax on Sophias terrace, ready to test three

USED DISTILLATION EQUIPMENT: CROWN PRINCE MOHAMMED BIN SALMAN SAYS
ALCOHOL WILL NEVER BE LEGAL.

decanters of "Riyadh Red Lantern 2018," a fitting name for her current renegade concoction.

Sophia has produced a semi-dry late vintage white and a dry red cabernet. To go with the wines are fasoleb'tut', a Romanian bean puree with spicy paprika, and sticky Polish potato bread, which Janusch says is more difficult to make than all of the wines put together.

I can't decide which wine I prefer. The semi-dry white with potato bread seems like the best pairing. Without question, Sophia's terrace is the best bar in the city.

Crown Prince Mohammed bin Salman says alcohol will never be legal, not even for the foreign tourists who are supposed to frequent the classy new resorts planned at the Red Sea. "A foreigner who wants to drink should go to Egypt or Jordan," MBS suggests. If one believes the estimates of the former US consul in Jeddah, prohibition will merely keep prices on the thriving black market sky-high and won't stop Saudis from enjoying their whiskey and other intoxicating beverages.

EXPAT COMPOUND IN RIYADH: NO ABAYAS, NO SEPARATION OF THE SEXES, AND BIKINIS AT THE POOL.

I have to think about Abdulaziz, who, in the end, got me home safely. Before I left his party-mobile with the Lady Gaga soundtrack, he showed me a few images from out in the desert: men and women in their early twenties sitting in Jeeps, holding drinks, and sporting an impressive collection of firearms. He and his friends like to do a little shooting in the desert, Abdulaziz explains.

When every aspect of life is ritualized, even death and burial, people develop the need to escape the monotony. They will want to taste existence in all of its abundance, and do something that's completely different.

THE CROWN JEWELS:
OIL, POWER, MONEY

A POOR BEDOUIN ERRAND BOY WORKS HIS WAY UP TO BECOME
SAUDI OIL MINISTER AND ONE OF THE MOST POWERFUL
ECONOMIC POLICY MAKERS IN THE WORLD. THE UNLIKELY STORY
OF ALI AL-NAIMI IS ALSO THE STORY OF HIS NATION.

Shortly before the birth of his youngest son in a Bedouin goat-hair tent in the desert village of Ar Rakah, approximately where the bustling center of the oil town Al Khobar is now located, the pearl diver Ibrahim Ali al-Naimi decides to leave his wife Fatima. The young Bedouin woman is left alone to care for five children. Fatima is petite, barely four foot eleven inches tall. She was married at fourteen. The only thing her youngest son Ali will keep of his father's is the name of his tribe, Naimi.

Where the future boss of Saudi Aramco, the world's largest oil company and the most profitable corporation of all time, was born, time has stood still for centuries. The summer of 1935 is scorching hot in the eastern Arabian Peninsula, and the winter nights are bitterly cold. The farmers and Bedouins, cut off from the rest of the world, barely eke out a living.

Ali al-Naimi is four years old when he gets his first job. He tends to his family's sheep, but he can't count. Every day, when he comes home, one or two lambs are missing, so his uncle builds a trap to snare the wolf that is killing the lambs grazing in the dunes. The wolf is caught in the trap; he is shot and skinned. The kids each get a chunk of wolf's meat, which tastes salty.

The predator's meat is believed to protect children from evil spirits or djinn. They appear in different forms. Some of them are shape-shifting and hide their true intentions in order to inflict as much damage upon humans as possible. Ali is given a wolf's tooth, which his uncle hangs around his neck. It is meant to bestow strength upon him.

The only girl among the five children is weak and eventually dies. "We were survivors," writes Naimi.

"THE MOST IMPORTANT MAN YOU'VE NEVER HEARD OF"

Naimi, as he is known to the world, tells this story in his 2016 autobiography, which he publishes at the age of eighty-two. They were hard times, but not unhappy, he writes. The hardship made people tough. Naimi, who had just gone into retirement, was for a long time one of the most powerful men in the world. The Bedouin has nearly seventy years of experience in the oil industry. Following his career as CEO of Aramco, he served as minister of petroleum for nearly twenty-one years.

The ministry of petroleum in Riyadh is a major power hub in the global economy. From here, markets can be stimulated or throttled. No other country has the capacity to either withhold or deliver hundreds of thousands of barrels of oil in a single day. Long-time Federal Reserve Chairman Alan Greenspan once called oil minister Naimi "the most important man you've never heard of."

At a panel discussion at the Center for Strategic and International Studies in Washington, Naimi, with his white hair, white moustache, and three-piece suit, looks like a friendly grandpa on a family visit. But that impression is soon proved wrong when Naimi starts talking about his work. He recalls the crisis of 2014, when the price of a barrel of oil fell from a hundred dollars to under thirty, lower than any point in the previous decade. The Saudi economy fell into a crisis whose effects are still felt today.

THE MUMBLING MINISTER

"I'll be honest," says Naimi, "there was no strategy. No one in OPEC wanted to curtail production, but they expected Saudi Arabia to do so. We said, 'No, why us?'" Shortly thereafter, Aramco flooded the oil market in order to secure its market share through oversupply. No other oil corporation can produce so cheaply and yet remain so profitable. That was Naimi's strategy, pure and simple.

Whether true or not, his admission in Washington is significant because, during his tenure as minister, he never talked publicly about his strategies. For journalists, it was always difficult to interpret his mumblings and cryptic, half-formed sentences. It was impossible to gain any substantial insights into Saudi tactics on the oil market.

Naimi is only three years younger than the kingdom itself. His story is also the story of how an isolated tribal society was transformed into a modern nation with powerful global influence within the span of a lifetime.

Around the time that King Abdulaziz assumed the throne in 1932 and united the four regions—Hejaz, Najd, Eastern Arabia, and Southern Arabia—into a single state, oil was discovered in the emirate of Bahrain, a tiny island nation just off of the Saudi east coast. Today, the two countries are linked by sixteen miles of causeways and bridges.

The Saudi king desperately needed money to develop his young nation. He had to make up for a decline in visits by well-off pilgrims to Mecca and Medina, the country's largest source of income at the time. The First World War made clear that oil would remain a key resource in warfare—and in industry—for the foreseeable future. King Abdulaziz immediately began to prospect for oil, even though it was absolutely unclear whether any of it lay beneath his kingdom.

One year later, in 1933, the Riyadh government signed a concession contract with an American exploration firm, Standard Oil Company of California, SoCal—known today as Chevron. Geologists from San Francisco headed out to the desert in search of the black gold. The company was granted "exploration rights in an area of 961,000 square kilometers (371,000 square miles) for sixty years." That year, the concession was transferred to a new subsidiary, California-Arabian Standard Oil. CASOC was the precursor to Saudi Aramco.

THREE YEARS OF FAILURE

CASOC's head geologist, Max Steineke, was an optimist. Born in 1898 to German immigrants, he grew up in Oregon in precarious circumstances as one of nine children. At twelve, Steineke went to work in a California lumber mill. A schoolteacher noticed him and made sure the boy received a good education. He ended up majoring in geology at Stanford.

In 1935, Steineke began drilling in eastern Saudi Arabia, near the village of Dammam. The geologist was supported by a handful of local Bedouins. In their leader, Khamis bin Rimthan, Steineke found a kindred spirit. The two men complemented each other perfectly. "They always seemed to know where they were and where they wanted to go," said Steineke's coworker, the geologist Thomas Barger, recalling their early days in the Eastern Province.

For three years, Steineke calculated, collected, and measured, to no avail. The project was plagued by setbacks. Wells collapsed; drills seized up deep in the rock. The head office in San Francisco wanted to pull the plug on the project and ordered Steineke to return to the United States.

THE DISCOVERY OF OIL IS A GAME CHANGER

The geologist asked his bosses for a little more time. He said that he at least wanted to wait for the results of Dammam #7, a very deep well where the drilling was proceeding very slowly.

In March 1938, Steineke struck oil at a depth of 1,440 meters. During further exploration of the area, Khamis bin Rimthan and Steineke discovered the Abqaiq Field in 1940, a vast reservoir of billions of barrels of oil.

AT DAMMAM OIL WELL #7: SHEPHERDS, CAMEL DRIVERS, AND FARMERS SUDDENLY ALL FOUND WORK IN THE OIL INDUSTRY.

The discovery changed everything: the kingdom, the politics of the region, and therefore, the world.

Before the Bedouin boy Ali al-Naimi made it to the Aramco boardroom, life threw a number of curve balls at him. The firm hired his nine-year-old brother as an errand boy. His brother brought Ali to the company-run school. There, the boys were taught English and math. Ali's big brother worked afternoons.

From the very beginning, Aramco played a central role in the education of young Saudis. Shepherds, camel drivers, and farmers suddenly found work in the oil industry. The company built schools, set up colleges, and sent its employees out into the world to attend the best universities.

When Ali's brother fell sick and died in 1947, Ali took over his position in the company. As an office boy, he was the family's only breadwinner—at age twelve. His monthly salary was ninety riyals, enough to cover the expenses of a modest household. But just nine months later, the labor ministry enacted a law prohibiting children under eighteen from working. Ali insisted that he was already eighteen, claiming that a genetic defect prevented him from growing facial hair. Nobody believed his story, and he had to leave the company.

CHEAP OIL FOR AMERICAN PROTECTION

Those early years in Saudi Arabia were uniquely dynamic. New opportunities constantly presented themselves to the nation and its people. One such moment was on February 14, 1945.

President Franklin D. Roosevelt was returning to Washington from the Yalta Conference in Crimea. The Second World War would only last another six months. In Yalta, the terminally-ill president and the other Allies agreed to partition Germany when the war was over. While passing through the Suez Canal, Roosevelt received King Abdulaziz bin Saud onboard the heavy cruiser, USS Quincy. Their two nations had only established diplomatic relations in 1939. It was the first-ever meeting between a US president and a Saudi monarch.

At first glance, the two statesmen couldn't have been more different. Roosevelt was highly educated, widely traveled, and president of the world's most advanced nation. The sixty-nine-year-old Saudi king had never even set foot in a school. He'd never traveled farther than Basra in Iraq, and he ruled one of the poorest countries in the world.

Yet Ibn Saud and Roosevelt were both shrewd strategists. They seemed to instinctively sense the boundless opportunities that a partnership between their nations could offer in the long term.

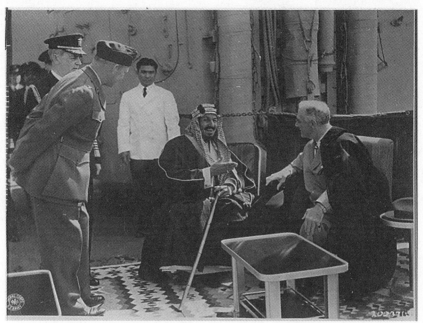

US President Franklin D. Roosevelt and Ibn Saud at their first and only meeting: The heads of state seal the historic alliance between the two countries. (Photo courtesy of National Archives.)

The two men hit it off immediately. In several treaties, they laid the foundations of today's alliance. The US offered Saudi Arabia military protection from its enemies, and in exchange (though it wasn't put so explicitly), the Saudis guaranteed the Americans unhindered access to cheap oil.

MAKING THE BOSS LOOK GOOD

Life continued to have some twists and turns in store for Ali al-Naimi. Back then, Saudi Arabia was the place to make your dreams come true. The Bedouin boy who put shoes on his feet for the first time at age nine was soon attending the American University in Beirut. He transferred to Steineke's alma mater, Stanford, to study geology and economics. At thirty, he was again hired by Aramco and asked by a higher-up about his career goals. Naimi didn't hesitate: "president of the company."

OUT OF THE DESERT

My Journey From Nomadic Bedouin
to the Heart of Global Oil

"THE MOST IMPORTANT MAN YOU'VE NEVER HEARD OF": LONG-TIME MINISTER OF
PETROLEUM ALI AL-NAIMI'S BIOGRAPHY (LEFT). AS A YOUNG ARAMCO EMPLOYEE
(CENTER, AMONG WORKERS): THE FATE OF THE NATION IS TIED TO A SINGLE COMPANY.

By the 1970s, the oil boom was in full swing. And in 1984, Ali
al-Naimi was in fact appointed president. In 1988, he was named
CEO of Saudi Aramco, as the company was then called. The
firm was already the single biggest producer of crude oil in the
world. At the beginning of 2020 the country exports up to 10
million barrels per day. The Saudi reserves are estimated to be at
least 265 billion barrels, making them the second largest in the
world after Venezuela, even if no one knows how much oil really
lies underground.

Over the years, the Saudis gradually bought the Americans'
shares in Aramco, until 100 percent of the company was in Saudi
hands. Aramco's profits are the highest of any company on the
planet. Simply put, Aramco is Saudi Arabia's crown jewels, the
kingdom's most precious treasure.

OIL PROCESSING FACILITY AT ABQAIQ IN THE EASTERN PROVINCE: IN ONE WAY OR
ANOTHER, EVERY RESIDENT OF THE KINGDOM PROFITS FROM ARAMCO.

When Naimi is asked about the secret to his success, he answers
mischievously. "Hard work, luck, and always making the boss
look good." That's not always easy when the fate of the nation
is tied to a single company. Saudi Arabia produces no other
significant exports, except perhaps dates.

STATE WITHIN A STATE

Saudi Aramco soon evolved into a state within a state. Passing
through the company's well-guarded gates in Dhahran feels
like crossing a border, entering a different world. Different laws
apply here. Women have always been able to drive within the
huge company complex, even Saudi women. There is no strict
dress code. Women wear suits, skirts, and blouses, as they do
in multinational corporations. Saudi Aramco is an extremely
modern, well-managed company employing specialists from

around the world. Men and women work side-by-side as equals. Many of the workers are American. The functional, cuboid administration buildings might as well be in Washington or Chicago.

Behind another wall lies Dhahran Camp. This is where the Aramco staff lives. Basically, it's a modern, Western town where Saudi traditions and rules don't apply.

ARAMCO STAFF HOUSING AT DHAHRAN CAMP: A DIFFERENT WORLD.

The street signs are green with white lettering, just like in the US. The streets have names like Rolling Hills Boulevard and 7th Street. The traffic lights are yellow. The stone ranch-style homes with flat roofs, carports, and yards could be located in Virginia or Maryland. In Dhahran Camp there is a recreation center, a golf course, tennis courts, pools, international schools, and all types of restaurants. Kids play in manicured parks. Women jog in shorts and sports bras.

THE KING BESTOWS GIFTS, THE PEOPLE KEEP THEIR MOUTHS SHUT

In one way or another, every resident of the kingdom profits from Aramco. First, there are the company's 69,000 employees. They have families, drivers, maids, gardeners, and more. Their children attend excellent schools. Then there are the well-lit, multi-lane roads that reach even the most remote towns, and the universities with their student apartments and free libraries. Even garbage collection and sewage treatment are paid for by petrodollars. Without Saudi Aramco, there would be no huge residential palaces, since these too are subsidized by the regime. The well-equipped military wouldn't have its 150 F-15 fighters. There would be no glittering malls and no kids' amusement parks.

For many years an unspoken pact has existed between the Saudi people and the royal family. The king bestows gifts upon his subjects: free education, free healthcare, and foreign scholarships, and there is no income tax. In return, the Saudi population stays out of government affairs and refrains from public criticism.

A SUITCASE OF CASH

As the oil gushes from the ground, billions flow into the state's coffers. The monarchy invests huge sums to ensure that the economic and political development of the country goes according to its agenda. Money talks. This just about sums up Riyadh's ability to shape war and peace in the Middle East and elsewhere. And it explains how the Saudis control the fate of politicians across the region. Countries like small, fragile Lebanon are on the Saudi payroll. Under President Omar al-Bashir, the Republic of Sudan benefited from Saudi financial support. The same goes for Bahrain and geostrategic allies like Pakistan and Djibouti.

In Riyadh in December 2018, for example, the Saudi crown prince handed Tunisian prime minister Youssef Chahed a check for $830 million. It's one way the kingdom supports the troubled economy of its North African brother nation. At the same time, it ensures that the Tunis government will show its loyalty to the Saudi king, if he should one day ask for it. Unsurprisingly, a large number of Tunisians aren't great fans of this particular Saudi policy, which aims to keep the autocratic system around them in place.

In 2013, the Egyptian defense minister Abdel Fattah el-Sisi staged a coup against the democratically elected head of government in Cairo, Mohammed Mursi. Sisi appointed himself president, and Riyadh shored up Sisi's power with a five-billion-dollar infusion of cash. It was in the kingdom's interest that Mursi go and Sisi stay.

Mursi was a high-ranking member of the Muslim Brotherhood, an Islamist movement founded in 1928. The Muslim Brotherhood's objective is to install Islamic republics all across the Middle East. Unlike the Saudi royals, they believe in democratic participation by the people within a Sharia-based framework of law. This is why the rulers in Riyadh consider the Muslim Brotherhood to be the greatest threat to the stability of their absolute monarchy. If free elections were held in conservative Saudi Arabia tomorrow, it's very likely that the Muslim Brotherhood would emerge victorious.

Petrodollars also support Saudi Arabia's humanitarian efforts worldwide. The kingdom is a fantastically generous donor to the

United Nations. At one point, Riyadh landed on the UN list of countries believed to have committed war crimes. UN inspectors said that the Saudis shared responsibility for the deaths of more than five hundred children in Yemen, where Riyadh had been waging a bombing campaign against the Houthi rebels since March 2015. Saudi diplomats told the then UN Secretary-General Ban Ki-moon that Saudi Arabia would cancel its pledged financial support for urgent UN humanitarian projects if the kingdom wasn't removed from the list.

Secretary-General Ban was distraught. He complained publicly about the objectionable pressure coming from the Saudis. Riyadh's ambassador vehemently rejected the charge of blackmail, but the UN urgently needed the Saudi money. Ban finally gave in to the kingdom's demand because otherwise "millions of other children" would suffer severely. The South Korean diplomat said it was one of the most painful decisions of his career.

When the Saudi crown prince ordered American arms worth astronomical sums in March 2018, it was oil money that was paying the bill. The deal for planes and weapons is said to be worth more than $100 billion. At a joint press conference, President Trump held up a poster in front of the cameras like a trophy. He gleefully pointed to images of fighter bombers and helicopters, and triumphantly announced that contracts worth more than $12.5 billion had already been signed.

Seven months later, the fear of high oil prices and the loss of lucrative business prevented the president from imposing sanctions on Crown Prince Mohammed bin Salman after the brutal torture and murder of Saudi journalist Jamal Khashoggi, even though the CIA said there was ample evidence that the crown prince personally ordered the killing.

Buying the obedience of politicians with money and gifts is generally considered offensive around the world, yet the leadership in Riyadh seems to get away with it. The kingdom promotes its agenda with sums of money that countries with tax-based budgets, or organizations with membership fees, simply can't compete with. What or whom should the king and his crown prince fear if they can use their financial clout to pressure the representatives of the most respected institutions in the world to forgo their principles?

NO OIL, NO POWER

The world is changing. The ongoing instability of oil prices means Riyadh can no longer depend on fossil fuel as a reliable source of income. In effect, the country is living well beyond its means.

Recently, the Saudi budget was in the red for the first time in history, prompting the government to dip into its $700 billion in foreign reserves to cover its $200 billion deficit. In the era of climate change and electronic mobility, nobody knows how much longer oil will remain a sought-after commodity. When the price of oil falls, Riyadh's power will decline.

Crown Prince Mohammed bin Salman is well aware of his nation's predicament, which is why he is avidly determined to save the "crown jewels." His plan is to restructure Saudi Aramco as quickly as possible. To remain viable, profits must be generated less and less by oil production, and more and more through the development of renewable energy.

To do so, the heir to the throne requires a new source of cash. MBS decided, therefore, to float the state oil giant Saudi Aramco, the treasure chest of the kingdom, on the stock exchange.

In absolute terms, Aramco makes a higher annual profit than Apple or Amazon, and the initial public offering in December 2019 was the biggest of all time. More precisely, the crown prince had planned to offer 5 percent of Aramco's shares on the capital markets. He asserted that Aramco was worth the princely sum of two trillion dollars, which is why he expected to raise $100 billion from the sale of shares.

How exactly the young ruler arrived at this high valuation of the company remains his secret. Analysts at Bloomberg say a valuation of around $1.5 trillion would have been more realistic.

The IPO failed to live up to expectations by a long shot. The Aramco offering raised $25.6 billion—a fraction of what Prince Mohammed had hoped for. The shares were not listed at either of the major exchanges in New York or London as one would expect in the case of such an extraordinary event, but in Riyadh, on the country's own stock market, Tadawul. The sale was not organized by international banks, as is usually the case, but by two Saudi financial institutions and the British HSBC. Investors came primarily from Saudi Arabia and neighboring countries.

Shortly before the historic IPO, a grave incident occurred that surely had a psychological impact on the process. On the morning of September 14th, 2019, nineteen high-tech combat drones and missiles descended upon the east of the kingdom. With a high degree of precision, they hit the most important state oil processing facilities in Abqaiq and Khurais. The attack was planned and implemented with a professionalism of which only a modern army is capable. No people were harmed, but within a few minutes the kingdom's oil production—the country's sole economic foundation—was reduced to less than half of its normal daily output.

DAMAGE TO AN INSTALLATION AT ABQAIQ OIL REFINERY AFTER THE MISSILE ATTACK IN SEPTEMBER 2019: THE COUNTRY'S SOLE ECONOMIC FOUNDATION.

This act of war struck the proud kingdom at its heart, even if the facilities regained their normal level of production within a few weeks. The strike revealed how vulnerable the country is, despite the American defense systems it spent billions on.

Satellite imagery suggests that the combat drones were launched from an Iranian military base. Since Tehran and Riyadh are bitter enemies, analysts believe Iran wanted to retaliate. The Islamic Republic denies responsibility.

Riyadh was among those forces which exerted massive pressure on President Trump to pull out of the so-called nuclear deal or Joint Comprehensive Plan of Action (JCPOA). The Islamic Republic signed the pact with the West in July 2015 following lengthy diplomatic negotiations. The agreement was intended to prevent the construction of Iranian nuclear weapons. In exchange, Iran would be freed from political and economic isolation.

Ironically, the Saudis had felt threatened by exactly those Iranian missiles which—once the nuclear deal had failed, in part due to their decisive influence—were being deployed against them for the first time. Trump's breach of the agreement was a heavy defeat for the Iranian government.

For a public offering to succeed, you need to tell a good—and credible—story. Investors need to believe that your company has a bright future ahead of it. Yet Aramco's books have never been independently audited. No one knows how large Saudi Arabia's oil reserves really are, how high the company's profits really have been, or exactly how all that money is being spent. To outsiders, the Aramco money machine is a black box.

The public offering, originally planned for 2018, failed due to insufficient transparency. At the end of the day, a certain amount of murkiness is clearly an integral feature of Riyadh's business model.

In any case, former oil minister Ali al-Naimi's recipe for success should also work for his successor. Since September 8, 2019, this role has been filled by Prince Abdulaziz bin Salman, an older half-brother of Crown Prince Mohammed, a son of King Salman's first wife. There's no question that the new Minister of Energy, Prince Abdulaziz, will work just as hard as the legendary Naimi, and perhaps he'll get lucky. But he will certainly find it more difficult to make his boss—Crown Prince MBS—always look good.

BANDAR, THE BLACK PRINCE: SAUDI ARABIA'S SECRET WEAPON

AS ONE OF THE GRANDCHILDREN OF IBN SAUD, WITH A SUDANESE
CONCUBINE AS HIS MOTHER, PRINCE BANDAR BIN SULTAN
UNEXPECTEDLY RISES TO BECOME ONE OF THE MOST INFLUENTIAL
DIPLOMATS OF THE POSTWAR PERIOD. PRINCE BANDAR HAS BEEN
DEEPLY INVOLVED IN THE GREAT CRISES OF WORLD POLITICS, FROM
THE IRAN–CONTRA AFFAIR TO THE WAR IN SYRIA—ALL THE WHILE
PURSUING A SINGLE GOAL.

When I visit Prince Bandar bin Sultan in his palace in January 2018, he is sitting in a large sand-colored armchair, smoking a supersized cigar. Bandar's face is broad, with brown sparkling eyes; the skin on his hands is dark and contrasts with his white *thawb*; he is wearing sandals. His face still features his trademark closely cropped beard, now grown gray.

Bandar's eyes are fixed on two monitors, each one the size of a small movie screen. One of them is dedicated solely to CNN. The other simultaneously shows a dozen international channels from Moscow, Washington, Beirut, Tripoli, and elsewhere. This is Bandar's world. Bandar himself can usually be found in one of those places he's now watching on TV. In one way or another, the prince has been a player in just about every international crisis of the past four decades. If there is one person who knows the answer to my questions—how did the Cold War end? How did extremism emerge in Afghanistan? Why did the US occupy Iraq? Why did Syria's President Bashar al-Assad win the war?—it is this veteran of the diplomatic front lines, Prince Bandar bin Sultan.

A businessman I'm friends with has arranged this meeting between us.

At two in the afternoon, a chauffeur in a black limousine picks me up from my flat in the center of Riyadh. The drive takes half an hour. Bandar's palace lies just outside the city. At the end of a long wall, heavy green gates open and the car rolls into a private park. The compound covers a large area, and the palace is an endless maze of marble corridors decorated with mosaics, hand-carved wooden doors, fountains, chandeliers, flowers, and greenery.

Prince Bandar is sixty-eight years old when we meet. He has spent twenty-two of them as Saudi Arabia's ambassador to the US. Until April 2014, Bandar headed the Saudi secret service, and for some time afterward continued as secretary general of the Saudi National Security Council. Prince Bandar has armed rebels in South America and Central Asia, and most recently in Syria. He has arranged some of the biggest arms deals in history in the service of His Majesty, and sometimes attends peace negotiations for uprisings that he himself helped to incite.

We talk for four hours, a blink of an eye in this breathless life. However, I leave with an understanding of how Prince Bandar created a kind of mutual love between Riyadh and Washington, representatives of two systems that are fundamentally incompatible. Like a pair of newlyweds—each of whom secretly wishes that they had married someone else but keeps up the sweet talk—they stay euphoric on an exorbitant dowry, which is increased every time disappointment threatens.

LOYAL AND KIND, BRUTAL AND DESTRUCTIVE

The image of the incompatible couple aptly describes the time Bandar spent in Washington, during which several American presidents succumbed to his charms. Bandar, who was educated in the US, was able to convey the sense of a common cause even after the great catastrophe that was the attack on the World Trade Center on September 11, 2001, when fifteen of the nineteen attackers turned out to be Saudis.

"I did as many favors as I could for the Americans, during a time when I didn't need them, so that they would owe me a favor when I did," Prince Bandar tells me. The diplomat explains the strategy of his success to me while blowing clouds of smoke into the air from his Cuban cigar.

Those who have witnessed Prince Bandar's life describe him as a dazzling personality: he is attentive and kind, loyal and funny, and particularly clever. Bandar fights for his causes with charm and passion, and is a brilliant negotiator. When money, a lot of money, is concerned—as is often the case in Bandar's affairs—his checks never bounce. But they also say that Bandar is a dangerous manipulator, a daredevil, who becomes menacing, brutal, even destructive, where His Majesty's ambitions are concerned.

Bandar would probably not reject this characterization. Back when he was doing his MA in International Politics at Johns Hopkins in Baltimore, he embraced the Italian political philosopher Niccolò Machiavelli's belief that those who act in the interest of the general public must not be held responsible for the moral cost of their deeds. You might say that good and evil do not exist for Bandar—only the mission matters.

Prince Bandar's mission was quite clear when King Fahd sent the then fighter pilot to DC as his emissary: he had to win over the US as a reliable protector of the kingdom and carve their bilateral relationship in stone.

A MAGIC FORMULA OF MUTUAL DEPENDENCE

His uncle, King Fahd, supposedly told him: "The US is our most important ally, and our biggest threat!"

"Why a threat?" I ask. "Because," explains Bandar, "you can't fully trust them, and they might attack you anytime. Like they did with Saddam Hussein, for instance." If you want to learn how politics is done in the Middle East, Prince Bandar bin Sultan will teach you.

US PRESIDENT GEORGE W. BUSH WITH HIS CONFIDANT PRINCE BANDAR (2002):
GOOD AND EVIL DO NOT EXIST—ONLY THE MISSION MATTERS.

(PHOTO COURTESY OF NATIONAL ARCHIVES AND RECORDS ADMINISTRATION.)

In the 1970s, Saudi Arabia becomes a rich country. Yet it remains vulnerable. The army on its own would probably be unable to defend against a large-scale attack, even though the majority of the Saudi arsenal consists of cutting-edge Western technology. Hardly anything can be done here without the Americans' support: when a Saudi F-15 jet fighter takes off for an attack on Yemen, the plane and the bombs are American. American mechanics maintain the jet and carry out repairs on the ground. American technicians update the targeting software and other encrypted technology. The Saudis aren't even allowed to touch any of it. The pilot himself was probably trained by the US Air Force.

The kingdom can therefore only consider itself safe as long as the largest military power in the world backs its regime. The tie that binds the US and the kingdom, this incompatible couple, consists of one simple but magic formula of mutual dependence: affordable oil on the one side, weapons and military support on the other. This makes them inseparable. Oil-rich Saudi Arabia is the main reason why, in the West, cars and machines have kept running, and why homes have stayed warm in winter. In exchange, Riyadh enjoys the protection of its ally, the US.

But the importance of fossil energy like oil is in rapid decline. And thanks to fracking, the US is becoming increasingly independent of foreign production. The price of oil remains at a relatively constant low.

The glue that has been keeping the two powers together for decades is still holding, but it isn't as effective anymore as it once was. Differences are no longer simply ignored, even if they have been there all along. Many in Washington, London, Paris, and Berlin are now asking themselves: Does this partnership still make sense?

FROSTY RELATIONS WITH WORLD LEADERS

The houses of Prince Bandar's various family members are distributed across the compound, yet the extensive corridors and the paths running through the park keep them connected with each other. Bandar's children live here, too. Princess Reema is an art expert educated in Washington. Under the leadership of King Salman, she has risen to become the most prominent female politician in the country. She was briefly a sort of minister for sports, and in her father's footsteps, has just been named the first female ambassador—the first one in the history of the country. She is now Saudi Arabia's representative plenipotentiary in DC. Her younger brother, Prince Khaled bin Bandar, an international businessman, is always dressed like an English gentleman in waistcoat and high collar with a silk handkerchief in his breast pocket. The forty-three-year-old studied at Oxford and is currently the Saudi ambassador in London. Before that, he represented the kingdom in Berlin.

On the day of our meeting, Prince Khaled is in Riyadh—then still being the ambassador to Germany—and joins our conversation. At the time of my visit, the relationship between Germany and the kingdom is fairly frosty. The young crown prince Mohammed bin Salman's ruthless style of leadership is being followed in Germany with some concern.

The Saudis, in turn, make short work of critics abroad. In August 2018, MBS recalled his ambassador to Canada. The diplomatic relationship is on its last legs following a tweet from the minister of foreign affairs, Chrystia Freeland, in which she denounced the arrest of the civil rights activist Samar Badawi and demanded her release.

The topic of Iran also touches a nerve. Germany was one of the leading negotiators of the nuclear deal with Iran. Saudi Arabia is outraged at its rival's rising political stock. Ambassador Prince Khaled bin Bandar argues that Iran poses an existential threat to the region, with its expansionist military influence in Lebanon, Syria, and Yemen. Indeed, Iran supports many of the kingdom's adversaries, including militias such as Hezbollah in Lebanon and the Houthi rebels in Yemen—and this on Saudi Arabia's very own doorstep.

American diplomats like to say that the Saudis are, as far as Iran is concerned, "paranoid, but not crazy," meaning that Riyadh may overrate the threat from Iran, but that there are good reasons for their concern. The tension that characterizes the relationship between Riyadh and Tehran dominates today's conflict situation in the Middle East and beyond.

FIERCE GENERALS

In Prince Bandar bin Sultan's living room are framed photographs of eight children and his wife Haifa, a daughter of King Faisal. On the walls and console tables there is a veritable procession of photos of celebrities from all over the world, signed with their regards. Among them are Prince Charles, Mikhail

Gorbachev, Ronald Reagan, and the former US secretary of state Colin Powell. What is remarkable is that Bandar manages to be friends with very different people simultaneously, some of whom have spent their lives trying to avoid being in the same room with each other—like the Nobel Peace Prize winner Nelson Mandela and the British "Iron Lady" Maggie Thatcher, who once called Mandela's party, the ANC, a terrorist organization. Both were members of Bandar's inner circle.

"Gone Fishing" with Vice President Bush—the beginning of a lifelong friendship.

PHOTO OF BANDAR'S COLLECTION OF CLOSE POLITICAL CONFIDANTS (WITH PRESIDENT GEORGE W. BUSH): "THE BEGINNING OF A WONDERFUL RELATIONSHIP."

Bandar is a brilliant raconteur. The stories he tells, stories others know only from history, are his life: he was personally involved in them. There is, for instance, the story of his trip to Moscow in 1988 to meet the Soviet leader Mikhail Gorbachev on behalf of President Ronald Reagan and King Fahd. The war between the Afghan *mujahideen* and the Soviets had been ongoing for more than eight years, and Bandar went to warn the Russians that Saudi Arabia would, if the Soviets didn't finally withdraw their troops, double its financial support of the insurgents. Gorbachev, he says, received him with a regiment of fierce-looking generals and commanded the Saudis not to interfere and to stop supporting the terrorists. Afterwards, Gorbachev ushered him into his office, embraced him warmly, and kissed him: "The generals don't want to accept that we can't afford this war anymore. Tell King Fahd that I'll be out of the country by March 1989."

And so it happened: the Soviets withdrew. That scene marked the beginning of the end of the Cold War.

THE GRAY AREA BETWEEN DIPLOMACY AND SECRET OPERATIONS

I've been writing about crises and wars around the world for nearly twenty years. I have reported from the Balkans, Central Asia, Africa, and the Middle East. If you travel through those places on the trail of Islamist fighters, you'll keep hearing the suggestion that "the Saudis" have given them money, sent them weapons, "bought" politicians. But at no point do those vaguely named actors appear in public. Emissaries from the Gulf states such as Prince Bandar are not accountable to any parliament and report only to their master, the king. They are active in that gray area between diplomacy and secret service activities, outside all protocol and under the radar of international observers, but their money, their connections, and their interests make themselves felt everywhere.

For example, what does peace in Afghanistan have to do with Saudi Arabia today? A lot, because the Saudis and the US, strictly speaking, invented the Taliban back in the 1980s, and a man called Prince Bandar was deeply involved in that development, too.

In 1979, the Soviets marched into Afghanistan. Moscow planned to create a satellite state there, part of its long-term goal of advancing toward Pakistan and the Arabian Sea. These were tense times during the Cold War between East and West. The Americans saw a chance to bring the Red Army to its knees by wearing it down in a guerrilla war on the Afghan battlefield. At the same time, the Saudis wanted to prevent the communists from establishing a foothold in a region that Riyadh considered to be, in the broadest sense, within its zone of influence.

From 1980 onwards, the Saudi secret services and CIA agents supported the Afghan insurgents, who in turn fought the Red Army from the safety of Pakistani territory. Only in those days they weren't called the "Taliban," but the *"mujahideen."*

The plan worked: the Americans delivered weapons and the Saudis delivered contacts, as well as Wahhabism for the madrasa textbooks. Active Qur'anic schools in the refugee camps recruited ever more youths prepared to deliver their homeland from the fight with the Soviet "infidels." We can thus call the Taliban the children of the *mujahideen*.

The intention was to keep the Islamist guerrillas active for no longer than necessary. That they were left behind after the withdrawal of the Soviet army is an accident of history. Among the *mujahideen* were all kinds of foreigners who belonged to the personal militia of al-Qaeda founder Osama bin Laden, and who subsequently became the seed from which global militant extremism grew.

RELIGIOUS FUNDAMENTALIST MAULANA NOOR MOHAMMED IN HIS CHALDARA QUR'ANIC SCHOOL IN QUETTA, PAKISTAN, AUTHOR(2007). ONLY PAKISTAN AND SAUDI ARABIA HAD OFFICIALLY RECOGNIZED THE TALIBAN'S EMIRATE.

Riyadh has also exerted a certain amount of influence in other wars in the Arab region, for instance in Libya, Iraq, and Syria. As a financier and negotiator, Saudi Arabia is a heavyweight player in almost all conflicts in which Islamist groups are involved. When the Arab Spring spread to Syria, the Saudis initially offered their backing to President al-Assad. The chief negotiator was once again Prince Bandar, since 2012 head of the Saudi secret services.

"We told al-Assad: Improve your relationship with your people. They want only reform, not a coup or a new government," the Prince tells me. "He wouldn't listen." The Saudis demanded that Damascus give up its close ties with Iran. Al-Assad should stop the arms being delivered by Iran to the allied Hezbollah militia in Lebanon, which were being transported across Syrian territory. That was Bandar's price.

Riyadh sees itself threatened by the military axis that connects Tehran to Damascus and Beirut. The kingdom wants to destroy the alliance and thereby weaken Tehran's influence.

But al-Assad declined the deal. The US had already made a similar offer, but the Syrian leader believed that Tehran, rather than Riyadh or DC, was his life insurance. And so war was declared.

Consequently, Saudi Arabia and Qatar armed anyone willing to fight the Syrian regime. "I was there quite often," Prince Bandar told me on that day in his palace in February 2018. "We armed the Free Syrian Army. It went totally wrong."

Bombed-out secret service quarters in Damascus; a father's memento of his killed daughter; uniformed student at the University of Damascus in front of an oversized portrait of al-Assad; author Susanne Koelbl and Syrian soldiers, on their way to the front lines in the divided city of Aleppo.

Two things went wrong above all: Bandar had reassured the rebels that the Americans would intervene in the war at a certain point, and President Barack Obama himself had warned President al-Assad that he would consider a "red line" to have been crossed should al-Assad deploy poison gas against civilians. Prince Bandar and the rebels saw this as a clear sign that the US would soon come to their aid in Syria.

However, when on August 21, 2013, hundreds of civilians died in a poison gas attack in Eastern Ghouta, near Damascus, Obama retreated. "We showed the Americans irrefutable proof," says a close confidant of Prince Bandar's, who has hitherto followed our conversation in silence.

In Riyadh, the story goes that President Obama tried to phone King Abdullah. He wanted to explain why he would not bomb Syria. But the king refused to take the call from the ally who had apparently broken his promise. However, it should be noted that at the time the Russians and Americans did agree on a UN resolution compelling Syria to join the Chemical Weapons Convention. Subsequently, around 95 percent of Syrian chemical weapons were destroyed under the UN's supervision.

Nevertheless, for the first time, Bandar is unable to keep his word to his partners on the battlefield. The prince is enraged. For him, this is the worst-case scenario.

FALLING OUT WITH THE US

The Iranians consequently redouble their operations, and the Russians too come to Damascus for support. Together, Tehran and Moscow prevent al-Assad's downfall. Now the Iranians are sitting exactly where Riyadh doesn't want them—in Damascus.

The US's great game is no longer working. In the past, Prince Bandar had known four US presidents, ten US secretaries of state, and eleven US national security advisors, and had had an excellent working relationship with most of them. But Obama wouldn't allow himself to be seduced, either by Bandar's charm or by his arguments. He had other plans for the Middle East.

The Democratic president wanted to extricate the US from the wars in Iraq and Afghanistan, and didn't want to be drawn into yet another conflict. A nuclear treaty with Iran was designed to prevent the country's nuclear armament. Obama's aim was to normalize relations with Saudi Arabia's equally resource-rich rival.

There was a rift. According to Bilal Saab of the Emirati newspaper *The National*, Bandar became persona non grata in the political circles of the Obama administration. King Abdullah recalled his front man from Washington. But the prince remained the king's personal emissary for special missions until Abdullah died in January 2015.

Bandar's ascent to become one of the most influential members of the ruling family and an agent for state affairs of all kinds has something of the fairy tale about it. The diplomat is the child of a black slave from Asir, a province in the far south of the country, and the then governor of Riyadh, Prince Sultan bin Abdulaziz bin Saud. Khizaran, Bandar's mother, entered the household as a maid and soon became the prince's mistress.

HIS GRANDMOTHER TAUGHT HIM ABOUT POLITICS AND WOMEN

When she gave birth to the boy, Khizaran was sixteen, Prince Sultan twenty. Prince Sultan was one of the seven sons of the nation's founder Abdulaziz and his favorite wife, Hassa Bint Ahmed al-Sudairi.

Under Islamic law, all sons are born equal. Nevertheless, Khizaran and the newborn were initially paid off and required to leave the palace. Only when he was eight years old did the little prince manage to get his father's attention. Bandar was allowed to visit Prince Sultan when the latter was sick in bed. During that visit, the father pulled his son onto his bed. It marked the beginning of their relationship, and Prince Bandar spent the rest of his life trying to impress his father.

Prince Bandar was eleven when his life underwent a fundamental change. His grandmother, Hassa al-Sudairi, perhaps the most influential woman in Saudi Arabia, decided that from now on the boy and his mother were to reside in the palace. By then, Bandar's grandfather Abdulaziz had been dead for some years.

Hassa was pious and strong-willed. Bandar adored her. She reciprocated his affection and taught him about politics, how to deal with women, about the country's history, and to honor his grandfather. Most of all, she gave him the feeling that he was special. "She was the most influential figure in my life," Bandar once told the *New Yorker*.

Unlike other royals, Bandar wasn't sent to a prestigious elite university. At the age of sixteen, he enrolled at the Royal Air Force College in England, hoping to prove himself as a fighter pilot. He flew risky acrobatic maneuvers until, one day, he sustained a serious back injury in a crash. He had to give up flying.

DAREDEVIL ASSIGNMENTS

It is more or less a coincidence that Lieutenant Colonel Bandar ended up in Washington getting involved in the trade negotiations concerning F-15 fighters. Saudi Arabia wanted to buy sixty jets for $2.5 billion. During Jimmy Carter's presidency, Bandar managed to gain political support for the deal, so it went through. Bandar's career as ambassador to the United States began shortly thereafter. He was barely thirty years old.

It was perhaps the mixture of charm and bravado, coupled with the aura of an "oriental prince," that gave Bandar extraordinary access to the right people. No one was better equipped to take advantage of what in the Middle East is called *wasta*: the generating of opportunities through unofficial contacts, with all negotiations taking place under the table.

Bandar's support of the insurgent *mujahideen* against the soldiers of the Red Army was bold. During George Bush Sr.'s presidency, Bandar was a familiar face in the Oval Office, and the Bush family soon came to consider him one of their own. In the US, this earned him the half-mocking, half-reverential nickname "Bandar-Bush."

There is a photograph of Prince Bandar and President George W. Bush which speaks volumes. It was taken in August 2002. The president is sitting in an armchair, wearing cowboy boots, chinos, and a shirt, gesticulating as he explains something to Bandar, who is sitting slightly higher than him, on the armrest of a matching chair. Bandar is wearing jeans and a blazer. His eyes are on Bush, and he is listening attentively.

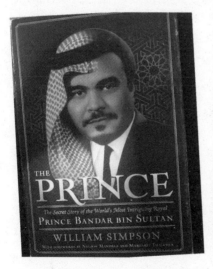
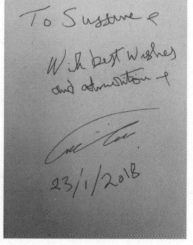

PRINCE BANDAR'S DETAILED BIOGRAPHY ABOUT HIS COLORFUL LIFE AS A DIPLOMAT—
WITH A PERSONAL DEDICATION TO THE AUTHOR.

It is these networks of trust that allowed Prince Bandar to negotiate the impossible, such as when many members of the Bin Laden family were able to leave the US discreetly and in an orderly fashion after the attacks on September 11, 2001, when the al-Qaeda founder's wider family circle stood accused of being complicit in the attacks.

To this day, the families of the victims of the attacks in New York suspect that Saudi civil servants may have taken part in this act of terrorism. They have clues pointing to their involvement—and have many unanswered questions. They want to sue the Saudi government. In March 2018, nearly seventeen years after the attacks, a federal judge in New York unexpectedly allows the case to proceed, which Riyadh tried to prevent with all its might.

The plaintiffs accuse the kingdom of having facilitated the evolution of al-Qaeda into a terrorist organization. The group, they say, was only able to carry out those attacks because they had the financial and operational backing of organizations directly controlled by the state. The kingdom, for its part, considers itself, too, a victim of terrorism. After all, it argues, al-Qaeda's aim is the downfall of Riyadh's royal family.

The accusations may be unfounded. At least, it has been impossible to prove them, not least because the Bush administration redacted twenty-eight pages of the US Congress's "Joint Inquiry into Intelligence Community Activities before and after the Terrorist Attacks of September 11, 2001" for reasons of national security.

The relevant passages were finally made public in July 2016. They concern phone connections between the hijackers and Saudi civil servants in the US Abu Zubaydah, a key figure in the al-Qaeda network, inexplicably had a number stored in his phone which belongs to the company that manages the Saudi ambassador to the US's villa in Aspen, Colorado. The firm is owned by Prince Bandar.

Unfortunately, there is no opportunity for us to discuss this during our conversation in Prince Bandar's palace. His Royal Highness is in a talkative mood, but a dinner engagement beckons. Yet during these four hours of conversation, I learn how

Bandar's system in Washington worked for such a long time, and how Prince Bandar finally failed during the war in Syria in the face of Barack Obama, as with the change in administration came a change in attitudes. And so, his second working thesis thus proved itself to be true: you can't trust the Americans.

SEVEN DATES A DAY
KEEP THE DEVIL AWAY

THE LUSCIOUS FRUITS OF THE DATE PALM ARE DELICIOUS AND
NUTRITIOUS—AND THEY WARD OFF SATAN.

My central European body isn't accustomed to the nightly plunge
in temperature in the Saudi desert. I've been in bed with a fever
for the last two days. My landlord, Colonel Hasan, is concerned,
so he sends over his Ethiopian housekeeper to check up on me.

Mariam is a brunette with her hair tied in an artful topknot.
She brings me soup and unroasted coffee containing ginger,
and a lot of dates in a heavy crystal bowl. Not too long after, Mr.
Hasan phones me for the second time that day, to ask me how I
feel again.

Though I'm just his tenant, Mr. Hasan pities me because I'm a
Western traveler stranded in a foreign land. According to his
view, I am in need of his male protection and support, and right
then I'm feeling too feeble to rebel against his intensive care.
Meanwhile, Mariam's spicy ginger coffee tastes amazing, like
medicinal firewater.

I've never been a big fan of dates. Here, though, the gooey brown
fruits are offered to guests as if they were epicurean delights like
fine wine or gourmet pralines, especially if they originate from
your host's very own farm. Apparently, the nuanced qualities
of the "Sukkary" from Al-Qassim Province, Saudi Arabia's
heartland, and the "Klalas Al-Ahsa" variety from Al-Ahsa in the
east are as distinct as those that distinguish a Tuscan Brunello
from a Grand Cru from Saint-Émilion.

Mr. Hasan advises me to eat three dates today. They contain
vitamins and crucial trace elements like magnesium. It will pep
you up, he says. "A sacred fruit, a gift from Allah to mankind."
Mr. Hasan never hesitates to bring up Allah, in the hope that the

lost soul residing in his building will somehow find her way to the virtuous path of Islam.

THE KINGDOM IS HOME TO MORE THAN 25 MILLION DATE PALMS: "WE COULD RETURN TO THE DESERT AND SURVIVE ON DATES AND CAMEL'S MILK."

It would not be wrong to say that part of the Saudis' strength and national pride rests in the knowledge of the life-sustaining energy of the date. More than twenty-five million date palms grow in the kingdom. The nourishing fruit has even had an impact on international relations. In protest of America's support of Israel against the Palestinians in the Yom Kippur War, King Faisal—the third ruler since the founding of the modern Saudi kingdom—cut off the supply of oil to the West. That was in 1973, at the beginning of the oil crisis. Secretary of State Henry Kissinger, just a few months in the job, hotfooted it to Riyadh to convince the monarch to lift the embargo. Kissinger's most persuasive argument was typically American: he threatened to send in troops to occupy the Saudi oil fields if the Arabs didn't back down.

King Faisal coolly turned away the visitor from Washington: "You're the ones who need the oil. We come from the desert. Our ancestors lived on dates and camel milk. At any time, we can return to the desert and subsist on dates and camel milk."

The oil crisis was a distressing time for the West. The German government banned driving on Sundays. The Palestinian conflict and Saudi oil shock were already impacting people's lives in the Western world. Older Saudis remember the story well and love to retell it, as Mr. Hasan proudly does again today.

He makes me promise to eat seven dates per day starting tomorrow. In any case, it has to be an uneven number. As is well known, seven per day ward off the Devil and heal every malady.

Lo and behold, within one week I feel a lot better.

Picnic and bonfires: The people of Saudi Arabia enjoy the intense quiet of the desert.

Oasis in the endless desert, untouched nature: Since the fall of 2019, travelers have had the opportunity to explore the enigmatic kingdom. Travel visas can now be obtained online and picked up directly at the border.

Social revolution with the help of public transportation: The new subway in Riyadh is a contributing factor in reducing gender separation.

BEDOUIN ROMANTICISM IN MODERN TIMES: THE SHAMMAR TRIBE PRESERVES THE HERITAGE OF THEIR ANCESTORS IN THIS MUSEUM.

SERVANTS FOR EVERY OCCASION: MILLIONS OF LOW-WAGE WORKERS FROM ASIA AND AFRICA MAKE LIFE EASIER FOR SAUDIS. NOW THEY ARE SUPPOSED TO LEAVE.

LADY AT THE WEDNESDAY CLUB: AN EXCLUSIVE GROUP OF SAUDI MEN, THE FIRST GENERATION OF ELITE SCHOLARSHIP STUDENTS WHO WENT TO IVY LEAGUE SCHOOLS IN THE US, MEET WEEKLY TO DISCUSS CURRENT AFFAIRS. THE PHOTO WAS TAKEN ON MAY 4, 2011, TWO DAYS AFTER OSAMA BIN LADEN WAS KILLED IN ABBOTTABAD, PAKISTAN. HIS VIOLENT END WAS THE THEME OF THE EVENING.

"WHAT IS NORMAL?": A SAUDI WOMAN IN THE HOME OF RELATIVES IN EASTERN SAUDI ARABIA.

The new religion is entertainment, nationalism, and sports: At a Tamer Housni concert in Jeddah, the young Crown Prince Mohammed bin Salman is portrayed as the biggest pop star of all.

At the check-out counter, in banks, at the lingerie store: Women now work and are visible in public. Riyadh understands that women are a catalyst for the economy.

UNTHINKABLE JUST A SHORT WHILE AGO: MUSIC, A MIXED AUDIENCE, AND OFFICIALLY SANCTIONED ENTERTAINMENT IN JEDDAH. FEMALE BRAND AMBASSADORS FOR A MASCARA BRAND AT ONE OF THE FIRST POP CONCERTS IN THE COUNTRY'S HISTORY.

FROM RESPECTED MEMBER OF THE ESTABLISHMENT TO TRAITOR: JAMAL KHASHOGGI (MIDDLE LEFT) IN THE CAVES OF TORA BORA IN AFGHANISTAN AT THE END OF THE 1980S WITH OSAMA BIN LADEN (2ND FROM LEFT) AND HIS ARAB MUJAHIDIN.

"FINALLY, WE CAN BREATHE": WOMEN AT THE 2018 COMIC-CON FESTIVAL IN JEDDAH. UNDER THE ABAYA THEY WEAR T-SHIRTS AND JEANS LIKE OTHER YOUNG PEOPLE AROUND THE WORLD.

PHOTO TAKEN DURING THE AUTHOR'S LAST MEETING WITH KHASHOGGI IN JEDDAH (2016).

MISSILE ATTACK ON ARAMCO'S OIL PRODUCTION, SEPTEMBER 2019: ABQAIQ

THE ATTACKS OF THE OIL PROCESSING FACILITIES OF ABQAIQ AND KHURAIS, IN SEPTEMBER 2019, CRIPPLED FIFTY PERCENT OF THE KINGDOM'S OIL PRODUCTION.

ASIR, NEAR THE YEMENI BORDER, SAUDI ARABIA

CAMP BASTION, HELMAND, AFGHANISTAN

GIRLS SCHOOL IN JALALABAD, AFGHANISTAN

PRISONER REFUGEES IN TRIPOLI, LIBYA

WITH STUDENTS IN BURAYDAH, SAUDI ARABIA

ON THE WHARF IN WONSAN, NORTH KOREA

WITH PRESIDENT BASHAR AL-ASSAD, DAMASCUS, SYRIA

WITH US TROOPS IN HELMAND, AFGHANISTAN

WITH TRIBAL VILLAGERS IN PAKTIA, AFGHANISTAN

ON THE MEDITERRANEAN COAST IN SABRATHA, LIBYA

NEAR THE NEW NEOM AIRPORT, SAUDI ARABIA

WITH THEN VICE FOREIGN MINISTER FU YING IN BEIJING, CHINA

WITH ULTRA-CONSERVATIVE MEN IN BURAYDAH, SAUDI ARABIA

WITH THE TALIBAN IN QUETTA, PAKISTAN

IN MUZAFFARABAD, DISPUTED KASHMIR, PAKISTAN

WITH US MARINES IN HELMAND, SOUTH-AFGHANISTAN

THE ROYALS: A TERRIFYINGLY NICE FAMILY

BEHIND THE WALL OF RIYADH'S PALACES, SAUDI PRINCES BATTLE FOR WEALTH AND POWER. IT'S NOT FOR THE FAINT OF HEART.

It is disturbing to see the richest Arab of all time (according to *Forbes*) after he's spent nearly three months in detention. Prince Al-Waleed bin Talal is sitting in a room in the Ritz-Carlton in Riyadh. The sixty-two-year-old, a high-ranking member of the ruling family, is being detained by his cousin and his cousin's father, none other than young Crown Prince Mohammed bin Salman and King Salman bin Abdulaziz.

Prince Al-Waleed bin Talal is emaciated, gray, and nervous. But the billionaire gives an interview wherein he plays down the awkward situation, trying to make everything appear less humiliating than it obviously is. On the night of November 4, 2017, Prince Al-Waleed was summoned from his private desert camp to the royal court in Riyadh, then forcibly taken to the Ritz. That night, more than three hundred princes, politicians, and businesspeople went through the same ordeal.

PRINCE AL-WALEED AT THE END OF HIS DETENTION IN JANUARY 2018: HOW THE ACCUSED WERE SELECTED REMAINS UNCLEAR.

The operation was carefully planned for months. The country's borders were closed, the airport was shut down, and the five-star Ritz-Carlton was converted into a luxurious jail. Prince Al-Waleed's cell phone was confiscated. He was accused of having committed serious crimes: money laundering, bribery, extortion; all, in his words, "misunderstandings" between himself and the government.

NIGHT OF THE LONG KNIVES

In November 2017, I traveled to Riyadh to find out what lay behind the so-called anti-corruption campaign.

Why were certain princes like Al-Waleed locked up? Why were hundreds of billionaires and politicians forced to hand over their assets, while others were not?

The prisoners at the Ritz had one thing in common: for decades, they had all operated within the orbit of the ruling family. But the reason why some fell into disgrace and were imprisoned remained unclear. More important, perhaps, is the question of why others were spared. Up to that point, most royals had believed they stood above the law and enjoyed immunity for whatever they did simply because they belonged to the ruling dynasty. But one night changed everything.

The sprawling House of Saud was in uproar—and in a state of fear. No one felt safe from the grip of the new ruling pair, the King and MBS. Although a reformer, MBS turned out to be the iron fist and mastermind behind the Ritz crackdown.

Five days after what will go down in history as the Saudi "Night of the Long Knives" I talk to the culture and information minister at the time, Awwad al-Awwad, in search of answers. I meet al-Awwad shortly before midnight at his office in Riyadh's Digital City, an area of huge cubist buildings illuminated in white and green, Saudi Arabia's national colors.

Awwad al-Awwad is in high spirits, but also exhausted. The "clean-up operation" made headlines around the world, and al-

Awwad had to make sure that the sparse reports being published within the kingdom were distributed to the right outlets at the right time.

Al-Awwad is not a prince. He worked his way up the ranks after earning a doctorate in finance law in England. Now the forty-six-year-old is helping Prince Mohammed bin Salman "drain the swamp" back home. He considers my question about the legal grounds for the mass detention rather strange. Al-Awwad says he believes that this incident is the dawn of a new era of justice.

"It's finally happening!" he says. "Someone has summoned the courage to clean up and put an end to the culture of theft! Don't you see it? The people are dancing in the streets!"

What does not fit into the picture, and what he does not mention, is the wealth of the current monarch and how it was acquired. King Salman's net worth is estimated at $17 billion. Allegedly, the money comes from the profits from his media empire. Crown Prince Mohammed's assets are thought to be worth $3 billion dollars. In late 2016, he bought a $500 million yacht. The year before, he purchased a French castle, Chateau Louis XIV, for about $300 million, not to mention the most expensive painting in the world, the *Salvator Mundi* by Leonardo da Vinci, which he bought in 2017.

When asked about his private expenditures of $1.25 billion over the past two years, the heir apparent told CBS he did not like to talk about his private life. "I'm a rich person and not a poor person. I'm not Gandhi or Mandela. I'm a member of the ruling family."

TEMPORARY FIVE-STAR PRISON: THE RITZ-CARLTON. AT LEAST ONE OF THE DETAINEES AT THE RITZ, A GENERAL, DIDN'T SURVIVE THE ORDEAL.

Internationally, Prince Al-Waleed was the best known of the hundreds of detainees at the Ritz being asked to pay a high price for their freedom. There were reports of torture and men carrying out "special procedures" to get the prisoners to agree to transfer a portion of their wealth to the state. The torturers were rumored to speak English amongst themselves, which suggested that they were foreigners and had been recruited solely for this operation, possibly by private American security firms.

When pressed on this point, the government said that such claims were unfounded and that the attorney general had prepared the indictments in accordance with Saudi law. The accused could receive their attorneys' counsel at any time. There was, however, the possibility of reaching an out-of-court settlement. If this was unsuccessful, the cases would be brought before a court. At least one of the detainees at the Ritz, a general, didn't survive the mistreatment. He had been a key player in the former king's power structure, a system which now had to be removed.

Some of the inmates at the Ritz managed to prove their innocence and walk free within a few days. Upon his release, Prince Al-Waleed weighed $6 billion less. This payment represented the tacit agreement between Al-Waleed and the state, reported the *Wall Street Journal*. Before his arrest, Prince Al-Waleed's net worth was estimated at $18 billion. The prince remained silent on the matter. The details were confidential.

Not a single case went to court. Not a single attorney spoke out publicly. The families of the detainees kept their mouths shut— except for the younger brother of Prince Al-Waleed, Khaled. He expressed his outrage in public and was immediately locked up. Burning questions, such as who was really harming the country and how much money was stolen or paid in compensation, were left unanswered, and it remained unclear whether innocent people had been detained.

King Salman and his son seized billions of dollars—money that family members and courtiers had been filling their own pockets with for decades. Officially, the amount exceeded $100 billion. The kingdom is in economic trouble and in dire need of cash.

It is not known what kind of assets were seized. Among the new "crown jewels" were the biggest TV channels in the country, media outlets with influence reaching far beyond the country's borders. They had previously been independently run by Saudi businessmen, but were now forced to work under the auspices of the government. The billions collected in the course of the "anti-corruption campaign" are to be managed by the state's Public Investment Fund, under the command of none other than Crown Prince Mohammed bin Salman. Thanks to the Ritz operation, he has come closer to achieving his goal of controlling the country's entire wealth.

There's clearly more to the whole affair than fighting corruption. The action was intended to consolidate King Salman's rule and secure the succession of his favorite son Prince Mohammed to the throne. In short, a demonstration of power aimed to intimidate the sprawling House of Saud and its minions, and to crush potential resistance. Nothing like this had ever happened in the country's history. You could say that the royal family ceased to exist as it had up until that fateful November 4th.

Even so, the royals continued to appear together as if nothing had happened. In the media, the ex-prisoners palled around with the king and the crown prince, praising their superb leadership and pledging their loyalty to the throne.

At the opening of Janadriyah, the annual national cultural festival, Prince Al-Waleed was seen cheerfully chatting away with King Salman, just three weeks after the monarch had laid his hands on a considerable chunk of Al-Waleed's wealth. The businessman made surprising comments such as "It might be shocking for many, but my relationship to him [Prince Mohammed bin Salman] is even stronger [than before the arrest]. I've forgiven and forgotten everything."

In 2006, a US diplomat then stationed in Riyadh described the special family dynamic of the royals in a report for the State Department. "Saudi Arabia is like the Ford Motor Company. The family name is on the door. It's the only country in the world that was created by one family and that's named after it." Nearly all key positions—governors, ministers, high posts in the secret services—are occupied by royal highnesses. At the end of the day, there is no choice but for them to get along with each other.

The influence of the Saudi middle class is negligible. There is no parliament to speak of, just the Shura, an advisory body consisting of twelve committees with no legislative power whatsoever. Representatives of the people can raise their concerns there. The last king, Abdullah, ruled that there should be a certain number of women among the 150 representatives. Since 2013, thirty of them have been female.

The House of Saud has grown tremendously since the country's founder, Abdulaziz bin Abd ar-Rahman Al Saud—"Ibn Saud"—conquered the Arabian Peninsula in the early twentieth century. Elderly Saudis joke that Abdulaziz always fought with two swords while he was forging the nation: one of steel and one of flesh. What they mean is that he subjugated and dispatched tribal leaders who stood in his way with the sword of steel, then married their widows and sired a large number of children—with the sword of flesh.

Ibn Saud had more than eighty direct offspring, forty-five of them sons, thereby expanding the House of Saud that rules today. Today, there are well over fifteen thousand princes and princesses. Prince Al-Waleed bin Talal is one of the founder's many grandsons.

THE ROYALS' DEPICTION OF THE UNIFICATION WARS: THE NATION'S FOUNDER, IBN SAUD, WAS CONSIDERED AN HONEST, HUMBLE MAN.

Direct descendants receive a fixed allowance from birth. It ranges between $200,000 and $270,000 per month for his children. Grandchildren get $27,000, great-grandchildren $13,000, while their children get a piddling $8,000. When princes and princesses marry, they are given between one and three million dollars for the construction of a residence. The portfolio of the royal allowances adds up to two billion dollars, a little less than 1 percent of the country's annual budget of around $240 billion.

In 1996, Prince Al-Waleed bin Talal spilled the beans about the top-secret list of royal allowances in a confidential conversation with William Fowler, the former US ambassador in Riyadh. Fowler cabled a memo on the subject to his superior. Fifteen years later, WikiLeaks published the confidential State Department correspondence—as part of the Cablegate documents—for all the world to read.

Fowler's report revealed further details about the royals' internal rivalries—for example, how a handful of princes in top government jobs received much more money than the rest. Huge sums are allocated outside of the official budget, flowing toward, for example, development projects around the two Holy Mosques in Mecca and Medina, which, as Prince Al-Waleed revealed, amounted to $5 billion per year at the time.

That's not all. Of the national daily oil production of eight million barrels, one million barrels were set aside, the proceeds from the sale of which were divided up between five or six princes, as Al-Waleed told the US ambassador. In the mid-1990s, that amounted to $20 million per day.

Saudi Arabia didn't always have a reputation for corruption. The nation's founder, Ibn Saud, was considered an honest, humble man who led a puritanical life following *Wahhabi* principles. It was well known that, when he was traveling through the country and saw a poor man, he would sometimes stop, get out of the car, and press a gold coin into the man's hand. Ibn Saud died in 1953. "King Saud—who succeeded Ibn Saud on the throne—and his brother King Faisal—who in turn succeeded him—are also reported to have been squeaky clean."

Back then, the nation was developing quickly, and the oil boom demanded rapid change. King Faisal—who took the throne in

1964—founded various institutions to run the country: a defense ministry, an interior ministry, a health ministry. He left the job of running the ministries to his brothers.

But the oil boom encouraged greed: day-to-day corruption on the part of hospital directors, construction bosses, and top state officials who would buy hospital beds, heavy machinery, and office equipment at normal market rates then charge the administration sky-high prices for the goods and pocket the difference. For a long time, this was the way things worked here. Everyone in the hierarchy added his signature to claim his share of the contract.

Princes used to seize plots of land and register them under their names. They either took the land away from the residents outright, or they bought it for a symbolic pittance if, for example, they had insider knowledge that a big construction project was planned for the site. When the time was right, they sold it to the state at the highest possible price, realizing huge profit margins.

A few princes have discovered the phenomenally lucrative business of so-called "commissions." The British corruption expert Nicholas Gilby claims that "for fifty years it has been standard practice between Saudis and British officials to pay bribes to ensure weapons deals."

It begins with Saudi middlemen offering contracts worth billions to foreign sales representatives of Western arms manufacturers in Saudi Arabia in exchange for a commission fee. They also work for influential princes. Two names come up again and again: the former crown prince Sultan, who served as defense minister for decades since 1962, and his half-brother, the former king Abdullah.

A "commission" of between 7.5 percent and 15 percent is pocketed by the middlemen and passed on to the Saudi princes. According to Gilby's research and a BBC documentary, in this fashion around £500 million ended up in the accounts of Prince Abdullah over several decades. They negotiated voluminous deals: the Prince brokered the purchase of British communications equipment for the one-hundred-thousand-strong National Guard. The middleman was Abdullah's brother-in-law.

BRITAIN'S BIGGEST ARMS DEAL EVER

In 1985, London and Riyadh signed the largest weapons contract in British history: the Yamamah project. Yamamah means "dove," but there was nothing dovish about it.

Huge covert financial transactions were an integral part of the deal from the start. Saudi Arabia agreed to buy 132 fighter jets from Britain, including comprehensive services, over ten years. The price: £43 billion. Concealed in the price were "commissions" worth around £6 billion, as was later unearthed by British investigators.

The invoices that defense contractor BAE submitted to the British Ministry of Defense included vaguely defined line items, such as "support services." The amount set aside for kickbacks was the difference between the actual cost and the money reimbursed by the Ministry of Defense. BAE managers forwarded the money to the middlemen, who passed it on to the Saudi princes and those in their close circles.

The arms deal was negotiated by then British prime minister Margaret Thatcher during a meeting with the Saudi ambassador to Washington, Prince Bandar bin Sultan. However, when Britain passed a new anti-corruption law in 2002, informants gave tip-offs and British journalists pounced on the case. The Saudi diplomat Bandar bin Sultan has since been accused of having received $1 billion in bribes for the Yamamah project over at least a ten-year period, in installments of £30 million per quarter. The funds were declared as marketing expenses.

The kickbacks ended up in Bandar's account at Riggs Bank in Washington. A Riggs employee told the BBC that the Saudi ambassador never distinguished between his private accounts and the embassy accounts.

When I meet Prince Bandar at his Riyadh palace in January 2018, he brings up the subject on his own. He seems displeased that the whiff of corruption has stuck to him. Nothing about the allegations is true, he says. He didn't personally profit from the deal.

"So, what happened?" I ask.

Prince Bandar puffs on his cigar. Unfortunately, he can't divulge further details. That would disclose too many state secrets. Then he tells me a surprising tale: the money was invested in arms for the Contras (the US-supported Nicaraguan rebel group fighting the left-wing Sandinista government in the 1980s), and for the *mujahideen* fighting the Soviets in Afghanistan. "Write that!" he enthuses.

"That's a new version of the story!" I reply. It can't be verified quickly, but I promise to write it. Well there, I've done it.

It will not be surprising if the colossal corruption case is never fully cleared up. In 2006, then British prime minister Tony Blair personally scuttled investigations by the Serious Fraud Office, the British anti-corruption authority. "If it had gone ahead, it would have involved the most serious allegations and investigation being made of the Saudi royal family. I don't believe the investigation would have led anywhere, except to the complete wreckage of a vital interest to our country," Blair explained later.

Riyadh put the British government under immense pressure. The Saudis threatened to end cooperation on counterterrorism if the investigations were not ceased immediately.

For the official investigator, Robert Wardle, it was a bitter moment. "They told us that if we continue British lives would be put at risk," Wardle explained in an interview. Judging by his expression, he didn't wish to shoulder that responsibility.

Still, a little later, during court proceedings in the US, the weapons manufacturer BAE was forced to admit its responsibility for the kickbacks. To avoid a court ruling, BAE offered to pay a fine of $400 million. Those responsible in the British government escaped unscathed.

THE KINGDOM'S FRIENDLY FEMALE FACE

Of the fifteen thousand Saudi princes and princesses, two thousand are considered filthy rich. All of the princes I meet in Riyadh have received top-shelf educations. They hold degrees from the top private universities in the world—in Britain and the United States.

PRINCESS ALJOHARAH TALAL ALSAUD AT A START-UP BUSINESS COMPETITION IN RIYADH(2018): ROYAL HIGHNESSES ATTEND MANY SPECIAL EVENTS AS GUESTS OF HONOR.

The older royals feel more connected to the traditional way of life than the younger generation. They still remember the mud villages where their parents grew up, and nearly all of them spent their youth in the kingdom. The younger royals often become acquainted with the outside world early in life. They live here, there, and everywhere.

Islam plays an important role in the lives of both old and young. Yet in none of my conversations with members of the royal family does religion ever come up as a crucial issue. These days, the alliance between the Sauds and the ultra-religious Salafis who strictly follow the teachings of Abd al-Wahhab seems purely strategic.

The royals I meet include the owner of a golf club, a young IT specialist and comic artist, a long-time director of the secret services, a hobby chef, and a lady—Princess Reema bint Bandar, who was educated as a museologist. She is the daughter of Prince Bandar bin Sultan, former ambassador to the US, who has since taken over that key position herself, becoming the first female ambassador in the history of her country.

I met Princess Reema several years ago in the open-plan office of the so-called Mass Participation Federation. With high ceilings, high doors, and wooden floors, the space looked more like a ballroom than an office. Back then, Princess Reema was running the newly founded organization, which was supposed to jolt the unathletic Saudis into action and transform them into a sports-loving nation. Reema encouraged women to publicly participate in sports, making them more visible. The mood of her staff was positive, almost euphoric.

The princess wore blue slacks, high heels, and an elegant dove-blue coat that resembled a kimono. A silk scarf was casually draped over her head. She had just organized the first-ever soccer game women were allowed to attend as spectators.

Reema bint Bandar was born in 1975. She's an energetic woman, a natural beauty, and is playing a leading role in the social revolution sweeping the country. Reema is the kingdom's best-known female politician.

Reema's mother is an art lover who presides over a collection of extraordinary artifacts. Her enterprising diplomat father has connections in the highest political circles around the world. Reema attended college in the US, and upon her return to Saudi

Arabia in 2005, she managed the Riyadh branch of the British designer department store Harvey Nichols.

"I can't believe that all of this is really happening here," she told me. I could sense her excitement about the latest developments which were enabling so much more freedom of movement for women. Crown Prince MBS is ten years younger than Princess Reema, and her cousin. He hired her to transform the promenade in Jeddah into a second Venice Beach. Her job was to somehow fill the expansive boardwalk with life.

Princess Reema is the benevolent face of the new kingdom. She's educated and modern, a successful businesswoman, divorced, and a single mother. She has a socially-minded, creative, and strong personality. At the World Economic Forum in Davos in 2018, she defended the kingdom, complaining that, despite everything, media coverage of her country was unfair. The media was cultivating a critical undertone, not acknowledging how many people were working hard to reform Saudi Arabia.

A few months later, in June 2018, Princess Reema appeared on CNN and explained to Americans how sensational it was for Saudi women to finally be allowed to drive, something she herself had already done on a regular basis while living in the US. She did this very elegantly, stressing that Crown Prince Mohammed had granted this right to all women. At the same time, her uncle, the crown prince, had ordered the arrest and imprisonment of the very activists who had fought for the right to drive for years. During their detention they suffered mistreatment and humiliating sexual abuse: "We're taking control, but we're taking control collectively, this isn't a singular activity, this isn't an anomaly, this is our current state and this is our future state. This isn't something you go back from."

BATTLE FOR THE THRONE

For a long time, unlike in other royal families—those in England or Sweden, for instance—there are no clear rules on succession in the House of Saud. The transition following the death of a Saudi king has always been a moment of potential instability.

King Abdullah meant to settle his legacy during his lifetime. He arranged for his half-brother, Crown Prince Salman, to succeed him on the throne, and decided that his even-younger half-brother, Mukrin, who ran the kingdom's secret services until 2012, should be next in line after that. Back in 2006, Abdullah created a council of thirty-four family members to monitor the succession process. Future kings must be confirmed by a majority in the council.

In 2014, King Abdullah was diagnosed with lung cancer. His end was in sight, and members of the royal family began to spy on each other. Phones were tapped, cameras and microphones were hidden in palaces. *The New York Times* reported that those close to King Abdullah purchased a Chinese device that could identify the number of every phone within a radius of three hundred feet.

In January 2015, Abdullah fell into a coma. His sons and the royal court attempted to keep his condition secret from the rest of the family and the public.

According to the *Times,* Khaled al-Tuwayjri, responsible for the king's finances, said that Abdullah was resting, but by that time the king had already passed away.

When Salman learned the truth, he went after the chief of the royal court, who had been dismissed; witnesses reported hearing loud punches in the hospital corridor. Al-Tuwayjri had long been disliked by most family members, especially King Abdullah's siblings. He was among those later detained at the Ritz.

During his first week in office, the new king, Salman, began to purge the upper echelons of competitors in the family. Two of Abdullah's sons, Prince Turki and Prince Mishaal, were detained. As governors of Riyadh and Mecca respectively, they had been two of the most powerful men in the country. Prince Turki, a politically ambitious man, had hoped to contain the rise of the already influential Prince Mohammed. He had warned his American and Chinese contacts about his cousin's fierce temperament.

Turki and Mishaal were brought to the Ritz on November 4. Prince Turki still hasn't been released as of the time of this book's printing. His military advisor, Major General Ali al-Qahtani, was the one detainee who didn't survive the harsh treatment in the five-star prison.

At the end of April 2015, Crown Prince Mukrin, in a surprise move, was stripped of his title. In his place, King Salman installed his nephew, Interior Minister Prince Mohammed bin Nayef, a favorite of the Americans with twenty years of experience in national security under his belt. The CIA valued Prince Mohammed bin Nayef for his hard line in the fight against terror.

Next, King Salman put his favorite son, Prince Mohammed, into position to eventually ascend to the throne; he named him deputy crown prince. He had broken the unwritten rule that the Saudi crown is always passed on to one of the nation's founder's sons—from one brother to the next, a geriatric succession line. For the first time, one of Ibn Saud's grandsons is in line to become king.

THE SILENT COUP

It didn't take long for Crown Prince Mohammed bin Nayef's political career to come to an abrupt end. In a confidential conversation on the night of June 20, 2017, King Salman forced the CIA's darling to resign. The king named his son Mohammed bin Salman crown prince. If MBS becomes king, Salman's branch of the family will determine the fate of the kingdom for generations. Other branches would be excluded from power for the foreseeable future.

That evening, King Salman summoned Prince Mohammed bin Nayef to the fourth floor of his palace in Mecca. The two men were alone in the room, but various sources provided matching reports on the gist of the conversation.

The king said, in effect, "I'd like you to resign because you haven't followed our advice and gotten treatment for your addiction [to prescription medication]; this dangerously impairs your ability to make decisions."

The fifty-seven-year-old interior minister was shocked. He had suffered from chronic pain since a suicide bomber blew himself up next to him in 2009. His body was riddled with shrapnel. He had kept the pain under control with strong medication. But no one had ever expressed doubts about his sharp intellect or his decision-making abilities. In fact, in February 2017, former CIA director Mike Pompeo awarded bin Nayef the George Tenet Medal in recognition of his "excellent intelligence performance in the domain of counterterrorism and his unbound contribution to realize world security and peace." Prince Mohammed bin Nayef never imagined having to yield to a man as young and inexperienced as Prince Mohammed bin Salman, a man trusted by very few to lead the kingdom through the most difficult time in its history: a period of low oil prices, a war in Yemen, growing influence of Saudi Arabia's arch-rival Iran, and the deterioration of relations between the Gulf states.

There are two versions of the story of Crown Prince Mohammed bin Nayef's abdication. The first goes like this: A letter from the king, written by advisors to Prince Mohammed bin Salman and addressed to the thirty-four members of the succession council, claimed that the interior minister was addicted to pain medication and that "we have tried for more than two years to motivate him to undergo treatment, without success." He should, therefore, be relieved of his post, and MBS should take his place, the letter argued.

The letter was read to the members of the council over the phone. All but three of them said they supported the proposal. Envoys were sent to the council members to gather their signatures.

That night, Mohammed bin Nayef was detained alone in a room—no phone, no access to his staff or his family. Even his bodyguards from the Ministry of the Interior were removed. Recordings of phone calls made to the council members who voted against him were played back to make clear to him how little support he had within the family.

At dawn, Mohammed bin Nayef capitulated. All it had taken, apparently, was a short meeting with the king. The powerful man who had carried the title of crown prince agreed to step down and sign the required documents.

The source of the second version of the story is a high-ranking Saudi official who talked to Reuters. According to this version, the story of intrigue against the interior minister is "a complete fantasy, worthy of Hollywood." Mohammed bin Nayef's removal from office was in the national interest, he says: Bin Nayef "experienced neither pressure nor a lack of respect. The reasons for his dismissal are confidential."

When he left the king's residence in the morning, Mohammed bin Nayef was surprised that his adversary and successor, Prince Mohammed, was waiting for him to say goodbye. He kissed his hands and embraced him.

It was a disconcerting farewell. The scene was part of a meticulously rehearsed production, with TV cameras capturing the moment. The footage, showing Prince Mohammed supposedly paying his respect to the ex-crown prince who had resigned moments before, was fed to the media; it suggested perfect harmony. Over the next few days, it was broadcast nonstop on all channels in Saudi Arabia and throughout the Gulf.

From that moment on, Mohammed bin Nayef had lost all political power. He was banned from leaving the kingdom, and forced to live under a kind of loose house arrest. The silent coup had succeeded, and MBS was set to become the next king.

Following the Saudi Night of the Long Knives, *Forbes* removed Prince Al-Waleed and several other Saudi billionaires from its list of the world's richest people. Their assets can no longer be reliably quantified and, besides, it is unclear how much of their wealth they still control, according to *Forbes*. The media now only talk about the total wealth of the House of Saud. With $1.4 trillion to their name, they are without a shadow of a doubt the wealthiest family in the world, sixteen times richer than the British monarchy.

Competition within the royal family used to be all about getting the biggest piece of the pie for oneself. Recently, *Forbes* created a new kind of list. Alongside the richest people on the planet, there's now an index of the world's seventy-five most powerful people. As a new entry, in eighth place: Crown Prince Mohammed bin Salman.

THE FAUSTIAN PACT
OF DIRIYAH

THE RISE OF THE HOUSE OF SAUD BEGAN IN A MODEST ADOBE SETTLEMENT—DIRIYAH. THE MYTH OF THE HEROIC ORIGINS OF THE SAUDI NATION WAS BORN HERE. THE KING'S SON, PRINCE SULTAN, UNDERTOOK THE RESTORATION OF THE HISTORICAL CAPITAL OF THE FIRST SAUDI NATION. NOW IT'S OPEN TO THE PUBLIC.

One of my first visits to Saudi Arabia was in spring 2011. The Arab world was in a state of upheaval. In Tunisia, Jordan, and Egypt, angry citizens had chased away their autocratic rulers or else toppled their governments. I was traveling with the landscape architects Richard and Jens Bödeker, a father and son team. They were heading to meet their favorite client, Prince Sultan bin Salman, a son of the former governor of Riyadh who is now the king.

On the way to Diriyah, Richard Bödeker—who passed away in November of 2019—explained his strategy for dealing with his royal clients. "Don't go to your master if you're not summoned. He will lose respect for you and you will lose your independence." On that day, Prince Salman had summoned him and, of course, the Germans show up on time.

Prince Sultan bin Salman's so-called farm lies several miles northwest of the capital, in a place called Diriyah. It's a kind of suburb, but is still thought of as the heart of the kingdom. It is there that the first Saudi state was founded a long time ago— in 1744.

It's no accident that Prince Sultan created his paradise on earth there, in Diriyah, where everything began. The history of Diriyah is also his history, the history of the Sauds and their kingdom. The myth of Diriyah is the myth of the Al Saud.

We veered away from the highway. The prince's property is at least as long as a soccer field, and the mud walls surrounding it were higher than the palm trees growing in front of them. Several massive gates opened slowly in succession. The driveway leads directly to a sprawling main house with a patio and several terraces. While a modern home, it is built in the traditional mud-brick adobe style.

DINNER AT THE FARM OWNED BY PRINCE SULTAN (CENTER RIGHT) WITH GUEST OF HONOR, LANDSCAPE ARCHITECT RICHARD BÖDEKER (CENTER LEFT), AND THE AUTHOR (LEFT). HIS ROYAL HIGHNESS IS UNPRETENTIOUS, GOOD HUMORED, AND SERENE.

Servants line up and offer us water and fresh lime and mango juice. Prince Sultan greets the Bödekers like old friends. Hands are shaken, cheeks kissed. Prince Sultan is slender and tall, nearly six foot six. His moustache is trimmed short. His Royal Highness looks very relaxed. He tells me about his recent vacation in the Swiss Alps, where he went paragliding. Saudis love to escape the heat of the desert and spend time in the refreshing climate of the Alps in Europe, especially during the summer months, when temperatures can easily reach 120 degrees in Saudi Arabia. Many wealthy Saudis own a chalet in Switzerland, France, or Germany—often formidable mansions or impressive castles—for just this purpose.

Prince Sultan chats in a light mood. He appears unpretentious, relaxed, yet focused. With his pleasant down-to-earth nature, he comes across very differently from his dynamic half-brother, Crown Prince Mohammed bin Salman.

Elegant and solicitous white-vested attendants serve stewed lamb and refill our drinks. They seem to be able to anticipate our wishes before we even know them ourselves. The prince entertains us with a firsthand account of the magic of the old royal city of Diriyah. The previous year, UNESCO declared the settlement a World Heritage Site. Now, under the supervision of Prince Sultan, Diriyah is being carefully restored: the administration building, the palaces, an old public bath.

At the time, Prince Sultan was minister for tourism, and therefore also responsible for the nation's archeological heritage. He is eager to tell the kingdom's history anew—in other words, the story of how the desert realm became, thanks to his family, what it is today: an oasis of progress.

The days of oil sales driving development in Saudi Arabia are numbered. Prince Sultan is painfully aware of this, which is why tourism is slated to become one of the kingdom's next big sources of employment. For the very first time, the government intends to open up its archeological treasures to international tourists. In Prince Sultan's opinion, the exciting history of the royal family and their desert kingdom has the potential to become a magnet for visitors, turning tourism into an important source of income.

The founding myth of Saudi Arabia is, in fact, a riveting story, and it goes like this: An ancestor of Prince Sultan, a certain Mohammed bin Saud, reigned over a rather modest territory in Diriyah, a largish adobe settlement, until he sealed an alliance with a radical religious cleric in 1744. Together, they forged the first Saudi state.

Back then, in central Arabia, competing clans were constantly skirmishing with each other. People yearned for solidity, for serenity. An authoritarian religious doctrine in cahoots with the central military power in the area presented an attractive alternative to the constant threat of being ambushed or killed.

In the beginning, Mohammed bin Saud only imposed the strict new religious order upon his small area of control. Then he swiftly expanded his rule to one region of central Arabia after another. In that sense, the early Saudi state was a huge success.

Nevertheless, Mohammed bin Saud eventually failed. You could even say he ended up being a victim of his own success. The Saudi-controlled area included Iraq and parts of the Gulf Coast, even the Hejaz, home to the pilgrimage sites in Mecca and Medina. Both cities were kept under the control of the Ottoman Empire, and the Sultan in Istanbul wasn't very pleased—to say the least—about the brazen takeover of his territory. He deployed his Egyptian vassals to take care of the invaders from Diriyah.

The Sauds did not have a chance against the more modern Egyptian cannons. By 1818, it was all over. The Saudi leaders were executed. Their date palms were cut down, destroying the livelihood of the local population. The seat of the Saudi government was in ruins. The first Saudi state had been annihilated.

A second Saudi state was soon to rise. This time it was based in Riyadh, and suffered a fate no better than the first one. However, in 1902, Prince Sultan's grandfather, Abdulaziz, reconquered today's capital with a stroke of tactical genius—and a mere forty warriors, or so goes the story. His men snuck along each of the walls of the home of the man ruling Riyadh at the time and killed him as he was leaving the house in the morning. At the Masmak Fort across the street, the point of a spear hurled by one of the attackers remains stuck in the entrance door.

Prince Sultan's tale is still echoing in my mind when he says, "Why don't you come by another time?"

THE HISTORIC GOVERNMENT SEAT OF DIRIYAH: STROLLING THROUGH THE NARROW ALLEYWAYS OF OLD DIRIYAH IN THE COMPANY OF HIS ROYAL HIGHNESS (LEFT).

RENEWING THE OLD CLAIM TO POWER

A few days later, I am indeed walking through the narrow alleyways of old Diriyah in the company of His Royal Highness.

Workers are hammering away. Beams are being chiseled out. The embellishments of heavy wooden doors are being carefully preserved and mud walls reinforced. The original inhabitants constructed their buildings out of a mixture of clay and sand from the riverbed of the Wadi Hanifa.

Prince Sultan shows me the walls of the Saud family's old Salwa Palace. Geometric openings in the walls are an indication of a sophisticated system that allowed air to circulate through the building to make the heat bearable. The architecture of Central Arabia, of the so-called Najd, Prince Sultan explains, was primitive but highly functional.

With pride in his voice he adds, "We are honoring our past, because it is our promise to our future." What at first sounds like a catchphrase is nothing less than a demonstration that the House of Saud is renewing its old claim to power in politically turbulent times.

The story of the rapid rise of the ruling family wouldn't be complete without a look at the role of Mohammed bin Abd al-Wahhab. The puritan religious leader doesn't stand in the historical spotlight as do the Al Saud, who take care of all matters of worldly governance. In a symbiotic relationship, the Al Sheikh, as al-Wahhab's family soon came to be called, rule over the morals and souls of the kingdom's subjects. The influence of these uncompromising religious reformers over the Saudi people is at least as momentous as that of the monarchy.

Abd al-Wahhab was born the son of a judge from Al-Uyaynah, a town thirty miles northwest of Diriyah. He lived from 1702 or 1703 to 1792. Through his studies and travels as a scholar, he adopted an extremely rigorous interpretation of Islam, teaching what he considered the true depiction of the early Islamic communities in Mecca and Medina and the life of the Prophet's companions as the model to follow, in line with the Qur'an and the Sunnah which had been transmitted mainly through an oral tradition. This inspired the theologian to demand a complete reform of religious life.

He believed in the idea of the unity of God as the sole creator, sustainer, and master of all the universe, meaning He would not tolerate the veneration of saints or tombs or stones and plants, by means of which many people indeed had found solace. The Sheikh ordered trees that had become objects of worship to be cut down.

In the struggle for ideological dominance, Abd al-Wahhab sanctioned the killing of "infidels." He defended the death sentence for Muslims if they didn't follow the one and only "true Islam," labeling them as apostates. To this day, his teachings are often referred to by extremists throughout the Muslim world to justify atrocities they commit in the name of Islam. Contemporary Saudi theologians are quite unwilling to discuss this particular issue, since the so-called Wahhabiya remains the official doctrine. They usually call it an "abuse" of the true teachings of the Sheikh and are eager to end the conversation quickly. But it's just not that simple.

From the beginning, the theologian's teachings polarized and divided communities wherever he preached his puritanical concepts. In Huraymila, a city in Najd, where Abd al-Wahhab lived for some time, he barely escaped an assassination attempt. Subsequently, he fled to his birthplace, Al-Uyaynah, where the local ruler called for the death of the rabble-rouser. In the end, the emir of Al-Uyaynah spared Abd al-Wahhab's life but forced him to leave his territory.

THE SOCIAL CONTRACT BETWEEN THE KING AND HIS SUBJECTS IS NULL AND VOID

The cleric then found asylum with Mohammed bin Saud in Diriyah. The leader recognized the immense power of Abd al-Wahhab's movement, which turned people into either passionate supporters or equally fanatical opponents. Saud believed he could harness this energy for his own political gain.

It's hard to say when the symbiosis between the religious fundamentalists and the modern state of Saudi Arabia began to wither. It happened, at any rate, long before Prince Sultan studied political science in the United States or when he became the first Arab astronaut, flying into orbit in the Space Shuttle Discovery in 1985. Sultan was twenty-eight at the time. That was when he fundamentally altered his thinking, he says. During the launch and the return to earth, he prayed nonstop: "You see the earth and recognize how small you really are, just a tiny speck in the universe."

In the 1980s, famous Saudi religious leaders like Abdulaziz bin Baz were still teaching their students that the earth is a disc at the center of the universe and that the sun revolves around our planet. Prince Sultan had to ensure Bin Baz that he had seen with his own eyes how the earth rotated on its own axis.

Nevertheless, Bin Baz became even more powerful. From 1994 until his death in 1999, he presided as Grand Mufti, the highest religious authority in the country. The preacher had lost his sight at the age of sixteen and apparently wanted believers to perceive the world as he imagined it.

I ask myself again and again how the politics of such a modern state can be compatible with the ultra-conservative world view of the *Wahhabis*. The assertions made by Saudi religious scholars that driving damages women's fertility or that the earth is a disc can easily be disproven with some quick online research.

When Prince Sultan's father Salman ascended to the throne in January 2015, he issued a decree only weeks later that many considered outrageous. After nearly eighty years, he abruptly stripped the much-feared religious police of all their power. These days their powers are limited to cautioning people for incorrect behavior.

But why did the king make this decision? And why then? There has always been an unspoken agreement between Saudi citizens and the monarchy: the king bestows prosperity like a benevolent father, and in return, the king's subjects stay out of politics.

This unwritten social contract is showing cracks. The low oil prices of recent years have left a gaping hole in the budget. The country's foreign currency reserves are dwindling. The state has run out of generous handouts for the people, such as bonuses and special allowances, and has to search for new sources of income. Young Saudis, however, expect the good life to go on. They want prosperity, jobs, and more freedom.

The Salafist ideology that maintained social stability in the country for so long is now getting in the way of urgently needed progress. A modern economy focused on tourism, the service industry, and trade can only function in an open society, something not really compatible with pure Salafist thought.

The royal city of Diriyah, with the Sauds' magnificent Salwa Palace in the At-Turaif district, lies on a limestone plateau. From there, the city drops into the valley of Wadi Hanifa and spreads across a plain known as Al Bujairi. It was here that Abd al-Wahhab once lived with his clan.

AL BUJAIRI HERITAGE PARK IN RIYADH: YOUNG SAUDIS EXPECT THAT THE STATE WILL CONTINUE TO PROVIDE OPPORTUNITIES FOR A GOOD LIFE.

Perhaps some historical truth is reflected in this geographical differential: Today, Al Bujairi, the site of Abd al-Wahhab's mosque, is used as a public park. The elegant complex includes restaurants, terraces, and souvenir shops. And yet this place is given far less historical importance than the At-Turaif government district on the other side, a monument in the Sauds' first seat of power.

Naturally, the reformer Abd al-Wahhab will always remain an integral part of the glorious founding myth of this nation, even though the unbridled violence of terror groups like al-Qaeda and the Islamic State would be unthinkable without his teachings of intolerance toward dissenters and members of other faiths.

His extreme views no longer fit with the image Saudi Arabia now wants to create for itself, of a young, modern economy. Prince Sultan's brother, Crown Prince Mohammed bin Salman, has decreed a moderate Islam. The country must change. Nothing less than its future is at stake.

THE ROYAL CITY OF DIRIYAH: THE SAUDS' MAGNIFICENT SALWA PALACE IN THE AT-TURAIF DISTRICT LIES ON A LIMESTONE PLATEAU AND DROPS INTO THE VALLEY OF WADI HANIFA.

THE MAGIC SCENT OF WOOD AND SWEAT

OUD COMES IN THE FORM OF RESINOUS WOOD OR AS OIL. TOP-QUALITY OUD IS WORTH ITS WEIGHT IN GOLD AND IS ONE OF THE MOST PRECIOUS FRAGRANCES IN THE WORLD.

In the Kingdom of Saudi Arabia, a successful celebration doesn't just mean that you handpicked the lamb at the market and had it prepared by the best cook. It's the little things that make a party great. One of them is the scent of bakhur—incense produced with the resin of the agar tree. I know about this from Tarek, who I first met when he was my tour guide on a trip to the desert. Since then, he sometimes accompanies me on my jaunts through the city.

Once a year, Tarek's mother visits the big bazaar in Riyadh to buy the precious wood, the resin of which exudes a bittersweet fragrance when burned on a lump of glowing coal. A good host like Tarek's father is waves the chalice of smoking resin under the sweaty armpits of his guests at the front door. The aroma is called Oud and is derived from the most expensive fragrant essences. The female guests perfume their loosened hair with the scent of the resin. Men like to place the smoldering chalice beneath their floor-length robes for a few minutes so that really everything smells good. According to Bedouin tradition, this is the way to safely rid your body of pests of all kinds.

TRADITIONAL OUD BURNERS.

The balsamic-spicy scent, which contains a hint of sweat, has been treasured by Arabs for its aphrodisiac effect for two thousand years. The West discovered Oud only recently. In 2002, Yves Saint Laurent used the scent for the first time in his men's perfume, M7. Animalistic, woody, and yet modern, is how the famous perfumist describes its character.

Oud is the Saudi equivalent of refined Cuban cigars or a bottle of Veuve Clicquot champagne. For a special occasion like the family reunion to which I have been invited, a host will splurge on a few ounces of quality oud. The finest-quality form of these noble scented woodchips cost upward of $50,000 for a two-pound batch, which also encourages a thriving and lucrative copycat market.

Oud is obtained from the trunk of the agarwood tree, and I am told the best quality comes from India and Vietnam. But the fragrance only reaches perfection, explains Tarek's father, a trained chemist who used to work for the oil company Aramco, when the resin interacts with a rare fungus, *Phaeoacremonium parasiticum*, which settles on the tree's bark. This uncommon

OUD CHIPS CAN BE WORTH THEIR WEIGHT IN GOLD.

mixture of tree sap and mold spores is therefore the source of one of the most expensive oils in the world.

Tarek's mother allows me to accompany her on an oud-buying trip to the bazaar. We enter the shop she has been frequenting for years, an elegantly decorated square room. The counter is draped in red velvet. The Oud wood is stored in ornately decorated glass jars with gold trim. We learn the store has a new owner.

He is a lean man with high cheekbones, arching, bushy brows over dark eyes, fleshy lips, and a high forehead. The new shopkeeper presents my seventy-two-year-old shopping companion with a selection of agarwood, then wafts the smoke of numerous samples in our direction. He offers coffee, sesame cookies, and a comfortable chair.

Finally the merchant opens a precious-looking box, carved and decorated like a treasure chest.

"I offer these goods only to my most exceptional customers," he whispers mysteriously. The wood's scent is beguilingly strong. Intoxicated by the alluring scent and the special treatment,

FEMALE CLIENTS IN A SCENT SHOP IN RIYADH: THE MERCHANT OPENS CARVED BOXES
AND LAVISHLY DECORATED TREASURE CHESTS.

Tarek's mother buys ten ounces of the treasured woodchips for
3,400 riyals, almost $1,000.

Back at home, Tarek's father, the chemist, quickly establishes
that his wife has been conned. The wood doesn't contain any
precious resin. It's been doused with cheap scented oils. Tarek
hasn't seen his mother in such a state for a long time. With two
of her five sons in tow—Tarek and the younger Hashim—she
marches right back into the store and demands her money be
returned to her immediately.

"I have never sold such goods," the seller boldly claims, wrinkling his brow. Tarek's mother hisses back that if the man denies making the sale a second time, she, in turn, will deny what her sons are about to do to him.

The proud Arab woman's eyes shoot hot arrows of anger out from under the narrow slit of her black veil. Tarek stands closely behind his mother. He is six feet tall and broad-chested. Next to him, his only slightly less impressive brother, Hashim, pulls himself up to his full height. All of a sudden, the salesman's demeanor changes as he abruptly remembers his "error" and hands Tarek's mother her money back.

She turns on her heel and storms out of the store to buy her Oud from the competitor next door.

That evening, the entire family gathers for dinner as planned—two dozen people, aged six months to seventy-nine years. The house is filled with the exotic resin scent of the agarwood tree. Tarek's aunt Adila presses his mother for the address of the Oud dealer where she has been a customer for years.

But the hostess just smiles mysteriously and says: "Trade secret, my dear."

QATAR: MY BROTHER, MY FOE

People perceive the tiny emirate of Qatar and the bigger Kingdom of Saudi Arabia as a single entity. For years, the border was inconsequential. But life has become hard for people living near the frontier since the Saudis cut diplomatic ties in 2017.

The white desert on the way to Salwa is empty, vast, and uninhabited. The sand seems to stretch to the sky. Once in a while a vehicle drives in the opposite direction on the four-lane highway.

Until recently, trucks lined up along the road and jammed the exit to Tamani, a larger settlement thirty miles from the Saudi border crossing to the mini-emirate of Qatar. The trucks carried fruit, rice, and camels.

It is six o'clock on a Sunday morning, a normal workday in the Saturday-to-Thursday week. I'm traveling with Fahd, an electrical engineer from Riyadh. We met at a lecture in one of the new cultural institutions in the capital. The topic was the portrayal of the Orient in European painting. The speakers presented pictures of lascivious women reclining, scantily clad, on upholstered furniture, such as Jean-Joseph Benjamin-Constant's *Odalisque*. Another painting—*Intérieur Oriental* by Théodore Chassériau—shows a topless dancer. Both works are by nineteenth-century French artists.

The Saudis are astonished by this view of the Arab world. After the lecture, Fahd and I talked about how we see each other's cultures and how they portray people, especially women. I found out that Fahd works in Salwa, the last Saudi city before the frontier to Qatar. As a technician, he is responsible for maintaining the equipment of the city administration.

What interested me was how Saudi Arabia decided, overnight in June 2017, to designate Qatar its mortal enemy, and what that meant for the people impacted by the sudden divorce. Fahd offered to take me along on his next trip.

ROAD TO THE END OF THE KINGDOM: WHERE CAMEL TRADERS, TRUCKERS, AND FAMILIES USED TO PASS THROUGH, IS NOW AN EERIE, DESOLATE LANDSCAPE.

BLOCKED BY PYLONS

Like a lot of family men, Fahd commutes from Riyadh to the Eastern Province every week. Fahd says that barracks are being built in Salwa for soldiers meant to secure the border. We drive past rows of new buildings which stand in rank and file.

We cruise toward the border crossing. It's closed. Concrete pylons block the way to the toll gate. Salwa is the only official crossing along the thirty-seven-mile land border that connects Qatar with the kingdom.

I get out of the car, German passport in my hand.

"What are you doing here?" asks a man in a white robe. Not so long ago, it was easy to cross this border. They would just wave you through.

The man is a security officer in civilian garb. He seems suspicious. I answer that I hope to travel to Doha, the capital of Qatar. The man gives me an incredulous look and raises his hand, making it clear that no one is getting through. Losing patience, he commands me to step back.

POWER, BETRAYAL, WOUNDED PRIDE

Qatar is a small, bulbous peninsula that protrudes into the Persian Gulf. If you believe Saudi Arabia's state-controlled newspapers, Riyadh would be happy if the tiny nation fell into the sea. In fact, Saudi Arabia is planning to physically cut off the emirate from the Arabian Peninsula by digging a canal.

The kingdom plans to spend up to $750 million, with a section of the waterway possibly to be used later as a nuclear waste dump. What better way to express contempt for your neighbors?

But what's behind all this?

Officially, Saudi Arabia justifies its sudden about-turn with the accusation that Qatar supports extremism and shelters terrorists, from the Taliban to Hamas to the Muslim Brotherhood.

Without a doubt, Qatar does extend its hospitality toward international figures who could be classified as radical—people like Khaled Mashal, a leader of the Palestinian organization Hamas. The Taliban keep an office in Doha. But it was set up with the consent of the international community to encourage negotiations between the Afghan government and the US. The opposing parties actively meet there.

High-ranking members of the Muslim Brotherhood, an Islamist movement that was founded in Egypt in 1928, live in Qatar. Riyadh sheltered the Brotherhood for many years, until they classified it as a terrorist organization in 2014. Hardly any other country has done more to promote the rise of the radical Islamist Taliban than Saudi Arabia.

There must be another reason for the break with the "little brother"—an old conflict. Relations between the ruling families in Doha and Riyadh have been toxic for years, and it's all about power, betrayal, and wounded pride.

The Saudis question whether the emir, Tamim bin Hamad Al Thani, really holds the reins in Qatar. They suspect that his father, Sheikh Hamad bin Khalifa Al Thani, is pulling the strings. Saudi Arabia, like other Arab countries, hasn't forgotten an old feud with the father, who abdicated in 2013 to install his son on the throne.

In 1995, Sheikh Hamad overthrew his own father, a plot that the Saudis tried to sabotage. A counter-coup, orchestrated by Riyadh, failed because a traitor squealed. Sheikh Hamad hates the Saudis, say long-time diplomats who were stationed in Doha and met the former ruler. He rarely misses an opportunity to irritate his neighbors, apparently.

This became all too clear in a leaked phone recording, probably from 2002, between the emir and the former Libyan dictator Muammar Gaddafi. Hamad Al Thani trash-talked the monarchy in Riyadh and predicted the imminent collapse of the kingdom. In twelve years at the latest, the kingdom would be finished. The emir acknowledged that he himself was actively promoting the destabilization of Saudi Arabia through various channels. And there was always disagreement over how the Muslim Brotherhood should be handled.

For Riyadh, the fate of the former Egyptian President Husni Mubarak was an eye-opener. The autocrat was considered a loyal Saudi ally. During the Arab Spring in 2011, after nearly thirty years in office, he was toppled by the Egyptian people. The political wing of the Muslim Brotherhood assumed power in Cairo as democratically elected representatives of the people.

Losing power the way Mubarak did is every autocrat's nightmare. Which is why Riyadh now persecutes supporters of the Brotherhood as if they were a terrorist organization.

By contrast, the young Qatari Emir Tamin bin Hamad Al Thani believes the Brotherhood is the great hope for Islamic countries in the Middle East. The Muslim Brotherhood are often well-educated and hold many important posts in Doha. The government of Qatar lacks manpower and consciously hired them as functionaries when the nation underwent rapid development into a complex, modern state in the second half of the twentieth century. Still, the strategy doesn't come without a certain dose of irony, as one of the primary aims of the Muslim Brotherhood is to do away with the Arab monarchies.

A DEEPFAKE SPEECH

Emir Hamad Al Thani seems to believe that his small nation isn't prone to democratic uprisings. Barely 2.7 million people live in Qatar, and only 300,000 of them are actually born Qataris. Qatar enjoys the highest per capita income in the world. The Saudis, however, rule over a population of thirty-two million, many of whom aren't doing well economically, especially the young.

The final break between the Thanis and the Sauds came on June 5, 2017, thanks to an allegedly inflammatory speech by Emir Tamin bin Hamad on May 23. A speech, it was soon revealed, that he never delivered.

Credible evidence exists suggesting that Russian hackers produced the fake speech, in which Tamin bin Hamad seems to praise Hamas and Hezbollah militants, appeals for an improvement of relations with Iran, and then goes on to predict a short Trump presidency. In short, the purported speech was tantamount to a declaration of war against Riyadh.

The following day, the Saudis canceled all flights to the neighboring country and closed the border. Qataris in the kingdom were given fourteen days to pack their things and leave the country. This was exactly what the hackers had hoped to achieve with their cyberattack. Shortly thereafter, the FBI found that they intended to break the fragile alliance between Qatar and Saudi Arabia and to drive Qatar into the arms of Russia's ally Iran. And that's exactly what happened.

Fake news or not, the Qatar scandal came in handy for Riyadh. The Saudi leaders had long been irritated by the influential TV channel Al Jazeera, where, every day, the young emir and opposition groups share their views on international politics— views which are very different from theirs. Together with its allies Bahrain, the United Arab Emirates, Egypt, Senegal, Mauritania, Djibouti, the Tobruk-based Libyan government and the Hadi-led Yemen government, Saudi Arabia severed its diplomatic ties with Qatar.

AHMAD SEES HIS FAMILY EVERY THREE MONTHS

Like Saudi Arabia, Qatar is a friend to the United States. An estimated 10,000 GIs are stationed at the huge Al Udeid Air Base. And yet Emir Tamin maintains pragmatic relations with Iran, Saudi Arabia's archenemy and rival in the region. Qatar shares the largest natural gas field in the world, South Pars, with the Iranian Republic. The emirate sits on an estimated 15 percent of worldwide gas reserves, making it by some estimates the richest country on earth.

At the end of the day, this row between "brothers" is about personal sensitivities and old hostilities. But it's also about strategic alliances in the Arab world. Insiders say that neither of the ruling clans is happy with the situation. Influential members of the Qatari ruling family are believed to be looking to reshuffle the Al Thanis's leadership.

But what does the end of diplomatic relations mean for the camel traders and butchers of Tamani? For the gas station operators on Salwa Road? For the teahouses? And what of the Saudi-Qatari families that have been torn apart?

In Salwa, my companion introduces me to Ahmad. The Saudi doctor is married to Amira, a manager at Qatar Airways. The couple lived together in Doha. But since the hostilities began, Ahmad sees his family only every three months.

For three years he's worked in a hospital in Salwa. Before the scandal, Ahmad got into his black-and-white Hyundai in Doha and drove to work in Saudi Arabia every day. He'd be back at night, in time for dinner. As the crow flies, his house is just thirty-five miles from his workplace.

Now Ahmad has to travel for at least nine hours when he wants to see his wife and son. He takes a flight to Kuwait, then another to Qatar, then a bus from the airport.

The doctor sits nervously on a chair in the emergency room in Salwa Hospital. The thirty-three-year-old is afraid of losing his job if his story is published and seen as criticism of Riyadh's radical policies toward Qatar. The subject of Qatar is taboo in the kingdom, like so many other subjects.

Nobody talks about it openly. Newspapers don't write about it, but for the Eastern Province, the punitive action against Qatar is a heavy blow to the economy which affects not just the emirate, but also the Saudis themselves. Trade between the nations has collapsed.

LIFE HAPPENS ELSEWHERE

Food is a whole lot cheaper in the kingdom than in Qatar, so a lot of Qataris used to travel there to buy groceries: fresh vegetables, eggs, lentils, rice. They were especially fond of visiting Al-Ahsa, the old oasis city 120 miles south of the border. Today, the hotels there are starved for customers, as are the hundreds of shops in Souk Qaisariya, the city's labyrinthine bazaar.

The decline has hit the traders of Salwa Road particularly hard. Tamani was the biggest camel meat market. The animals were often slaughtered on the spot. The meat was fresh and cheap.

Now the camel pens are abandoned, the hotels and tearooms empty. There's no life in Tamani anymore.

Along the highway, the sand is piling up around the abandoned gas pumps. Before heading back to Riyadh, Fahd and I drink tea at one of the last two remaining service stations. Fahd says the two nations might find common ground again. Here, sometimes things turn around, and suddenly fortunes change.

In late 2018, Crown Prince Mohammed bin Salman spoke at a conference for international investors in Riyadh about how the "strong economies" of the Gulf would grow together and blossom in the coming years. The Mideast was the "New Europe," he said. Surprisingly, he included Qatar in his vision. Since relations were severed, the emirate hadn't been worth mentioning. That seems to have changed. Apparently, Washington has been pressuring Saudi Arabia to open the border.

"Something's happening behind the scenes," says Fahd.

"Hopefully," I think.

THE MAGIC OF BATHA

THE NEIGHBORHOOD HOUSING RIYADH'S LOW-WAGE MIGRANT UNDERCLASS IS BUZZING WITH ENERGY AND COMMERCE. THE SAUDIS' SERVANTS WHO LIVE HERE LEAD TOUGH, DEGRADING LIVES. BUT BATHA IS ALSO A PLACE THAT CAN BRIGHTEN YOUR DAY.

Among the mysteries of the Middle East belong the sudden turnarounds that occur in seemingly impossible situations. For example, the minor daily miracles that happen when you place your trust in a stranger. Like when your visa runs out and it's unclear if you can even leave the country legally, or when a strange infection assaults you and condemns you to your sickbed, or when—as is happening now—your hard drive (on which this book is stored) just gives up the ghost.

With adrenaline pumping through my veins, I ring an American neighbor's doorbell. He shrugs his shoulders. He knows a lot about corporate consulting, but not much about IT. I'm getting desperate. I won't be able to fix this problem on my own. I need help. I'm not sure what kind of help, but I have an idea where I might find it.

I jump in a taxi and tell the driver to take me to Batha, the area where the poorest migrants and domestic servants from Bangladesh, the Philippines, Pakistan, and India live. I show the Pakistani driver my hard drive and try to explain my situation by making hand gestures with the cable. He doesn't speak a word of English and I don't speak Urdu. Our combined knowledge of Arabic is limited to a few phrases. He doesn't really look like a tech guy, but that's of no importance. He's obviously someone who has to overcome adversity each and every day.

At some point, he nods and says: "Al Obaid." I don't know who or what Al Obaid is, but I have the feeling that things are taking a turn for the better.

Of the kingdom's thirty-two million inhabitants, a good ten million are expats, i.e., foreigners. Those from the West usually live in guarded residential complexes with tennis clubs and swimming pools. The rest live in Batha or even farther to the south, at the edge of the city.

These are the people who make your coffee, iron your clothes, clean the hospital restrooms, and bag your groceries. They drive the kids to school and your mother to the mall. They pick the trash up from the street, clean your house, change your baby's diapers. They're everywhere, and their sole purpose is to make the lives of Saudis easier. At night, they disappear into their cramped dormitories, often in windowless basements. They work long, grueling shifts, and they are always available for their masters.

Migrant workers usually leave their families back in their home countries. With their earnings in Saudi Arabia, they often pay for their children's education. For a monthly wage of about $350, they have to watch their kids grow up on Skype.

SAUDIS WOULD RATHER NOT GET THEIR HANDS DIRTY

The salaries of Saudi state employees are around ten to fifteen times higher than the pay of low-wage workers. A Saudi IT professional, chemical engineer, or college professor earns between $3,500 and $7,000 per month. On top of that come special allowances and bonuses that the king regularly doles out to keep his subjects happy. But such gifts are becoming less frequent, and one day they will cease altogether.

Saudis seldom work in private business. They prefer working for the state, by far the largest employer. In general, they don't like getting their hands dirty. Saudis usually show up at the office at about ten o'clock, take a long prayer break, leave punctually for lunch, answer their most important emails, go pray again, and then head home early. But soon, all that could be history. Since January 2018, Saudi citizens have had to pay taxes for the first time ever: a 5 percent value-added tax on most products and services.

What's more, the government wants migrant workers to head home, and in 2017 imposed a new levy of a hundred riyals per foreign worker, roughly twenty-five dollars per person per month. A fine must also be paid for any wives or additional family members. The charge goes up every year: by 2019 it had risen to two hundred riyals per month; in 2020 it will be three hundred, and so on until no Saudi family or company can afford to fly in a driver from Pakistan or Indonesia, feed and house them, and pay them a wage on top.

Riyadh wants to "Saudi-ize" the economy. All this means is that Saudi citizens will have to drive their cars and mow their lawns themselves. A lot of immigrants from the world's poorest countries have already been laid off. Up to three million have left the country.

In a nutshell, the state isn't as fantastically rich as it was a couple of decades ago. It's run out of money to give away. There aren't enough jobs to go around for the hundreds of thousands of young, expectant Saudis who graduate from college and enter the job market every year.

If the government has its way, young Saudis will have to work in the dreaded private sector, and at wages much lower than those paid by the state. They will have no choice but to work in less prestigious positions than their parents. Already, many Saudi women are forced to work because a single paycheck no longer feeds a family.

Someone who already understands all of this is Istar. I met the fifty-year-old the first time I used the Saudi version of Uber— Careem. Istar is one of the car service's "captains." Careem offers an alternative to the usual street taxis, which until now have been firmly in the hands of Pakistani drivers. The government wants more Saudis to drive taxis.

Istar also manages a cafeteria in a military hospital in As-Sulimaniyah District. He's tall, well-built, and wears a black T-shirt and jeans. With bonuses, he earns 15,000 riyals or $4,000 per month; not bad, but not great either. Nonetheless, Istar and his wife belong to the middle class. He has three sons—fourteen, nine, and three years old. His wife doesn't have a driver, so Istar drops the kids off at school every day and picks them up again. Five thousand riyals go to rent for the family's apartment near the airport. He does the grocery shopping with his wife between his hospital job and his taxi shift.

Istar's father is very well-off, a retired four-star general and businessman who made his fortune during the 1970s oil boom. He owns a palace in Jeddah on the Red Sea and another one in Riyadh. Yet he has fallen out with his five sons and three daughters. He has never shared his wealth. All of his kids rent their homes.

Istar's family doesn't seem to be the most loving bunch. "The family is like a hand," says Istar, spreading his fingers. "You can't cut off fingers without making the hand useless." His father is eighty-six years old, and is sick and frail. His children are waiting for him to die. Until that day, Istar will keep moonlighting for Careem six days a week. The gig earns him another two thousand riyals every month, sometimes three thousand (between five and eight hundred dollars).

BACK HOME EVERY TWO YEARS

The average income in Saudi Arabia is about $22,000 per year compared to around $32,000 in the US. There's a huge gulf between what domestics make (a few hundred dollars per month) and the salaries of state employees. In the kingdom, wages are paid in cash. Income tax is unheard of, but life is about as expensive as in the US.

Fresh fruit and vegetables are often imported from America or Europe and cost twice as much. For six organic eggs, you'll have to shell out ten dollars, at least at the upscale Carrefour supermarket in Olaya.

In Batha everything is cheap. Batha is Riyadh's oldest commercial district. It's in the south of the city next to the Al-Oud Cemetery, the public graveyard where the Saudi monarchs are buried— from the founding father Abdulaziz bin Saud to the latest ruler to die, King Abdullah. Beyond the graves begins the world of the precarious—and now unwanted—migrant workers.

My taxi is a white Toyota Corolla. The Pakistani driver has a grayish-red beard and wears a turban and shalwar kameez, the traditional male dress in his homeland. He has lived in Riyadh for thirteen years, in Batha of course. He travels home every two years, to the Pakistani tribal areas in Waziristan. He can't afford to make the journey more often.

The migrant workers have so many sad stories to tell, but some of them are doing alright. Some are warmly received and treated like relatives by their employers, but most of them have no such luck—largely due to the harsh *kafala* system.

Under this system, employers must sponsor their hired staff and monitor their movement. The process offers migrants no protection whatsoever from abuse. They are often at the mercy of their boss's mood, as was the case with Tuti Tursilawati. The young Indonesian woman came to Saudi Arabia in 2009 to work as a maid in a private household. Her employer, and sponsor, was a man named Suud Malhaq al-Utaibi.

VIOLENT BOSSES

Tursilawati dared to take the plunge into such a different country. Her upward-pointing eyebrows gracefully framed her almond-shaped eyes. The young woman from West Java Province wore her dark hair tied behind her neck, and when she laughed, her long front teeth would poke through her full lips. An Indonesian migrant newspaper published a picture of her after Tursilawati was arrested in Ta'if in Mecca Province.

The maid hit her employer with a stick and then fled; her sponsor had tried to rape her, Tuti Tursilawati told the court. She acted in self-defense after he had repeatedly sexually assaulted her.

In 2011, Tursilawati was sentenced to death and on October 29, 2018, she was executed. She was thirty-four years old. Appeals from high-ranking Indonesian politicians to spare the young migrant were ignored.

Tursilawati was the third foreign maid to be executed by beheading in Saudi Arabia in 2018.

There are videos showing maids jumping from balconies to their deaths as they run from violent employers. Women who managed to escape to a safe house in Lebanon told a journalist about how they were bullied, beaten, and sexually abused.

On construction sites, foreign laborers have to do the most dangerous work. Migrants often complain that they work hard for months without pay and are then powerless against their sponsors in the courtroom. Their employers keep their passports, and the police usually side with the Saudi citizens.

MANY LABORERS IN SAUDI ARABIA ARE POOR MIGRANT WORKERS FROM PAKISTAN, BANGLADESH, THE PHILIPPINES, AND SUDAN WHO WORK HERE TO FEED THEIR FAMILIES BACK HOME.

We drive along Olaya Street past the Ministry of the Interior. At night, all the windows are lit. The building looks like a spaceship out of *Star Wars*. The officials inside don't have to worry about their careers. The security sector is growing by the day.

We head down King Faisal Street to Murabba Park. Behind the park begins Batha. All around us, cars are honking at rush hour. We inch ahead. A group of men pushes their way through idling vehicles. They're carrying bags of fruit, sacks of rice, and bottled water.

People push and shove in Batha. They haggle, they run, they shout. Batha is dirty, loud, and overcrowded on weekends. But at the same time, this is one of the few places with any life in Riyadh. Men and women—with and without headscarves—walk freely together. The country's strict rules apparently don't apply here. Very few Saudis ever come to Batha.

THE STREET IS THEIR ALMA MATER

Batha is a parallel universe. This is where the others live.

We pass a fish market, gold dealers, vegetarian street food joints, and tea rooms. Spices are weighed and fruit is hawked. We reach an alleyway with nothing but tech and computer stores. The driver gets out and asks for "Al Obaid" at an old mall dating back to the 1970s. Second passage on the right. Al Obaid is a small camera store with the latest video equipment, Polaroid cameras, and pricey Nikon, Canon, and Panasonic reflex cameras.

I pull out my hard drive and the useless cables that are no longer activating the device. The Egyptian shopkeeper takes out various cords from a shelf beneath the cash register and tries to insert them into the drive one by one while plugging the other end into a power adapter. Nothing happens. He sends his employee, an Indian, into the storeroom. He comes back with another cable.

The Egyptian devotes his attention to another customer. The Indian and his Pakistani coworker continue the search, plugging and unplugging. Finally, the Pakistani heads to the shop next door and returns with another man who casts an expert eye on the hard drive, disappears for a moment, then comes back with a new cable with a knob in the middle and a British plug.

With a screwdriver, he pokes at the socket of the drive on which the chapters of this book are saved. I begin to lose hope. I feel I am on the brink of a heart attack. Yet the guy seems to know what he's doing. He splices the knobbly cable into two strands, stretches and bends them, and connects them with the hard drive's cable. And then it happens: the miracle of Batha! The LED begins to blink.

Hallelujah! The hard drive lives!

I'm relieved. No, ecstatic! I fetch *karak* for everyone—dark, sweet tea with evaporated milk.

The ingenuity of the people of Batha is astounding. Few of them have had any formal schooling, let alone a college education. The street is their alma mater. They support each other and pool their skills together into a higher system that somehow brings things together and enables them to solve the most challenging problems.

I pocket Al Obaid's business card as if it were made of gold, bow before the Pakistanis, and roam the streets for a bit.

A tailor has set up shop on a simple board and takes "walk-in customers." From a bakery made of bricks emerges a song by the famous Afghan bard Ahmad Zahir. The baker pulls a tamis flatbread out of the tandoor oven. It smells delicious and steams in the cool night air.

At first glance, Batha doesn't look like a place that promises much happiness. The lives of the men and women who earn a few riyals on these streets are filled with hardship and humiliation.

A shoemaker says he will repair my handbag with a few stitches. The bag is about to burst because I stuff my laptop into it several times a day. Ten riyals, $2.60. Financially, the shoemakers and fruit sellers can't be doing all that well. It can't be possible to feed a family this way.

A COBBLER ON THE STREET: NOT EVERYONE IN SAUDI ARABIA LIVES IN A PALACE.

This low-cost private sector with its tiny profit margins only functions because an army of relatives is doing the same thing, day in, day out. Here, in Qatar, in Dubai, and elsewhere in the Gulf. These people collect the crumbs of the well-off. Together, it's just about enough for the survival of their families back home.

For this reason alone, Batha is bursting with energy. The people's efforts flow together. Each one of them pursues a meaningful task, even if the world sees them as nothing more than uneducated laborers. They provide a lifeline for many others.

The people here know little about each other, but they help one another. They even help me, although I obviously come from an entirely different world.

HOW LITTLE KARIM TRIED TO SOLVE THE YEMEN CRISIS

THE BRUTAL WAR IN NEIGHBORING YEMEN CASTS A DARK
SHADOW OVER THE KINGDOM. MOST SAUDIS REFUSE TO DISCUSS
THE CONFLICT—EXCEPT FOR KARIM, AN ASTUTE ELEVEN-YEAR-
OLD BOY WHO ENGAGES ME IN AN INFORMED CONVERSATION ON
THE ISSUE.

Saudi Arabia has thirteen provinces, and every February, the Janadriyah Festival takes place near Riyadh to celebrate the nation's regional customs and traditions. With sword dances, camel rides, and culinary specialties, the huge, state-organized event lasts for two weeks and feels a bit like a World Expo for Saudi Arabia. Each province presents its history and architecture, its local products and crafts. Here you can find rare delicacies—rose essence from the city of Ta'if, honey from the forests of Raghadan, and palm frond baskets from Asir Province.

Janadriyah reminds me of medieval festivals in Europe where people dress up like maidens, blacksmiths, and knights. Only no one's in costume here. In the Middle East a lot of people still carry a dagger in their belt, at least on official occasions. The ubiquitous Bedouin tents are still the preferred accommodation for weekend trips out to the desert.

Karim accompanies me to the folkloric fiesta. He's only eleven, my friend Nora's son. We're going to meet up with her later. On the way, it begins to drizzle. As we pass through the gates, the heavens open up and rain comes down in buckets.

Karim and I flee to the Mecca Pavilion, where the holy city is presenting itself. We sit on thick cushions and drink *karak*. A large map shows exactly where we are in the fairgrounds. It's embedded in an even bigger chart of the Middle East, which shows the kingdom with all of its neighbors. When the boy notices the map, he spontaneously explains the security strategy of his country. "We're the biggest and strongest on the Arabian Peninsula and in the whole Middle East," he says. "Actually, we only have friends, and when they turn against us, the Americans help us out."

I'm impressed. I tell Karim that his dad couldn't have explained it better.

Karim comes up to just below my chin. His thick hair is parted down the middle. He wears jeans and an orange T-shirt with the slogan "I love KSA," short for the Kingdom of Saudi Arabia. In fifth grade, Karim speaks some English, which means he already belongs to the country's elite.

He points to Iraq, Iran, and Syria, because there you can find friends who sometimes turn against Saudi Arabia. And then to the south, to Yemen, where the kingdom and other Gulf states are waging a war against the Houthi rebels. "That's going to take a while longer," says Karim, looking annoyed, reflecting the mood of most Saudis. Everyone wishes this war had ended long ago or—even better—never begun in the first place.

Karim pauses his lecture and runs outside into the rain. He wants to buy sweet *sambusa*, baked dumplings.

Prince Mohammed bin Salman promised his subjects a rapid victory in Yemen back in March 2015, when he ordered Saudi troops to bombard Houthi positions. He optimistically dubbed the operation "Decisive Storm," echoing "Desert Storm" in January 1991, when the US liberated tiny Kuwait within a few weeks after it was invaded by Iraq.

In the effort to win the Yemen war quickly, the Saudis teamed up with other Arab states. Their most important ally was the United Arab Emirates. Together, they hoped to smash the Houthi rebel army and reinstate President Abdul Rabbo Mansur Hadi—who had been driven out of the Yemeni capital Sanaa—as the rightful head of state. As of today, the UAE has mostly withdrawn from the coalition.

The Houthis are a rebel group from the north of Yemen who adhere to the Zaydiyah, an autonomous branch of the Shi'ite confession. Theologically, the insurgents were inspired by the Iranian Revolution. Their conflict with the Sanaa government had been brewing for more than a decade. The Houthis, feeling neglected by former president Ali Abdullah Saleh, demanded more support for their region and ended up clashing with the central government in a series of skirmishes. In 2011, during the Arab Spring, the majority of the population rose up against President Saleh. The president made a big mistake: he handed over power to the weak Vice President Hadi while he traveled to the United States for medical treatment.

The Houthis filled the resulting power vacuum. In September 2014, in alliance with other tribes, they took control of Sanaa. Finally, in March 2015, Saleh's successor Hadi was forced to flee the country.

241

Riyadh sees the Houthis as a military threat. Already during Saleh's era, there were isolated battles between the Houthis and Saudi Arabia and their allies. For the Saudis, though, this war is mostly about neutralizing the influence of Iran on their doorstep.

Saudi Arabia feels increasingly surrounded by combat groups loyal to Iran. Riyadh fears that Tehran could exert influence over Yemen in the future, as they have already done in Lebanon through radical Hezbollah and in Iraq through Shi'ite militias. Furthermore, they worry that the Houthis could try to stir up segments of the Saudi population who are dissatisfied, or who reject the *Wahhabis*, to revolt against the monarchy.

THE $200 MILLION-PER-DAY WAR

In short, the Yemen war is a proxy conflict between the two big rival powers in the Middle East: Iran and Saudi Arabia.

Karim is back from the *sambusa* stand. His hair and T-shirt are soaked. He proudly holds up the hot, steaming dumplings that are filled with *khoya*, a soft cheese containing saffron and nuts. As we sample the sweets, we resume our discussion. He anxiously tells me he heard that fragments of rockets from Yemen came down near their flat in Riyadh last week. He was scared.

Over the past few weeks, there have, in fact, been repeated attacks on Riyadh with relatively imprecise missiles. I heard such an explosion from my apartment in Olaya. The rocket was shot down and blew up several miles away. Nonetheless, two people died in the attack.

The mid-range missiles always come at night. Blurry snippets of a video circulating on WhatsApp show the places where the rockets have come down. Since the attacks began, many Saudis fear that their country will be consumed by war and unrest like Syria, Iraq, Libya, and Yemen.

THE HOUTHI WAR PROFITEERS

Nobody here likes to talk about the war in Yemen. All news coming out of the country is distressing. At the end of 2018, Save the Children reported that 85,000 Yemeni kids had starved to death since 2015, mainly because the Saudi-led military alliance has blocked food shipments by sea and air, but also because the Houthis have stolen humanitarian food aid from the hungry. Three million Yemenis have become refugees. The bombings and the fighting have killed 100,000 people so far, 12,000 of them innocent civilians. Anyone who wants to know more can read up on the tragedy online.

On a daily basis, Riyadh media reports on so-called military progress. Pundits and TV hosts would have you believe that victory is close at hand. Therefore it's not surprising that a logically thinking eleven-year-old like Karim would ask,

"Susanne, why doesn't the war end, when we've almost won it for so long?"

One could answer: War is always harder to end than to start. Wars progress, and the interests of those involved change.

At the moment, for example, the Houthi rebels and their allies in Sanaa are the biggest profiteers of this human tragedy. Their leaders are living better than ever. Many of them have become multimillionaires as a result of black-market dealings. They drive expensive cars and live in big houses.

Meanwhile, hospitals hardly have any medicine. Millions of people in the countryside, including the Houthis' tribal areas, are on the verge of starvation. Nonetheless, the capital is a booming hub for those in power and their supporters. New buildings are shooting out of the ground. Supermarket shelves are full, like in the West, thanks to the smuggling, and there are enough rich people who can afford the food. Why should the Houthi leaders give in when the war is so profitable for them?

For Iran, it's opportune that the kingdom is bogged down by the war. The military operation costs Riyadh up to two hundred million dollars per day.

By contrast, Tehran has invested hardly anything in the war but is inflicting serious harm upon its archenemy. Iran has suffered virtually no casualties. Nor have they delivered expensive arms. They have only sent military advisors, helped smuggle weapons and munitions, and—as was established in a UN Security Council report—provided missiles.

Early in the conflict, Iranian military aid to the Houthi rebels was hardly worth mentioning. It consisted of statements of intent and a direct flight between Sanaa and Tehran. The Saudis assessed the threat from Tehran as being significantly more dangerous than it actually was. They wanted to send a signal: stay away from our territory.

In the meantime, though, the war has continued unabated for nearly five years, and cooperation between the rebels and Tehran has blossomed into a strong alliance. You could say that Saudi Arabia's prophecy that Iran's henchmen would be poised at its southern border in fact came true during the war.

Karim has eaten two sweet *sambusas*, but he's still waiting for an answer. He can't understand why a powerful country like Saudi Arabia can't bomb peace into existence so that its friend, the internationally recognized President Hadi, can return to office in Sanaa.

POWER SHIFT

"The kingdom might have made a mistake from the start," I begin carefully. Saudis are often sensitive about even the slightest criticism. "There are a lot of people who want to exploit this mistake. They want Saudi Arabia to lose as much of its money and reputation as possible until it finally gives up."

Saudi Arabia, through its vast wealth and exporting of its radical religion, has exerted influence around the world for decades. Riyadh buys political loyalty, whether in Lebanon, Bahrain, Egypt, or Sudan, and claims, as the guardian of the holy cities of Mecca and Medina, to be the center of the Islamic faith. For a long time, nobody dared to challenge the House of Saud.

At least until 2003, when the US-led Iraq War caused the first cracks to appear in the power structures of the Middle East. The removal of Saddam Hussein sent shock waves toward the autocrats in the region, including those in Riyadh. Might not the same thing happen to the king of Saudi Arabia one day? Then in 2011, during the Arab Spring, populations revolted against their corrupt rulers in Yemen, Tunisia, Egypt, and Libya. Dictators were murdered, forced to flee into exile, or were tried in court like the Egyptian President Husni Mubarak.

To escape a similar fate, King Abdullah showered his subjects with gifts. On a single Friday in March, the king handed out $93 billion.

Today, nothing is what it once was. The old Arab alliances have become brittle. Regional power relations have shifted, indeed most often in favor of Iran. Wherever the opportunity presents itself, Tehran tries to weaken the kingdom. Saudi Arabia's aggressive war in Yemen is just such an opportunity.

The murder of the journalist Jamal Khashoggi in Istanbul directed international attention toward human rights violations in Saudi Arabia and, eventually, toward the forgotten war in Yemen. In the US, people are asking themselves why American bombs are killing innocent children in Yemen. Germany, Denmark, and Italy have suspended arms shipments to Riyadh.

Crown Prince Mohammed bin Salman is signaling his readiness to enter peace negotiations. But the situation is tricky. The first round of talks between the warring parties under the aegis of the United Nations ended in mid-December 2018 with a ceasefire in the port city Hudaydah. Now, direct talks between the Saudis and the Houthis are taking place. But a more comprehensive, lasting treaty is still a long way off.

That's roughly how I sketch things out for Karim, and it doesn't make him happy. But his face brightens when he understands that there is a chance for peace at some point, because that is what the young leader of his country is pursuing in the meantime.

Outside, the downpour has stopped as suddenly as it began. We want to visit the Asir pavilion, representing that province, in the southwest of the country. We're meeting Karim's mother Nora there. Asir is known for its mild climate, spectacular nature, and Yemeni-influenced architecture, with its high, narrow houses, white windows, and meandering, jagged roofs. The province shares a short stretch of border with Yemen.

With some friends, problems can last a bit longer, Karim explains. Now in a more cheerful mood, he offers a tip on how more can be achieved in future negotiations: "The king should give the Americans more oil or money, then they'll help us more again."

I nod and mumble. That is what will probably happen. Then we move on, toward Asir.

RICHARD OF ARABIA: MAKING THE DESERT BLOOM

IN THE 1970S, RIYADH WAS A DUSTY CONCRETE JUNGLE. THANKS
TO THE GERMAN LANDSCAPE ARCHITECT RICHARD BÖDEKER,
THE CITY HAS BLOSSOMED INTO A METROPOLIS DOTTED WITH
GREEN OASES.

In the Qur'an, paradise is usually described as a garden: an
enchanting place with lots of trees, plenty of shade, and cool
streams running through it. Paradise probably looks a little
like the private country estate of Prince Sultan bin Salman bin
Abdulaziz Al Saud.

Prince Sultan is the oldest living son of King Salman. As the
first Arab astronaut to fly into space, he recently became the
chairman of the Saudi Space Commission. Before the gates
of the Saudi capital lies his farm, with its own man-made
waterscape and a "philosopher's path," where the prince takes
his evening strolls.

FIRST ARAB ASTRONAUT PRINCE SULTAN AND LANDSCAPER RICHARD BÖDEKER AT HIS
ROYAL HIGHNESS'S FARM IN DIRIYAH: "YOU NEED TO GET CONCRETE OUT OF YOUR
HEADS AND REPLACE IT WITH SOME GREEN."

BEHIND THE KINGDOM'S VEIL

247

Today, the prince is in an upbeat mood. In his white *thawb*, he sits at a long table surrounded by bougainvillea and anemones. Beside him, in the place of honor, sits Richard Bödeker, his German landscape architect, always a welcome guest at the house. The prince has visited Bödeker in Germany, where he has designed his own magical garden in the Neandertal valley near Düsseldorf. Bödeker sports black pants, a black shirt, and a black vest. Distinguished whiskers sprout from his ruddy cheeks down to his chin, the mad professor look. "Richard of Arabia," the prince likes to call him.

"How are you, Richard, my friend?" His Royal Highness asks. Bödeker groans. The gardener is eighty-five. For more than four decades, he has been making the extravagant garden fantasies of his Saudi clients come true. Bödeker runs his fingers through his whiskers. The things princesses and princes dream up, he says, they're straight out of fairy tales. It's his job to make those fairy tales a reality.

Some time ago, Prince Sultan purchased an estate near Ta'if, a relatively cool mountain town southeast of Mecca. Tomorrow, Bödeker will climb into Prince Sultan's small private plane and fly to Ta'if. The prince has hired him to create an oasis there, a botanical masterpiece complete with roses, lavender, and stone sculptures. His Royal Highness says he wants to pilot the airplane himself. Bödeker rolls his eyes.

Bödeker has had a huge influence on the appearance of the Saudi capital. When the gardener came here for the first time in 1973, Riyadh was a dusty city with six-lane highways cutting through it. "You need to get concrete out of your heads and replace it with some green," Bödeker complained to the chief city planner at the time. The Saudi officials were so impressed by the grouchy German that they continued to employ him over the following decades.

Nowadays, big thoroughfares like King Faisal and King Abdullah Road run partway through tunnels covered by parks designed by Bödeker. The oldest palace complex in the heart of the city was transformed into a sumptuous oasis of a hundred palm trees representing a century of the Saudi dynasty in power. The Diplomatic Quarter also resembles a lush oasis. Naturally, Bödeker also designed the German embassy's garden.

RIYADH OASIS: LANDSCAPE ARCHITECT BÖDEKER IMPLEMENTED THE LEADERS' VISION OF A GREEN CITY.

Swaths of green now permeate central Riyadh. Kids play in water playgrounds. The city employs an army of gardeners, most of them trained by Bödeker's staff. The German's secret for dealing with the Saudis is a combination of tolerance and fundamentalism. The Arabs are very conservative Muslims. Bödeker is deeply green. "I don't have any time for politics," he says. For him, it's about trees and gardens. When Europeans complained that women couldn't drive in Saudi Arabia, he always retorted that this would take care of itself one day. He was proven right.

The public beheadings that take place on Fridays don't diminish Bödeker's attachment to the country. Other cultures, even the Americans, execute dangerous criminals, he says. Here, many of those sentenced to death are pardoned.

FATHER AND SON AT THE FARM OF A CLIENT: THE LANDSCAPE TEAM OF BÖDEKER AND BÖDEKER HAS DEFINED THE SPIRIT OF GARDEN DESIGN IN SAUDI ARABIA.

Servants bring dessert on silver trays: rice pudding with rosewater and brittle, wild berry sorbet, pastries soaked in syrup.

Bödeker shares his office in Riyadh with several partners and members of his family. His son Jens joined the Saudi business a few years ago, as did Jens's wife Alexandra, also an accomplished landscape architect. Even together, they can hardly satisfy the Saudis' demand.

The Bödekers have come up with some pretty creative ideas. They broke a taboo when they used treated sewage to irrigate their green spaces. The water used by a Riyadh resident irrigates an average of six trees. The princes and oil magnates build their mansions wherever islands of green form in and around Riyadh.

But isn't there a limit? How much can a desert nation be made to bloom? Bödeker believes a lot more can be done. The prince's gardener and his team are now expected to perform the unthinkable: turn the valleys of Riyadh Province green, an area almost the size of California. Bödeker says it's feasible: "There are plants with 150-foot roots. That's where the water is."

Bödeker abruptly bids his farewell. He wants to get some rest at his hotel before his trip with His Royal Highness Prince Sultan to Ta'if, the city of roses.

BLUE GOLD

SAUDI ARABIA IS RICH IN OIL, BUT ITS REAL WEALTH LIES BENEATH
THE DESERT, HIDDEN IN ANCIENT AQUIFERS.

It's raining cats and dogs in Riyadh and it shows no intention of
letting up. Kids squeal with delight as they romp on the lawn
in front of King Fahd National Library. Men in *thawb*s get on
their knees to touch the small puddles forming on the paving
slabs. "Finally, nice weather," says a man taking a stroll through
the Olaya quarter with his wife. The veiled lady lifts her gloved
hands so that the sleeves of her abaya come in contact with the
moisture. Nobody thinks of opening an umbrella. It's the first
rain after a long, scorching summer.

As a central European, I'm less excited about the downpour.
It's late October. A rapid shift in weather often brings about a
sudden drop in temperature, this time from eighty-five to sixty
degrees. I'm wearing a thin summer abaya and sandals and
suddenly pine for a warm tearoom. The closest dry place is
the mall.

When it hasn't rained for months, the whole nation prays for
Allah to show mercy and send water down from the heavens. Not
many places on earth get as little precipitation as the Arabian
Peninsula—enveloped as it is by two vast deserts, the Nefud in
the north and the Rub' al-Khali in the south.

WATER WASTERS

Strictly speaking, humans can't survive in such an arid
environment. A few regions in the far south that are affected by
the monsoon see about twenty-five inches of rainfall per year. In
most of the country, including the Riyadh region, it's less than
four inches. And this small amount of precipitation is spread out
over a few months, mostly between December and April. Most
of the rainfall seeps into the desert sand immediately and can't

be used for irrigation. No grass grows here. Only a few insects and some rodents can endure the brutal climate. By contrast, in 2018, the US had an average of 34.6 inches of precipitation distributed over the year and some farmers still complained about the drought.

It might come as a surprise that, despite the Saudis' near-religious worship of rain, they were, until recently, the most reckless water wasters on earth. For decades, Saudi Arabia heavily subsidized water and supplied it to the population more or less for free. They flooded the fields of their private farms, soaked their golf courses, and regularly refilled their swimming pools.

That's over now. In January 2018, the state began sending its citizens water bills that reflect the true cost. People were shocked. Suddenly, they had to pay about 2.5 US cents per gallon of tap water.

The Saudi government runs huge desalination plants, but the process is complex and expensive. The preparation of a cubic meter of fresh water in older facilities consumes up to ten kilowatt-hours of power if you factor in the energy used to pump it to the end user. For that, you could run ten loads of laundry in your washing machine. Due to the high energy consumption alone, the process is probably unsustainable in the long run.

The kingdom produces more than four million cubic meters of fresh water every day. That equals 142 liters or thirty-seven gallons per person.

EMPTY POOLS

Since he started paying more for water, Fahd, an electrical engineer, feels that his family's water usage has skyrocketed. After the price hike, he hired a company to check the pipes in his house for leaks. He warns the kids not to leave the faucet on while brushing their teeth. The pool, which his wife Maha would refill every Thursday in time for the weekend, has remained empty. "Swim at your friends' *istiraha*," Fahd says. His monthly water bill is about 1,000 riyals (around $250), 670 riyals for tap water, 330 riyals in wastewater charges. In the old days, he paid a total of twenty riyals per month. As an engineer, Fahd does well for himself. He earns 14,000 riyals plus 6,000 in special allowances per month, together about $5,300. But the additional cost pains him. The state's income from water charges still doesn't cover the true costs of water treatment. Desalination is simply too expensive.

WATER IN PUBLIC PLACES: FOUNTAINS ARE A NEW FORM OF OUTDOOR ENTERTAINMENT.

There were once huge underground aquifers, but in just a few decades, they have been largely sucked dry. In the 1970s, the government began to cultivate huge quantities of grain and vegetables with the aim of self-sufficiency. Circular fields the size of freeway intersections were cultivated. Seen from an airplane, the recurring circles form a psychedelic pattern stretching across the endless desert. The circles differ only in color, ranging from light green to dark brown, depending on what crops are being grown.

(COMPARISON OF HISTORIC AND CURRENT NATURAL SPRING)

NATURAL SPRING AT THE AL-AHSA OASIS: WHAT USED TO BE AVAILABLE IN
ABUNDANCE HAS BECOME A LUXURY FOR THE AVERAGE SAUDI FAMILY.

To irrigate the fields, the Saudis pumped vast quantities of groundwater to the surface. Apart from the scant rainfall, the aquifers are the country's only natural source of water. These subterranean reservoirs took tens of thousands of years to fill with water. Many of them are now depleted and will be no use to the next generation because the aquifers are replenished very slowly.

The fact that a place like the ancient oasis of Tayma still exists is a miracle in its own right. The huge palm forest in the northwestern Tabuk region has been inhabited by humans for six thousand years. Tayma was once an important trading center on the incense route to what is now Medina. The oasis is the only source of drinking water—or "blue gold" as the Saudis call it—within a radius of a hundred miles.

Earlier inhabitants of the Arabian Peninsula knew how to carefully conserve the precious resource. Their farms were fed by a sophisticated underground irrigation system. Caravans would stop in Tayma to fill up at the springs that never ran dry. The trading center flourished for a thousand years, from the sixth century BC until the fifth century AD. Some 80,000 palms stand proudly in Tayma today, kept alive by careful watering.

In Riyadh, the rain has stopped, and I wait for a while until the temperature has risen before returning outside. I buy a bottle of mineral water in the mall. A liter costs fifty cents. Gasoline at the pump goes for forty-five cents. I ask myself, what is more precious, oil or water?

FORBIDDEN LOVE AMONG
THE WAHHABIS

NONCONFORMISTS AND ATHEISTS ARE FORCED TO LIVE
CLANDESTINE LIVES IN SAUDI ARABIA. SECRET LOVERS JASEM AND
ASMA LIVE IN CONSTANT FEAR OF BEING DISCOVERED—AND THE
POTENTIALLY HORRIFIC CONSEQUENCES.

Jasem is a skillful dancer, easily the best at this 2017 New Year's
Eve party in Riyadh. In perfect time with the 1930s Cuban
rhythms blasting from the speakers, he thrusts his hips, first
to the right, then to the left. He nudges his partner away, then
gently pulls her back. Well before midnight, the dance floor is
filled with revelers shaking their stuff to the infectious DePhazz
lounge hit, "The Mambo Craze."

Jasem is a tall, lanky guy, almost a little too thin. His face, with its
protruding cheekbones, is as pale as an ancient marble bust. His
thick hair is parted straight down the middle.

Alcohol flows freely at the party. Wine, vodka, gin. A lamb roasts
on the spit in the elaborately illuminated garden with its islands
and niches of trees and shrubs. It's a diverse crowd. White and
Black, Americans, Romanians, Saudis, Germans, French. The
New Year's celebration in the Diplomatic Quarter is hosted by a
Western diplomat famed for his fantastic parties.

Asma and Jasem stand out, even in this colorful crowd. A math
professor, Jasem wears an English summer vest. A Bordeaux-
red handkerchief pokes out of his breast pocket. His dancing
shoes are welted Oxford brogues. His lover Asma, a student,
wears a skintight, cream silk jumpsuit. Her haircut is angular,
pageboy-style. Jasem twirls Asma, catches her. They float across
the terrace.

What looks so light and easy on the dance floor is in reality
rather complicated. Jasem and Asma are breaking just about
every rule of the traditional, religious world they live in. No one

can ever find out about their love affair and how they spend their days together, let alone their nights. They can never reveal how they really feel about the country and the culture, not even to their friends and family.

"Someone like me shouldn't exist here," says Jasem. Early in life he sensed he didn't fit into a society based on prohibition and guilt.

"I'm an atheist. I don't believe in God. I don't believe in sin. Or in absolute monarchy as a political system."

YOUNG SAUDI MEN STROLLING ALONG TAHLIA STREET IN RIYADH: THEIR GENERATION GREW UP IN A CULTURE OF CLOTHING RESTRICTIONS, SELF-SACRIFICE, AND FEAR OF HELL.

ATHEISM IS A CRIME ON PAR WITH MURDER

On January 2, I visit Jasem at his home. He lives at the end of a cul-de-sac in Al-Khozame, on Riyadh's west side. It's a modern, one-story, sand-toned house with a flat roof. Luckily for him, Brits and Indians live on his street. Foreigners pay no attention to their neighbors' family situations, Jasem says.

A small Jack Russell terrier with light-brown splotches around both eyes bounces through the door. The religious police always forbade the ownership of dogs. They say it is inappropriate for Muslims to keep them in the house. And besides, men use dog walks as a pretext to chat up and harass women.

Asma and Jasem did, in fact, meet while walking their dogs in Wadi Hanifa, the dry riverbed that has been turned into a recreational area. Asma has a Chihuahua.

We sit in Jasem's kitchen. He's wearing jeans and a polo shirt and has tied a kitchen towel around his waist. Jasem is kneading dark, aromatic dough. He's baking date bread for Asma and me.

On weekdays, Jasem heads a small research department at the university. His career is going well. He takes part in scientific debates on TV. Asma studies at the College of Arts and aspires to be a painter. Officially, she lives in a student residence, but she usually spends the night with her boyfriend.

Jasem's atheism and lackluster loyalty to the king are about as bad as being a murderer in Saudi Arabia. Punishments for blasphemy and insults of the prophet can lead all the way to death by decapitation.

Coffee is brewing on the gas stove. Jasem prepares a tray with blue-trimmed English porcelain and liqueur glasses. Asma's on her way, he says, sliding the baking dish into the oven.

FEAR AND SACRIFICE

Jasem's place is a typical well-to-do bachelor pad: sneakers in the entrance, a racing bike hanging on the wall. Some art in the staircase, leather sofas, a glass coffee table.

When we meet, Jasem is thirty-nine. He was born in 1979, the year that extremists occupied the Grand Mosque of Mecca and demanded that the Saud family abdicate the throne. As a result, religious clerics loyal to the regime were able to isolate Saudi

Arabia even more from Western influence. Saudi citizens were to adhere strictly to the "true Islam" preached by the *Wahhabis*.

Jasem's generation grew up in a culture of clothing restrictions, self-sacrifice, and fear of hell. Jasem didn't buy into any of that.

Maybe it began with his mother's divorce, he explains. He was eight years old at the time. She taught high school English. After the separation, she and her son moved to her parents'. His mother was the breadwinner of the house. Jasem's father remarried and wasn't particularly interested in his son from his first marriage.

The 1980s were hard years for single women. Jasem saw how his mother was given short shrift by officials, for example when she applied for a license to open her own small school. It was impossible for her to advance her career. Even his grandfather humiliated his daughter, blaming her for the failure of her marriage.

A NEW KIND OF MASCULINITY

Jasem says back then, although he didn't really understand feminism, as a young boy he knew that what he saw around him wasn't right.

One day his mother brought home a biography of the British mathematician and philosopher Bertrand Russell, winner of the 1950 Nobel Prize for Literature. The book opened up a new world for Jasem. The biographer mentioned in passing the name of one of the books that had won Russell acclaim, *Marriage and Morals*, a thin volume in which the philosopher defends a notion of sexuality far removed from Victorian notions of sin.

Russell emboldened seventeen-year-old Jasem to doubt the culture around him and to take individual responsibility. For Jasem, this was nothing less than a revelation and the key to a new way of thinking.

We're sitting in Jasem's small backyard. Amidst different grasses, irises and hibiscus are in full bloom, violet and red. The walls are high enough to keep prying eyes from looking into the garden.

Jasem's encounter with Russell inspired him to study mathematics and statistics. Ever since, he has been able to think for himself and see reality for what it really is.

"We men continue to be told the bigger, the better. That's masculine—the biggest, fattest pizza, the biggest car. But it's inflexible. None of that works anymore," Jasem muses. He's seen the economic data, the population statistics, the oil prices. Saudi Arabia is in the midst of a paradigm shift.

It's about fundamental questions: masculinity versus feminism, rigidity versus flexibility, security versus insecurity. Luxury is on its way out; cars are getting smaller; women are gaining more influence.

A WOMAN RISKS IT ALL

We hear a key in the front door. Asma pokes her head through the kitchen window. Jasem jumps up and kisses her, first on the mouth, then on her pageboy hair. He pulls the date bread out of the oven, distributes it over three ceramic plates, and fills our glasses with fifteen-year-old cognac.

It's four in the afternoon. Alcohol is, of course, strictly forbidden. Through the embassies, foreigners sometimes have legal access to deliveries from their home countries. The strong stuff is usually smuggled in from Bahrain, the United Arab Emirates, or Egypt. A bottle of top-shelf whiskey can cost $350 on the black market. And, of course, people distill and brew their own concoctions behind closed doors. But in this country, an aged French cognac is about as unconventional as Jasem himself.

"We're thinking about getting married," Jasem says, looking at Asma. He raises his glass and takes a tiny sip. Asma is silent.

A woman risks everything when she marries a man her parents haven't chosen for her. If the relationship were to be exposed, the punishment could be unthinkable. Asma's father could lock her up, force her to marry another man, even kill her. She carries the greater burden in this illicit relationship.

Asma is wearing a tight blue linen suit and boots. "I don't have control over my own life," she says. It racks her nerves to live in violation of her family's principles.

Asma says Saudi mothers tell their daughters that love is an unsettling feeling, that the senses cloud the mind and cause you to make bad decisions. Those who pursue love end up as unhappy as women in the West, as you can see in the soap operas running on every TV channel. In Saudi Arabia, women are protected by the wisdom of Islam and the traditions of the family.

Asma laughs, but she doesn't sound all that amused. She doubts her father would accept Jasem as her future husband. Only certain tribes and family arrangements are considered suitable for a union.

It would be Jasem's second marriage. The first one lasted only eight months. Naturally, the marriage was arranged by Jasem's mother. The bride was twenty-four, beautiful, had a college education, spoke three languages. Jasem wanted to do things differently than his parents, better. He wanted a marriage between equals. He didn't ask where his wife was going, when she was coming back, or whom she was meeting.

"Then something totally unexpected happened," he says.

One evening, when he came home from work, his wife was gone. She hadn't cooked. The fridge was empty. The young bride had expected a classic Saudi marriage with rules, commands, and total control by the husband. And when that didn't happen, she saw it as a sign of male weakness, Jasem explains. Subsequently, she "excessively" tried out her freedom. "We couldn't find the words to tell each other what we wanted," says Jasem. That all happened six years ago.

Jasem puts on some music. Jack Johnson's "Washing Dishes," a lazy foxtrot. It's winter and the sun has almost set. Jasem refills our glasses and takes Asma by the hand. For a few steps, the two of them sway together.

Outside, behind the walls, the world will remain hostile for the foreseeable future. All that remains for Asma and Jasem is the present moment.

BRAVE WOMEN

THREE FEMALE ACTIVISTS STRUGGLED FOR THE RIGHT TO DRIVE
AND FOR A BIT OF SELF-DETERMINATION. THEY WERE ARRESTED,
TORTURED, AND TRIED FOR ESPIONAGE. ONE OF THE WOMEN IS MY
FRIEND EMAN.

Eman al-Nafjan must have sensed they were coming for her.
Two weeks before she was arrested, the university professor
unexpectedly changed the profile picture on the WhatsApp
account she had been using for years. In place of the familiar
drawing of her face with shoulder-length brown hair and a broad
smile is the head of a scaly reptile with its mouth wide open.
Lodged deep in the animal's throat is a frog with an expression
of terror on its face. Evidently, the creature is fighting for its life.
Perhaps, this was her way of announcing impending disaster.

In 2018, on May 15, Eman al-Nafjan was indeed placed under
arrest, along with other well-known women's rights activists.
A few days later their faces appeared on the front page of a
pro-government newspaper. The headline read: "Traitors."
The layout resembled a wanted poster from the Wild West.
Government sources were quoted as saying that the women
faced prison sentences of up to twenty years or perhaps even the
death penalty.

At the time, al-Nafjan was thirty-eight and a mother of four,
a well-organized, caring woman. Her youngest daughter was
barely two years old. For ten years straight, al-Nafjan fought for
human rights in her country, especially for the rights of women.

ENGLISH UNIVERSITY TEACHER AND FORMER BLOGGER EMAN AL-NAFJAN WITH HER
YOUNGEST DAUGHTER: "ANYTHING IS BETTER THAN STAGNATION."

She was one of the kingdom's first-ever female bloggers. On
SaudiWoman.me she discussed social issues such as the true
meaning of *Wahhabism*, the ins and outs of divorce in Saudi
Arabia, and why secret second wives have become so popular
in the kingdom. Al-Nafjan attended college in Birmingham,
England. She lived in a house near Riyadh airport together with
her husband, an IT specialist, and their children. She taught
English at the university.

VIRAL CAMPAIGNS

Eman al-Nafjan had already spent time in prison in 2013 because
she filmed a woman driving a car in Saudi Arabia. The video
went viral around the world. One of the drivers was Loujain

al-Hathloul, perhaps the best-known Saudi woman's rights campaigner—and the second face on the newspaper's "traitor" poster. The third woman in this club of heroines was Aziza al-Yousef, a professor emeritus of information technology. Al-Yousef, an elegant woman, studied in the US in the 1970s. You could say she played a motherly role in the group.

Together, the trio waged a passionate struggle for equal rights. It is largely thanks to their work that women are permitted to drive in Saudi Arabia today. With their tireless activism, they kept up the political pressure and attracted media attention to the issues they cared about: they posted videos of themselves driving; they sent petitions to the royal family; they created viral campaigns on Facebook and Twitter. As a consequence, they are now paying a very high price.

EMAN'S FORMER BLOG: THE FIRST ENGLISH-LANGUAGE BLOG TO OPENLY DISCUSS QUESTIONS OF SAUDI FAMILY LIFE AND SOCIETY.

A good five weeks after the activists were arrested, Saudi women were officially permitted to get behind the wheel of a car for the first time. The historic occasion was celebrated worldwide—by the press, by foreign diplomats, and by the Saudis themselves. Yet the heroines who made it possible were absent. I asked myself, why the crown prince didn't utilize these national icons, beloved at home and abroad, to his own advantage by appearing arm-in-arm with them as a symbol of progress and collective change? Instead, he had them put behind bars.

Some observers said it was a deliberate move to instill fear in both the women and anyone who might be inspired by them. In an absolute monarchy, the people can have no voice. The ruler alone determines which rights are enjoyed by which social group. You don't tell a crown prince how to run the show.

MBS, the heir apparent, said the arrests were "100 percent" unrelated to the women's political activism—nothing to do with their driving before it was legalized or with their struggle against the guardianship law. Al-Nafjan, al-Hathloul, and al-Yousef struggled vehemently against Saudi legislation that gives men control over nearly every aspect of their wives' lives as if they were nothing more than underage children. In the meantime, the guardianship law has been extensively reformed.

CHARGED WITH ESPIONAGE

For Crown Prince Mohammed bin Salman, Eman al-Nafjan and her comrades in arms are not actually human rights activists. In October 2018, he told Bloomberg News that there was evidence in the form of videos and recordings of phone conversations that proved that certain women shared information with foreign intelligence in exchange for money. The crown prince said that investigations had conclusively shown that the women took part in an intelligence operation against Saudi Arabia: "They have a network, connection with government people, leaking information for the sake of these other governments."

These were extremely serious accusations. The punishment for treason is as harsh as it is for murder. With her probing questions, the Bloomberg journalist attempted to extract more precise details about the alleged collaboration with foreign powers from MBS. She wanted to know whether it was the women's contact to media and foreign embassies that ended up costing them their freedom.

Bloomberg: "These are espionage charges?"

MBS: "Yes, you can say that."

Bloomberg: "Does that mean talking to foreign diplomats and journalists?"

MBS: "Journalists, no. But intelligence, yes. Secret intelligence. We have some of them with videos. We can show it to you. Tomorrow we will show you the videos."

The videos were never released. Neither were the phone transcripts. To this day, the reasons for the women's incarceration and the exact nature of the charges laid against them remain unclear.

1,500 DISSIDENTS BEHIND BARS

I met Eman for the first time eight years ago in a Starbucks in the Diplomatic Quarter on Riyadh's west side. She was wearing an inconspicuous black abaya, a black hijab, black pants, and a black blouse. At the time, there was almost nowhere to meet publicly in Riyadh. Recently, countless cafes and restaurants have sprung up, and Eman is thrilled about this kind of progress. When King Salman and his son assumed power, Eman supported their course of radical transformation, even long after the crown prince began his harsh crackdown, and even though, well before Eman was jailed, some 1,500 journalists, clerics, and assorted dissidents had already been locked up. "Anything is better than the paralyzing stagnation we have had for many years," Eman said during one of our last meetings.

Would she still say that today? Probably not.

Eman, Loujain, and Aziza were friends. They first met on social media. In a country where most people don't know anyone outside their own family, Facebook and Twitter have opened up radically new opportunities for communication.

One time, the four of us got together for coffee: Loujain, Aziza, Eman, and I. Back then, Loujain was already living in the United Arab Emirates, where she was studying sociology at the Sorbonne University Abu Dhabi. The slim, dark-haired woman moved to UAE as a precaution after she spent sixty days in prison in 2014–15. Her crime: being filmed driving a car as part of one of the group's campaigns. She was not keen to relive the experience.

We took off our abayas, consumed coffee with cookies, and enjoyed the relaxed conversation. The women had blue rubber wristbands made bearing the words "I am my own guardian." This kind of social activism is utterly unconventional and provocative in a country like Saudi Arabia. Even so, the women were a long way from devising a political plot.

Eman al-Nafjan has been locked up for more than a year, probably in Dhahban Central Prison near Jeddah, a maximum-security facility where terrorists and political prisoners are kept. Since late 2018, some gruesome details have emerged. Allegedly, the women were photographed nude. They were accused of being "agents of Qatar," and chained to an iron bed frame and beaten.

One woman was told that all of her children had died. When she begged her abuser for a chance to see her children one more time before their funeral, it turned out that the kids were still alive. Just one more brutal way of breaking the inmates' spirit. Aziza's children are grown up. Loujain has no children. But Eman has four, so she was probably that woman—assuming that the story is true.

لامكان للخونة بيننا

قبضت رئاسة أمن الدولة على مجموعة تواصلت مع منظمات مشبوهة حاولت النيل من العقيدة والدين وإثارة الرأي العام

إيمان محمد القحطان   لجين هذلول الهذلول   عزيزة محمد اليوسف

محمد فهد الربيعة   عبدالعزيز محمد المشعل   ابراهيم عبدالرحمن المديميغ

تتطلب التحقيقات عدم الإفصاح عن اسمه حاليا

SAUDINEWS50

أخبار
السعودية

ACTIVISTS ARE BRANDED TRAITORS: "NOBODY IS ABOVE US, NOT EVEN GOD."

Their families, their friends, and even diplomats are at a loss as to how to support the women. If they keep quiet, no one will even hear about the prisoners' fates. If they publicize the case, the women could be punished again just for that, and their supporters might be targeted by the country's brash new foreign policy.

TORTURED AND ABUSED

Loujain's parents were deeply shaken after they visited their daughter in prison at the end of 2018. Her father tweeted that Loujain was tortured and sexually abused—in the presence of one of the crown prince's closest confidants, Saud al-Qahtani, former director of the royal court's media office. The parents' visit was three months after the brutal killing of journalist Jamal Khashoggi. Saud al-Qahtani is suspected to be one of the key players responsible for the murder.

A few days after Loujain's father tweeted about the brutal abuse of his daughter, his Twitter account was blocked, his voice silenced. Loujain al-Hathloul's parents have been banned from leaving the country.

When the US secretary of state and former CIA chief Mike Pompeo traveled to Riyadh for a state visit in January 2019, Loujain's sister, Alia al-Hathloul, appealed to him in an article published in the *New York Times*. Alia was living in Brussels and hoped that the high-ranking American official would broach the subject of Loujain in his dealings with the crown prince. The Americans are probably the only ones with any influence over the young prince. Alia al-Hathloul wrote how her sister was first held at an unknown location from May to August. Apparently, she was kept in a hotel, in solitary confinement. Loujain, known for her vitality and self-control, had, according to their parents, been unable to keep herself from trembling.

Alia recounted how their parents had seen Loujain collapse in tears and tell them that between May and August she had been repeatedly abused in a basement. According to her sister, they tortured her with electric shocks and waterboarding, after which they threatened to sexually abuse and rape, beat, or even kill her. Loujain showed her parents her upper thighs, still black and blue from the maltreatment.

During the holy month of Ramadan, Saud al-Qahtani personally tormented her all night, together with six other men, she told her parents. Afterwards, he had forced her to eat with him, even after sunrise—disregarding an important religious rule. Her sister wrote in the *New York Times* that Loujain confronted the men about it and one of them answered, "No one is above us—not even God." At least when it came to describing the state of affairs in Saudi Arabia, the statement seemed accurate.

Responding to a report on the case by Amnesty International, released in November 2018, the Saudi Human Rights Commission bowed to international pressure. Several delegates from the commission visited Loujain in prison. When she asked whether the organization could protect her from further torture, the delegates replied, "No, we can't." Secretary of State Mike Pompeo, the one person who could have had a positive impact, was obviously uninterested in even trying.

Al-Hathloul was also followed by hundreds of thousands of people on social media. Her arrest unleashed a storm of outrage on Twitter, Instagram, and Telegram Messenger. This is what makes the human rights activists truly dangerous, even to a ruler with absolute power.

During recent waves of arrests, even more influential activists were rounded up, the latest in November 2019. This too is part of the grand plan of "Vision 2030." All are to remain silent while the new kingdom comes into being. That is what the crown prince wants, a close confidant of the young ruler told me. Another close aide said that MBS believes the women are only interested in fame and want to make a name for themselves.

The end result of Crown Prince Mohammed bin Salman's transformation of Saudi Arabia could be a mix of the Chinese model and that of the similarly authoritarian United Arab Emirates: a society increasingly liberated from religious restrictions; a free-market economy in which those loyal to the king can become rich and, ultimately, absolute political control over the country.

There are signs that Eman, Loujain, and Aziza have all been subjected to similar forms of torture. Eman tried to take her own life several times while incarcerated. In the end, she was allowed to leave prison until the sentencing, under the condition that she refrained from telling anyone what really happened in jail. She has been banned from blogging or expressing herself publicly in any other way. No one knows whether the once vivacious woman will ever recover from the hardships she has endured. The IT professor Aziza is also back home. Now her son has been arrested instead. Loujain, on the other hand, perhaps the most resilient of the women, stated that she was not prepared to publicly deny that she was tortured. At the time of writing, she still remains behind bars.

In the summer of 2019, Reporters Without Borders, an international organization that campaigns for freedom of speech, awarded its "Prize for Courage" to Eman al-Nafjan. I had the honor of delivering the laudatory speech and could at least tell that audience about her jovial, unassuming personality.

Anyway, it is frustrating to realize that there is very little that I or anyone else can do to assist these three outstanding women—other than share their story.

"I AM MY OWN GUARDIAN" WRISTBAND. CERTAINLY UNCONVENTIONAL BUT A LONG WAY FROM A POLITICAL PLOT.

OSAMA BIN LADEN'S BOMB-MAKING INSTRUCTOR REVEALS ALL

BEFORE HE WAS JAILED AT GUANTANAMO BAY, KHALED AL-
HUBAYSHI, FORTY-FOUR, REMAINED FAITHFULLY BY THE SIDE
OF THE AL-QAEDA LEADER TO THE BITTER END. ONCE RELEASED
FROM THE PRISON CAMP, HE ATTENDED A SAUDI ACADEMY THAT
REHABILITATES EX-JIHADIS. NOWADAYS, HE'S A FAMILY MAN,
WORKING AS AN ELECTRICIAN, WHO TRIES TO SEE THE BEAUTY IN
LIFE'S SMALL JOYS.

When I meet the man who trained Osama bin Laden's bomb makers, he's just finished a day's work at the Saudi Electric Company. He already worked there before he signed up for the jihad, a decision that eventually led to his imprisonment at Guantanamo Bay, where Khaled al-Hubayshi was forced to wear an orange jumpsuit and a wristband marked "No. 155." For weeks, he was kept blindfolded and his hands remained tied behind his back. Most of his time was spent kneeling on the floor. Joining Bin Laden's war against America cost him five years of his life.

He invites me to his apartment in Jeddah on the Red Sea coast. Outside, the sun burns bright, but thanks to the dark curtains, not a single ray of light makes it into the house. Al-Hubayshi greets me wearing a white *thawb*, sandals, and a red-and-white *ghutra*. We sit on a large corner sofa in his living room. His face shows an ironic smile, not pretentious, but with a touch of humility, the expression of a person who has found new confidence after coming to terms with his failures.

BEHIND THE KINGDOM'S VEIL

KHALED AL-HUBAYSHI: AS A MUJAHID IN THE PHILIPPINES IN 1999, AS A TERRORIST DURING HIS TIME WITH OSAMA BIN LADEN IN THE TORA BORA CAVES IN AFGHANISTAN, AND IN HIS ORANGE JUMPSUIT AT GUANTANAMO AS PRISONER #155.

When the Pakistani secret service captured him in December 2001, while he was fleeing Afghanistan three months after 9/11, the then twenty-five-year-old lost everything in a single blow: his freedom, his dreams, his reputation. All that remained was his faith—which was both a positive and a negative. His faith helped him survive Guantanamo, but the very same set of beliefs had brought him there in the first place.

At Guantanamo, al-Hubayshi was kept in Camp X-Ray. Another al-Qaeda explosives expert, a friend, lost his mind there. "His name was Tarek Al-Masri, an Egyptian." The prison broke him. "Masri stripped off all his clothes, ran around like a wild man, and thought he was in the burning fires of hell."

That put fear into al-Hubayshi's heart. He could never be sure whether he would wake up in a state of insanity. "We simply didn't know what was happening to us."

Three other inmates taught him to speak English. An American guard taught him chess. "Some guards were pieces of shit, others were nice," he recalls.

One day, Defense Minister Donald Rumsfeld paid a visit. A reporter asked the politician why he kept people in cages. Rumsfeld answered that they weren't cages, they were cells.

"They were cages, like the ones used for training animals," al-Hubayshi says. Many years have passed, but the memories of his imprisonment are still fresh in his mind.

Al-Hubayshi's wife Alma enters the room. Al-Hubayshi was born in 1975. She is seven years younger than him, a brunette with bangs and amber eyes. Alma is dressed in a short black cotton dress, its sleeves dotted with reflective squares, and dark tights. The marriage was arranged with help from the Ministry of the Interior, which even paid for the dowry and wedding party, all part of the rehabilitation program that the Saudi government has developed for former jihadis like al-Hubayshi.

"I want you to learn English," Khaled tells Alma, looking at her amicably. "Life gets more interesting."

Alma is pregnant with their third child. She meets up with her sisters and sisters-in-law several times a week. Alma is Khaled's wife and the anchor of his new life. For her, what could be more interesting?

Al-Hubayshi is very different from Alma. He's a restless bundle of energy. He's a sensitive man with a quick intellect. He always wanted to do something special in his life, something meaningful. He came from a respected family. He attended college and earned a good salary at the power plant in Dammam, the capital of the Eastern Province. He'd had it all, but something was lacking. His days were monotone: he went to work, he went to the mosque, he visited his family. Nothing new ever happened.

CHE GUEVARA OF THE ISLAMIC WORLD

When al-Hubayshi was a teenager, Saudi organizations collected money from fans after every soccer match: a riyal for the oppressed Muslims of Palestine, a riyal for the *mujahideen* in Afghanistan, and so on. The Red Army had occupied the country, and influential Saudi imams would embolden young men to join the resistance against the Soviets during their Friday sermons.

By 1989, the *mujahideen* had managed to chase the Russians from Afghanistan. Among the fighters were a few thousand foreigners, volunteers from across the Islamic world. Many of them were Saudis.

The best-known leader among them was the son of a fabulously wealthy construction tycoon—Osama bin Laden. Newspapers celebrated the mujahid like a rock star.

Young men like al-Hubayshi revered the multimillionaire, who was living with his comrades in primitive conditions in Afghanistan. They loved the freedom fighter with the reverence that leftists in the West once had for Che Guevara.

"But in the end Osama betrayed us," al-Hubayshi says. By December 2001, about three hundred fighters were left, holed up with Bin Laden in Tora Bora in the mountains near the Afghan-Pakistani border. The Taliban government in Kabul had allowed the al-Qaeda leader to set up training camps in Afghanistan. In exchange, Bin Laden gave money to the ever struggling Taliban.

When the US launched their assault by air on Afghanistan in October 2001, Bin Laden was hiding with his men in Tora Bora. He told them that the fight against the Americans would take place on their soil, in their territory. Everything was prepared: the weapons, the cave hideouts. For five weeks, Bin Laden's men waited in their positions. Al-Hubayshi was one of them. But Bin Laden had misjudged the situation. Instead of US troops, Afghan fighters allied with the Americans ended up attacking Tora Bora. Al-Hubayshi recounts how at some point Bin Laden gathered his men and told them to flee to Pakistan. They should approach their embassies there. Bin Laden himself disappeared overnight. "He just abandoned us," says al-Hubayshi with bitterness. Today he is all too aware that he had followed a false hero.

AL-HUBAYSHI AT THE MOHAMMED BIN NAIF COUNSELING AND CARE CENTER:
"WHAT DO YOU FEEL?"

For days, the men marched toward the border through knee-deep snow, over the icy mountains. Many of them did not wear solid shoes and had no gloves, so their fingers and toes froze. On the other side of the border, they were captured by Pakistani forces and handed over to the Americans. Al-Hubayshi no longer believes that Osama bin Laden really cared about the protection of oppressed Muslims. "He wanted to be famous."

Alma leaves to fetch coffee from the kitchen. Al-Hubayshi says that his wife lives in a different world. She understands nothing of politics and knows nothing about the jihad. She cares about who marries who in the family and what dress she is going to wear at a wedding. "Sometimes I wish I was like her and knew nothing."

Al-Hubayshi was too young to join the war against the Soviets in Afghanistan. When he graduated college at twenty and entered his first job as an electrical engineer, the international jihadis of the Hindu Kush had moved on to the next battlefield, the Balkans, where a civil war had been raging since 1991.

In Friday sermons, al-Hubayshi heard that Serbs and Croats were slaughtering defenseless Muslim civilians in Bosnia. Worshippers heard about how the victims were flung into wells and the dead buried in mass graves. The imams reminded them of the "duty of jihad."

Ultimately, al-Hubayshi found the answer to his inner restlessness on a supermarket shelf, next to the chocolate. He saw a pile of VHS tapes about the Balkan War. He bought all of them and watched them the same day.

One of the tapes contained footage of the infamous massacre in Sarajevo's market square on February 5, 1994: women lying in their blood next to wooden market stalls; a woman whose head was missing; a man torn to shreds by a 120mm mortar shell; sixty-eight dead, 144 wounded. Another video told the story of the al-Mujahid, a group of Arab jihadis.

"THEY APPEAL TO YOUR EMOTIONS"

"I couldn't sleep anymore, knowing that Muslims were being killed and that women were being raped. I wanted to be one of those *mujahideen*."

Al-Hubayshi got in touch with a local recruiter, of which there were many at the time, via religious networks. The recruiter offered to put him in contact with the group in Bosnia. To al-Hubayshi's disappointment, the war came to a sudden end in October 1995. The American special envoy to the Balkans, Richard Holbrooke, had negotiated the Dayton Peace Accords, which were signed by the three warring parties. The treaty recognized Bosnia and Herzegovina as a sovereign state with Sarajevo as its capital.

As an alternative, the recruiter suggested al-Hubayshi join a separatist rebel group in the Philippines, the Moro Islamic

Liberation Front. He traveled to the island nation and lived with the fighters in the jungle. His teachers showed him images from Nigeria, where a group of "infidels" had burned a Muslim alive. The teacher asked him: "What do you feel?"

"They appeal to your emotions and your sense of responsibility," Al-Huybashi says.

He was trained to operate weapons: .30 and .50 caliber guns, 60mm mortars. "Kids' stuff," he thought. Then nothing much else happened. The *mujahideen* spent most of their time on their base. "I wanted to be involved in something important," al-Hubayshi says. And so he contacted his idol, Osama bin Laden.

In 1980, Bin Laden had attended King Abdulaziz University in al-Hubayshi's hometown of Jeddah. There, he met the charismatic Palestinian theologian Abdullah Assam. Assam inspired the tycoon's son to invest his private wealth in the struggle for Muslim liberation.

In 1988, the duo set up an organization, which they named "the base" or *"al-Qaeda."* Its objective was to topple the corrupt regimes of the Middle East. The victory over the Soviets in Afghanistan excited both men. Anything seemed possible. They wanted to change the world once and for all. They believed Islamic governments founded upon their ideas should take power in Muslim countries around the world.

THE HUMILIATED HERO

In 1990, Bin Laden returned to Saudi Arabia. His partner Assam, however, was killed in an attack in Pakistan. Around the same time, Iraq invaded its small, oil-rich neighbor, Kuwait. The Riyadh government asked the US for help: The Americans should step in for Kuwait and protect Saudi Arabia from an eventual Iraqi invasion. Bin Laden, for his part, offered the Saudi defense minister, Prince Sultan, his "holy warriors" to do the job instead and fix the problem. The conversation between the two men was short but had a long-lasting effect.

Bin Laden: "Within three months I can provide 100,000 well-trained fighters. You don't need the Americans. You don't need any non-Muslim troops. We will be enough."

Prince Sultan: "There aren't any caves in Kuwait. What are you going to do when they attack you with chemical and biological weapons or fire missiles at you?"

Bin Laden: "We'll fight them with our faith."

Prince Sultan did not trust the capabilities of Osama bin Laden's guerrillas. He considered the Americans, with their regular troops and high-tech weaponry, a safer choice. Saddam Hussein's army was decisively defeated in a short, brutal war—Operation Desert Storm—and forced out of Kuwait. US military stayed in Saudi Arabia. All bridges between Bin Laden and the monarchy were irrevocably burned. Osama bin Laden was humiliated.

He now lashed out against the royal family with utmost contempt and condemned what he believed was the country's dishonorable dependence on the United States. He declared that the Al Saud were unable to protect the holy sites of Mecca and Medina and that they had to ask infidels to do the job for them. Covertly, many Saudis seemed to agree with him.

BLACK OR WHITE WITH NOTHING IN BETWEEN

It was one of the rare moments in the country's history when realpolitik and Wahhabism became incompatible. Al-Hubayshi asks his two young daughters frolicking around in front of the sitting room to hush up. He closes the door. Back in the day, al-Hubayshihad listened to his heart.

"In a way, Osama bin Laden was a man of conviction," al-Hubayshi explains. "But it's not for him to decide on politics, nor for us." At the time he did not have it in himself to understand the scope of what went on. War changes people, he says. "It reduces everything to black or white, with nothing in between."

For Bin Laden, the US was the chief enemy propping up the "corrupt puppet governments" of the Middle East. At the top of his list of despicable regimes was the one in his home country, the Kingdom of Saudi Arabia.

The Riyadh government likes to point out that Saudi Arabia couldn't have anything to do with Islamist terrorism because the kingdom itself was one of the terrorists' primary targets. One could argue that this isn't necessarily a contradiction since, when it came to Islamist terrorism, the Saudis were the arsonists and the firefighters in one.

Today, their secret services crack down hard on extremists, at least if they are acting against the interests of the country. The Saudi General Intelligence Presidency is highly efficient, sharing the information it has gathered with its allies.

Nevertheless, the roots of extremism can be found in the *Wahhabi* ideology. To this day, there are still Saudi schoolbooks that stir up hatred against Sufis, Shi'ites, Jews, and Christians. Such downright fanatical intolerance is used to justify the unbridled violence that al-Qaeda and the Islamic State have unleashed upon the world.

CAUGHT IN THE TRAP

It can be argued that the founding story of Saudi Arabia was itself a jihad project. The key to the Al Sauds success in conquering the country in the early twentieth century was the so-called Ikhwan—"Brethren"—who were known for their brutality and fearlessness. Recruited from Bedouin tribes, the Brethren formed the first Saudi army.

In order to use them in their quest for power, King Abdulaziz settled them in oases and indoctrinated them with the radical, puritanical ideology of his ally, the religious leader Abd al-Wahhab. Armed with fanatic fervor and the firm desire to die as martyrs in the war against infidels, the Ikhwan could not be stopped. They took one region after the other by storm, until they had conquered most of the Arabian Peninsula.

Then something happened that is perhaps comparable to the current conflict between today's rulers in Riyadh and their rebellious jihadis. To consolidate his expansion, King Abdulaziz was forced to adapt his strategy. He had to make concessions to minorities and allies who followed a different interpretation of Islam. He welcomed modern technological achievements. The reactionary Ikhwan rejected such compromises—just as Osama bin Laden did later on. Like the future al-Qaeda leader, some of the troops revolted against their master. King Abdulaziz finally wore down the rebels among the Ikhwan through the deployment of modern weaponry in the great Battle of Sabilla in 1929.

Khaled al-Hubayshi believes that he fell into the same trap. The interests of the Saudi state mutated while he was living with the *mujahideen* in the far-off mountains of Afghanistan. "They said, join the jihad, and I went. When I came back, I was a terrorist."

FIVE-STAR TERRORIST REHAB

Perhaps the Saudis developed such a generous rehabilitation program precisely because they know they were the ones who opened Pandora's box in the first place.

The Mohammed bin Naif Center for Counseling and Care on the outskirts of Riyadh is a five-star facility for reintegrating extremists into society. There's a swimming pool, a movie theater, and an auditorium, as well as psychologists and religious teachers. At the Center, terrorists learn to become productive members of society once again.

Al-Hubayshi was one of the program's first participants after the Americans released him from Guantanamo in mid-2005 and sent him back to his home country. He was held for another year in a maximum-security prison near Riyadh. The de-radicalization process lasted through 2007.

Considerable resources are invested in the program, and it boasts a high success rate. Reportedly, only 3 percent of participants relapse into their old ways of radical violence. A decisive factor seems to be the inclusion of families in the exercise. After graduation from the Center, most of the inmates marry and have kids. They leave the Center with professional skills. After passing the "final exam," they receive a car, a job, and financial support for six months. To date, thousands of former extremists have completed the program.

مركز محمد بن نايف للمناصحة والرعاية
Mohammed Bin Naif Counseling and Care Center

FORMER AL-QAEDA MEMBER AL-HUBAYSHI: "I LEFT AS A HERO AND RETURNED AS A TERRORIST."

Critics say that Jihadism can't be defeated without getting rid of Salafism. Even in the case of model student al-Hubayshi, it isn't entirely clear to me whether he has really renounced jihad or if he merely abandoned the concept of attacking politically undesirable targets. "In the jihad, soldiers only fight other soldiers. The attacks on September 11, 2001, were wrong because they targeted civilians," he adds.

EXPORTING WAHHABISM

Jihadism played an undeniably central role in Wahhabism. Until seventy years ago, this extremely radical ideology was just a tiny movement within Sunni Islam. Saudi petrodollars enabled it to spread across entire continents, first Africa, and then Asia.

In the 1960s, through the concept of Islamic solidarity, King Faisal created a program that was initially intended to provide an antidote to the socialist nationalism of Gamal Abdel Nasser in neighboring Egypt.

From 1973 on, the kingdom invested 5 percent of its gross domestic product in such programs, for example, offering African students scholarships to take courses in Islamic Studies at the University of Medina and then sending them back to their home countries as ambassadors of Saudi Islam. In its missionary zeal, Saudi Arabia funded the construction of thousands of mosques, Qur'anic schools, cultural centers, and financed youth projects in many countries. Later on, with satellite TV channels and free websites, the kingdom provided its own brand of religious content to countless institutions. "We want Islam to be reborn—without nationalism, ethnic groups and political parties—but with the call of Islam and the call of jihad to defend our religion," King Faisal said in a speech in Mecca in 1968.

This was how, based on the Saudi model, small Islamic organizations sprouted up around the world.

When the US diplomat Farah Pandith traveled to eighty countries with at least partially Muslim populations between 2009 and 2014, she established that "in each place I visited, the *Wahhabi* influence was an insidious presence." In a 2015 op-ed in the *New York Times,* she wrote that da'wah, the missionary agenda originating from the Gulf region, had fundamentally changed local religious practice. For decades, da'wah, the call to

Islam, has been promoted by institutions like the Muslim World League and the World Assembly of Muslim Youth (WAMY).

WAMY was founded in Riyadh in 1972 and maintains offices in fifty-six countries, as well as an international network of hospitals, orphanages, and teaching institutes. According to the 9/11 Commission Report, these youth organizations openly financed the Islamic terrorism of Hamas and extremists in Pakistan. Ironically, for decades, the contact person for financial support of fundamentalist fighters from Kabul to Sarajevo was the emir of Riyadh, today none other than King Salman. Salman's deceased brother, the former defense minister Prince Sultan, was one of the most generous backers of the international jihad.

"YOU LEAVE AS A HERO AND RETURN AS A TERRORIST"

If there are such things as jihad celebrities, then al-Hubayshi knows them all. He recalls studying side-by-side with today's al-Qaeda leader, the Egyptian Ayman az-Zawahiri, in the Bin Laden Library of the Afghan training camp. A Saudi named Abu Zubaydah, number four or five in the al-Qaeda hierarchy, was his closest buddy. Today, Abu Zubaydah is forty-eight, four years older than al-Hubayshi. "A true friend," al-Hubayshi says. Abu Zubaydah once got him out of a Pakistani jail. Another time he provided him a new passport.

Abu Zubaydah was captured and brutally tortured by the Americans in secret prisons, including one in Poland. In total, eighty-three instances of his having been waterboarded have been documented. Abu Zubaydah remains in Guantanamo to this day.

Al-Hubayshi says they all started with the best intentions and all ended up as beggars, criminals, or murderers. When al-Hubayshi traveled to Afghanistan for the third time in May 2001, Osama bin Laden disclosed to him that he was planning an attack on America. They met in an inconspicuous concrete building in

Kandahar, a kind of bunker without electrical power. There was only cold water, he recalls. "Osama said we should get used to difficult situations."

Al-Hubayshi was sought after as an explosives expert. Not only did he know how to fire anti-aircraft missiles and rocket-propelled grenades, but he was also versed in building remotely triggered explosive devices. He knew how to detonate bombs with photoelectric beams and mobile phones. Al-Hubayshi was partly trained by Ahmad al-Almani, a blond Egyptian who carried out the bomb attacks on the US embassies in Dar es Salaam in Tanzania and the Kenyan capital of Nairobi that resulted in hundreds of deaths.

"To be taught by Ahmad was like going to college," al-Hubayshi says. Al-Hubayshi passed on his knowledge to Chechens, Libyans, anyone who was permitted to take the courses or who paid the organization a lot of money to do so. Bin Laden wanted to bind al-Hubayshi to the group, so the al-Qaeda boss tested his loyalty. Al-Hubayshi hesitated. He sensed that he had lost his way on his mission to do something good for Muslims. The Muslims in Afghanistan were fighting each other. The Taliban were battling against the so-called Northern Alliance, and Osama bin Laden was a wanted man around the world. Saudi investigators had also set their sights on al-Hubayshi. His last trip to the al-Qaeda base wasn't voluntary—he was escaping a prison sentence back home.

Alma enters the room. She smiles. Their daughters, Reema and Jawhara, jump toward their father. The couple discuss family plans, who is picking up whom and when for a wedding dinner.

I'm somewhat irritated by their antithetical lives: Alma, who has no clue what drove her husband to Afghanistan and what he might have done there, and Khaled, who isn't interested in weddings and the beautiful clothes you wear to them. Nonetheless, I sense gratitude and love in the house.

I ask Khaled what it's like to leave behind a life-or-death struggle alongside the greatest terrorist of all time, Osama bin Laden, for a small, ordinary life. "Who's Osama bin Laden?" Alma asks. I look at her in disbelief. "Is that a joke?" I ask. But Alma's face is serious. "How can you live in Saudi Arabia and be married to a former al-Qaeda fighter and not know who Bin Laden is?" I ask. Alma starts to cry and runs out of the room.

Khaled had told Alma that, earlier in his life, he fought as a mujahid against the infidels, and that the man he believed in had abandoned the group. Yet he had never mentioned the man's name. When Alma married Khaled seven years ago, she knew nothing about the groom other than his age and his name. She comes from Medina, 250 miles away from Jeddah. Nobody told her that Khaled had done time in prison. "He's a relative," her mother told her. "A good man." For most Saudis, al-Hubayshi's decision to join the jihad—which translates to "struggle on the path of God"—is not a disgrace. Neither is having been imprisoned by the Americans in Guantanamo.

I run after Alma and tell her how sorry I am to have offended her and that I just couldn't believe that someone in Saudi Arabia didn't know that name. Alma sits down again and says, "I'm not stupid. I care about other things. I don't watch the news; I watch other TV shows."

Her husband takes Alma's hand, nods at her, and says, "You know other things."

For a moment, al-Hubayshi is silent. His face looks relaxed. Maybe he is getting the best medicine against jihad, a sickness that inflicts the heart and is highly infectious and that some people never recover from.

Then al-Hubayshi says that the wives of other ex-jihadis ask their husbands about what it was like to be in Guantanamo and whether they were tortured. They want to hear tales of war and Osama bin Laden. But that wouldn't work for him.

"If she admired me for what I did and saw me as a hero, then maybe I'd already be fighting in Iraq."

BIRTHDAY WITH EVIL SPIRITS

LIKE KIDS AROUND THE WORLD, YOUNG SAUDIS WANT TO CELEBRATE THEIR BIRTHDAYS, BUT SARA'S PIOUS GRANDMA BELIEVES SUCH PARTIES ARE BLASPHEMY. THANK GOD THAT AN ISLAMIC SCHOLAR AT THE LOCAL QUR'ANIC CENTER HAS A QUICK FIX.

In Arabic, a birthday party is called an Eid Milad. For any six-year-old like Sara planning her first-ever party, it's a life-changing experience. If that isn't enough excitement, Sara's grandma cancels her attendance at the very last minute. She phones her granddaughter to inform her that a godly person like herself can't celebrate an Eid Milad. It's sinful, blasphemous, *haram*! Sara is heartbroken. Her mother, Nora, is dumbfounded. How can a little girl's birthday party be anything but innocent?

Nora calls her mom back: "Why are you doing this to Sara?"

Her mother is sixty-two. She likes to wear a gauze veil over her *niqab* as an extra precaution to prevent Satan or an evil djinn from touching her.

Nora's mother says a God-fearing Muslim cannot celebrate their birthday as "Eid" as if it were one of Islam's most important celebrations like Eid al-Fitr, the festival of breaking the fast at the end of Ramadan, or Eid al-Adha, the festival of sacrifice, celebrated a little over two months later. A person who celebrates their own birth as if it were a holy festival is an egotist lacking any kind of religious humility, she says.

Nora is at a loss. She's booked the playhouse near the Financial District, exactly as Sara wished. The cake has been ordered. Invitations have already gone out to friends.

Surely Allah wouldn't want her to call the whole thing off? Nora has no desire to hurt her pious mother's feelings, but also can't face disappointing her daughter. She consults an Islamic scholar at her neighborhood Qur'anic center. Nora returns home in a great mood. She has found a way to strip the event of anything hinting at the sacred without having to sacrifice the party. Instead of uninviting the guests, Nora simply reinvites them, this time to "Yom Milad," meaning just "birth-day," without the "Eid." In the Arabic world, no one actually says "Yom Milad," but the result—bringing together the family—justifies the linguistic clumsiness.

On the big day, kids from Sara's class come to the playhouse, twenty-three first-grade girls and four boys from the extended family. The kids sculpt Play-Doh, bake pizza, ride in electric-powered boats shaped like swans on an artificial lake, romp inside a foam-filled plexiglass cube—all the typical things six-year-old kids with well-off parents do on their birthdays in Riyadh.

I show up a little late. At the entrance, I pass twenty-six chauffeurs waiting in twenty-six SUVs for their young mistresses and masters to leave the party. On the steps, twenty-six nannies pass the time, most of them from the Philippines. In front of the play area is a pink table with Sara's twenty-six presents that will probably take the birthday girl days to open.

KIDS AND CAKE: AN ISLAMIC SCHOLAR AT THE LOCAL QUR'ANIC CENTER SAVES THE DAY!

Sara cuts the huge cream-sponge cake. Sara's photo is printed on it in icing. Everyone gets a small slice, even Sara's happy grandmother, who sits beside her granddaughter in a sea of children. Grandma has lifted her gauze veil and even her *niqab*. And there's not a djinn in sight.

Sara beams from ear to ear. Allah never wanted this fantastic celebration to be canceled because of one little word which—unlike the presents, the cake, and grandma—could easily be done without.

MARRIAGE, A STRAITJACKET

WEDDING CELEBRATIONS—ALWAYS LAVISH AND FULL OF SURPRISES—ARE THE HIGH POINT OF MOST SAUDI WOMEN'S SOCIAL LIVES. THE PARTY THE NIGHT BEFORE THE BRIDE MEETS THE GROOM IS ALSO A MARKETPLACE FOR THE NEXT ARRANGED MARRIAGE.

For weeks, I've been excited about attending Nazish's and Tamin's wedding. A wedding is the most significant event in the life of almost every Saudi woman. But what should I wear? Is it okay to wear black? Here, my wardrobe for festive occasions is limited to a blue suit and a dark sheath dress.

My friend Nora reassures me. Nazish is her cousin, so we'll be celebrating among relatives. The party is being held in the King Khaled Hall at the Holiday Inn in downtown Riyadh. The party begins at seven in the evening. Actually, two parties in two different rooms. One for the guys, one for the ladies.

At the women's celebration, 250 stunning ladies take their places on upholstered seats. They're wearing sexy, low-cut dresses with high slits and tight bodices and their faces are made up like models. Their long, blow-dried hair flows down their backs. These women must have spent the past thirty-six hours at the beauty salon.

Nora's sleeveless, floor-length dress is made of golden, pleated fabric, and is only tied at the shoulders. It looks like the robe of a high priestess and must be devilishly expensive. Nora bought it just for tonight. With my little black dress, my hair pinned back, and a pearl necklace, I probably come across like an uptight housekeeper to these women. Nonetheless, everyone is welcoming. Apparently, the women have filed me under "Western exotic."

Kisses and hugs are exchanged. Mothers, aunts, nieces, and cousins. All of them belong to the extended Dossari family, an old Bedouin tribe from the Najd in the heart of the Arabian Peninsula. At twenty-three, Nazish is no longer considered a young bride. Tamin is the son of her father's cousin. Here, they like to keep it in the greater family.

The tradition is problematic. The kingdom is struggling with a high level of genetic defects caused by marriage between blood relations. The phenomenon exists not only here, but throughout the Islamic world.

Since 2004, couples planning to marry have been required to undergo genetic testing. Over half of couples are advised to call off their wedding due to "genetic incompatibility." Because the quest for the ideal spouse usually takes place among cousins, the pool for a suitable life partner is normally quite small.

BEAUTY: GOOD TO HAVE, BUT NOT ESSENTIAL

The women flock to the dance floor. They take a lot of photos, but only of themselves. No group shots are allowed at weddings. Neither are pictures with the bride. Just selfies. It's taboo to photograph other women. Showing images of unveiled ladies damages their reputation, warns Nora, slicing her hand across her neck.

The future spouses are absent. Nazish is still at the beauty salon, being preened and primped for the big moment when she meets her groom for the first time. The whereabouts of the groom are unknown. We women celebrate alone, with the bride's three sisters, her 150 cousins, their mothers, and lots of aunts. It's worth the trouble because this is where sisters and mothers scout for the brides of tomorrow—for their sons and brothers.

Romantic notions about marriage, such as those in the West, are frowned upon. The idea that mutual attraction and the conviction of being soul mates could form the basis of a life together is seen by most here as a recipe for disaster. In Saudi Arabia, marriages are arranged by the family.

The bride must come from the right tribe and from a good clan—a family with influence and money—and should have an agreeable character. Beauty is welcome, but not a must-have.

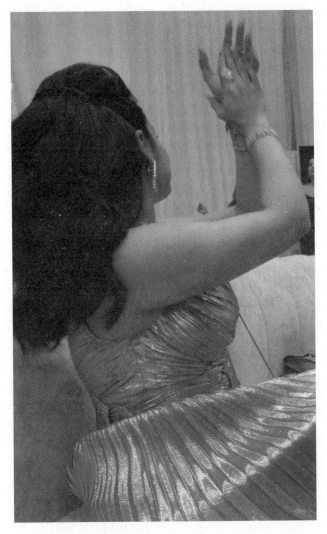

NORA AT HER COUSIN'S WEDDING. EVERYTHING HAS BEEN NEGOTIATED: THE BRIDE PRICE; IF SHE WILL HAVE A DRIVER, HER OWN HOUSE, OR A MAID; EVEN IF HER HUSBAND CAN TAKE A SECOND WIFE.

Nora says that Nazish has been stressed out for weeks, not only about the wedding preparations, but also because her life is going to change fundamentally. Tonight, she will move into her husband's family's house.

Just two generations ago, before the internet, before girls could read and write, brides were often still children, aged thirteen, fourteen, or fifteen. They would be accompanied to their new family by a *rabiah*, an older woman who would educate the girls about the wedding night, sex, and how to deal with their husbands. The *rabiah* would stay at the new house for a few days.

Today, young brides receive the Islamic wedding guide, *Tuhfah al-Arous*, which translates as "Treasure of the Bride." The booklet is a collection of quotations from the Prophet and his followers on the subject of marriage, and is intended to help the bride understand her partner spiritually, physically, and sexually.

According to the book, the husband should refrain from jealousy and making accusations against his wife. It also states that, for a man, water is the best perfume. The bride is instructed to be "modest and obedient. Let him see only that which he likes to see and smell. Never let him go hungry and do not disturb his sleep." The guide also answers "technical questions" in great detail. Before the first lovemaking session, the groom should perform two *rak'ah*, bowing in prayer, then hold the head of his spouse and say, "Bless my wife for me, bless me for my wife. Bestow me with her abundance and bestow her with my abundance." After that, he can "do whatever he wants."

ANGELS WILL CURSE THE WHOLE NIGHT

Saudi Arabia's equivalent of Dr. Ruth is the bestselling fundamentalist writer Abdul Malik Mujahid, author of books like Different Questions and Answers for the Muslim Woman. The Pakistan native immigrated to Saudi Arabia in 1980. In the book, he provides rather mundane, Qur'an-compliant answers to five hundred questions about birth control and hygiene as well as marital rights and duties—without giving any references. According to Mujahid, the wife is primarily responsible for fulfilling the responsibilities that come with marriage.

Question #247, for example, addresses what happens if a woman "does not show herself [to be] obedient in providing her husband with sexual pleasure." The answer: "Angels will curse the whole night." The bride also learns how many animals will be slaughtered when she gives birth—one for a girl, two for a boy. Pubic hair should be removed every forty days. She may not talk to anyone about sex with her husband. And she is not allowed to divorce simply because her husband starts to drink alcohol. Rather, she should show patience and pray.

At the wedding party, the bride finally drops by at midnight. Video cameras held by women record the festive moment of her arrival. The guests have put on their veils so that no one will be recognized in the footage.

Nazish walks through a gate of flowers toward a throne and sits there, surrounded by flower girls, accepting the guests' best wishes. She is wearing a white lace dress with a flowing train. Nazish looks happy. Half an hour later, Nazish disappears to be united with her groom. Dinner is served. By two in the morning, the party is over. The beauties pull their black abayas over their princess dresses and head home, unrecognizable and anonymous.

I want to find out more about what it means to get married in Saudi Arabia. Nora suggests meeting in a beauty salon she regularly frequents before weddings.

DO SAUDI WOMEN LOVE THEIR HUSBANDS? EVENTUALLY, YES.

It is midday. The beauty parlor is run by a Moroccan woman. Because it's just the two of us, we are able to make an appointment for a party makeover for Nora, who has to attend another wedding that evening. I play the bride.

First, they slide a white silk and batiste dress over me. Three women begin trilling loudly. They push me through the salon past a half-dozen customers. The staff, in green robes with gold trim and golden belts, chant evocative sayings, wishing the bride a happy life, one without darkness.

The ritual doesn't elicit a particularly joyful effect. It feels as if that darkness were threatening me, like in *Beauty and the Beast*, where the girl has to recognize the nobility of her hideous groom and overcome his repulsive exterior so that he can become the prince he truly is.

I ask Nora if Saudi women love their husbands. Eventually, yes, she says. "There is no such thing as love at first sight, just lust at first sight." The family selects the groom. Friends, employers, colleagues, and family members are quizzed about his character, his strengths and weaknesses. The family must all approve the selection.

If the families agree, a contract is signed that leaves no detail to chance. The agreement stipulates the size of the dowry, whether the woman will finish college and work, and whether she will have her own house, a personal driver, and a maid. The contract can also specify that the husband is forbidden from taking a second wife, which, according to Nora, is considered a very impolite demand.

The wedding celebration is arranged by the groom. If he doesn't have enough money, the wedding is a more modest affair in his own house, among close relatives. Many men go into debt to make the right impression. In Riyadh, a wedding can cost more than a single-family home. Typically, hundreds of guests are invited. Wedding planners are hired. Designers create the extravagant flower arrangements. Famous singers are booked. Photographers and videographers come to capture the special day.

THE AUTHOR ENDURES A BRIDAL MAKEOVER AT THE BEAUTY SALON:
GETTING MARRIED IS STRESSFUL.

BRIDAL MAKEOVER

Candlelight flickers on the spa's oriental tiles. Rose petals are
scattered around the room. A bathing attendant pours water over
my head and rubs oil into my hair. She scrubs me from head to
toe with soap, ridding my skin of every flake. She cracks an egg
on my head. This symbolizes a life without obstacles. Probably
also great for my hair.

Verbena oil and henna powder are rubbed into my bridal skin.
I feel like a Sunday roast, seasoned and poked, prepared for
consumption. The gentle string sounds of the *oud* emanate from
the loudspeakers, accentuating the ritual.

I am brought to the love Jacuzzi, a cold foam bath with rose
petals. Women wrap me in a gold-thread brocade gown. Three
of them work simultaneously on my perfection. They blow-dry
my hair, give me curly locks, primp my eyelashes, and paint my
lips red. On the top of my head, they fluff up a clump of hair and

pin on a golden crown together with an emerald diadem. The inlaid gem is attached to a golden chain and falls down over my forehead. Finally, I'm given matching earrings, and my bridal makeover is complete.

Amidst festive trilling and best wishes for a good life, the bride is sat on a throne in a candlelit room decorated with roses. The room fills with staff and customers. They all sing and clap. Peppermint tea is served, as are sweet and spicy baked goods. The roast is ready for carving.

MARRIAGE AS A CASTLE

"Getting married is stressful," Nora says. But she still loves to attend weddings, at least other people's, she laughs. For Saudi women, weddings are the high point of their social lives, along with funerals—the less joyful occasions.

Four weeks later, I bump into the young bride, Nazish. We sit next to each other eating cake at Nora's daughter Sara's birthday party.

"How's married life?" I ask. With a slightly tense smile, Nazish says, "It's a different life. Not always so easy." On her wedding day, her mother said, "Talk to no one but your husband about your relationship." It's as if marriage were a castle that had to be defended by the wife. Happiness sounds different.

Women forget about that silence later in life, a Saudi-British sociologist who studies marital relationships explains to me a few days later. She says older women speak extensively among themselves and are very open about sex. No detail is spared when it comes to talking about what happens in the bedroom. A favorite topic is their husbands' little failures. Of the castle that Nazish is so eager to defend, not a single stone remains.

ROOM FOR A SINGLE WOMAN, PLEASE

In the desert kingdom, you'll find hotels for every budget. Foreign women traveling alone are met with a warm welcome or at least curiosity. Saudi hoteliers find Westerners' preference for bright rooms eccentric.

According to prevailing Western tastes, a hotel is considered pleasant because of its central yet quiet location. Or because of its spacious rooms with large windows that let in plenty of light—preferably with a view of a park or famous landmark.

Saudis favor hotels with windows as small as the arrow slits of medieval castles. As a precaution, these openings are usually sealed off with thick, opaque curtains that reach from ceiling to floor and run along the entire wall. These are intended to prevent prying eyes from looking in. They are also meant to spare hotel guests the embarrassment of accidentally witnessing an immoral act beyond their four walls.

For the Saudi traveler, Jacuzzis are a favorite room fixture, and they usually feature prominently in hotel advertising. The Jacuzzi is typically photographed in full operation, brimming with foam and surrounded by flowers. Often a seductive trail of blossoms leads from the bathroom to the bedroom. On the bed there is always a pair of kissing swans made out of folded bath towels and framed by a heart outlined in rose petals.

On booking websites, hotels with underground parking garages get the best ratings from Saudi guests. It's not as if there aren't any parking spots in the spacious Saudi Arabian desert, but discretion is everything in this country. In other words, it's preferable if you can take the elevator directly from the parking garage up to your darkened room.

MR. SAYYED BUILT HIS NEW HOTEL IN THE OLD SAUDI TRADITION: TAKING ADVANTAGE OF A RECENT PHENOMENON IN THE KINGDOM—THE EMERGING TOURIST INDUSTRY.

Ideally, women—who aren't considered mature adults in this country—should not travel alone. If they do travel at all, they should at least be accompanied by their husband, father, or brother, so that they can give the appearance of being "family."

In most Saudi hotels and restaurants, there is a "family section," a poorly lit room or niche with a separate entrance. Women and children must take their meals here. The attractive areas are reserved for men.

Saudi concierges are a little surprised when a Western woman without a father, a husband, or a prince to accompany her requests a single room in a provincial hotel. But, since Saudi Arabia is going through a period of upheaval, it is exhilarating to try out the new freedoms. When a Western female traveler shows up in such a male-dominated place, people's curiosity usually has the upper hand. Frequently, the receptionists want to know everything about me: where I come from—America, Russia?— if I am married, my age, my husband's current whereabouts, whether I have children, and if so, how many. I am expected to disclose all of this information to a person whose English is no better than my Arabic, which is limited to a few sundry phrases. In the end, they always give me a room.

I am writing these lines in the Al Eairy Hotel on Makkah Road in the oasis city of Al-Ahsa in the Eastern Province, not far from the Persian Gulf. The Al Eairy has 143 rooms, all of them a little run down. But a night costs a mere thirty dollars, so who am I to complain?

Across the street from the hotel are the beautiful Mahasin Park and a mosque bearing the same name. To the left is a neighborhood filled with restaurants, suggesting the presence of human life, not always a given in this country, where nearly everything takes place behind high walls and thick curtains.

In Saudi Arabia, you'll find an endless number of modern mid-range hotels, including innumerable architectural experiments involving mirrored glass and concrete. I am content with the uneconomical roominess of the old Al Eairy. My suite is at least five hundred square feet. The overly bulky, veneered furniture and the flaking, gilded tables come across as a little shabby.

WELCOME TO OUR BEST ROOM. IT'S LARGE, IT'S DARK, IT'S PERFECT. EXCEPT WHEN YOU ARE A ROAMING WRITER WHO NEEDS LIGHT, A DESK, AND A WORKOUT AT THE GYM.

The bathroom tiles are probably as old as I am, and the crystal chandelier hanging from the ceiling has in all likelihood never worked. However, the veiled receptionist does everything to make me feel comfortable. She immediately changes the sheets after I pluck two suspicious black hairs from the bed.

There is an enormous TV in the room, but no desk. I've come here to write, though, so I build a podium by placing a little golden table on top of the nightstand. It's much healthier to work standing up anyway.

I jam the heavy drapes behind chairs on both sides of the room and, finally, the view through the liberated window opens up: the desert, a palm grove, and beyond that, the twinkle of the lights of Al-Mubarraz on the horizon.

Saudi Arabia can be magical, and it wouldn't be a kingdom if there wasn't any fairy-tale luxury in Al-Ahsa. At the best hotel in the town square, the InterContinental, a room costs 2,900 riyals per night, nearly $800—without breakfast, but including underground parking, an elevator taking the guests straight to the right floor, and a Jacuzzi.

SHEEP IN WOLF'S CLOTHING

THE NOTORIOUS WAHHABI SHEIKH SALMAN AL-OUDA IS ONE OF
THE MOST CONTENTIOUS CLERICS IN SAUDI ARABIA. I ASK MYSELF:
WHAT EXACTLY IS A GOOD SHEIKH?

Millions of young Saudi women follow strict religious rules that
prevent them from leading interesting lives. Virtually everything
is forbidden: meeting new people, exploring the world; nearly
every essential emotional and intellectual experience, in fact.
Meanwhile, educated young Saudi men drop everything and
head to war zones in countries they know nothing about,
ready to sacrifice their lives for jihad. How do such extremist
convictions infect people's hearts and minds?

Parents play a role, as do schoolteachers and the Qur'an centers
found in every neighborhood. All of these influences contribute
to an incredibly narrow perspective. One person in particular
has exercised extraordinary influence over the moral sense of
countless people in the kingdom for decades, perhaps more than
any other spiritual role model: Sheikh Salman al-Ouda.

PROMINENT SALAFIST SHEIKH SALMAN AL-OUDA IN FRONT OF HIS OFFICE IN RIYADH
(2013): HE KNOWS WHAT'S RIGHT AND WHAT'S WRONG—IN POLITICS AND IN LOVE.

Al-Ouda is preacher, couples' therapist, and philosopher all rolled up in one. His office in Riyadh promptly answers every question emailed in by supporters. At the time of writing, the cleric has more than thirteen million Twitter followers. Millions more subscribe to his YouTube channel. Al-Ouda holds the key to believers' souls, it seems. Somehow, he manages to retain his independent spirit, and sometimes his utterances are so provocative that the nation holds its breath in anticipation of the royal court's reaction.

NO PHOTOS WITH WOMEN

Al-Ouda knows what's right and what's wrong—in politics and in love. He knows who's virtuous and who's evil. He knows how to find the perfect wife or husband. He knows which perfumes are suitable, and he knows how to cut your fingernails according to Sharia law.

The man is an impressive phenomenon, whether you consider him to be the paragon of enlightenment or the Devil incarnate. When I met him a few years ago in his Riyadh office, he was wearing simple brown leather sandals. His white *ghutra* was perched loosely on his head, without the usual black cord. His beard, which blended directly into his frizzy hair, was cut uncommonly short for a sheikh from Buraydah.

Al-Ouda is a workaholic. His bulky desk, decorated with inlays, was covered in unfinished manuscripts and open books. The cleric has published countless tomes on religious subjects. The walls were lined with shelves holding encyclopedias and some worldly literature, like the biographies of US presidents and Robert Greene's self-help bestseller *The 48 Laws of Power*.

As he spoke, al-Ouda looked directly into my eyes and used the same animated gestures he does on TV: "Salam—welcome. Please, no photos with a woman. That could be used against me."

It's not easy to arrange a meeting with a famous religious scholar. Every time I tried to call, one of his sons or nephews rejected my request for an appointment. I would politely ask for a conversation with the sheikh to find out more about Wahhabism, the only true Islamic doctrine—a typical beginner's mistake.

People in the know advised me to never mention "Wahhabism" if I wanted to talk to a *Wahhabi*. Only critics of the ultra-conservative strain of Islam use the categorization. For most Muslims, the very term *"Wahhabi"* is derogatory. Even Saudi *Wahhabi* clerics refer to themselves as "Salafis" because they orient themselves based on the way of life and beliefs of the so-called exemplary companions (salaf saleh). At the end of the day, this means that all *Wahhabis* are Salafis, but not all Salafis are *Wahhabis*.

REBEL WITH A CAUSE

In a country where people can't meet in bars and have only recently been able to attend pop concerts, charismatic preachers like Salman al-Ouda have performed a role similar to that of rock stars in the West. Some imams are revered as idols. At the same time, the famed preachers are virtually unapproachable. At most, men can talk to them in person at the mosque. Women are only permitted to eavesdrop on a cleric through a dividing wall. They can later put a face to the voice by watching him on TV or YouTube.

Al-Ouda is considered a hardliner. He originates from the puritanical, xenophobic Al-Qassim region in the heart of the Arabian Peninsula, a place where the locals are proud of being the cradle of monotheism and the *Wahhabi* belief, the "true Islam."

Al-Ouda forbids believers from reading novels. Women shouldn't drive because it forces them to "exhibit their corporeality." Osama bin Laden cited al-Ouda as a religious authority to justify his own move into terrorism.

But al-Ouda is also a rebel. Again and again, he has revolted against the policies of the Saudi monarchy. In 1991, he criticized the government for allowing American troops into the country. It was the time of the Gulf War. Iraq had invaded Kuwait, and Riyadh wanted protection. Clerics allied with al-Ouda saw the stationing of "infidel" soldiers in the country as a "contamination." For them, it was a declaration of bankruptcy by the Saudi king, whose duty is to protect the holy sites in Mecca and Medina from the enemies of Islam. Alongside other religious leaders, al-Ouda called upon the Saudi people to rise up against their rulers.

Al-Ouda is one of the most influential leaders of the Sahwa or the "Awakening" movement, which promotes a form of political Islam that has been gaining ground in Saudi Arabia since the 1980s. Under the old agreement between the dynasty of the religious leader Abd al-Wahhab and the House of Saud, clerics are to keep out of politics. However, the Sahwa sheikhs reject exactly this traditional division of power, thereby directly challenging the monarchy.

The Sahwa movement is inspired by the Egyptian Muslim Brotherhood. In the 1950s and 1960s, many Muslim Brothers fleeing persecution by the Egyptian president Gamal Abdel Nasser took refuge in Saudi Arabia. They played an essential role in the modernization of the country. At first, Riyadh even promoted their activities to create a bulwark against Nasser's republicanism—until the Saudi rulers recognized that the ideas of the Muslim Brotherhood could eventually be used against them. Nowadays, Saudi Arabia classifies the Brotherhood as a terrorist organization.

IT'S ALL ABOUT LOYALTY

In al-Ouda's homeland, Al-Qassim, the Sahwa movement is especially popular among the young. In 1994, the sheikhs called on the people to protest against the government, resulting in the so-called Buraydah Intifada. Police cracked down on the demonstrations, and al-Ouda was jailed.

"That was a lesson," al-Ouda said during our encounter, sitting on a yellow brocade sofa in his spacious office. A close associate, a man with whom al-Ouda once shared a prison cell, served tea and sweets. After spending five years behind bars, al-Ouda was prodded by the interior minister to write a letter acknowledging his mistakes and promising never to repeat them. That was twenty years ago, but al-Ouda still isn't really free.

SHEIKH SALMAN AL-OUDA IN HIS OFFICE WITH THE AUTHOR: "PLEASE, NO PHOTO WITH A WOMAN—THIS COULD BE USED AGAINST ME." NOW HE IS ON TRIAL AND RISKS EXECUTION. HIS AND THE COUNTRY'S PRIORITIES HAVE CLEARLY SHIFTED.

"They follow every step I take, every tweet I write. I am harassed by their army of trolls. They have full control over me," he said. Al-Ouda lowered his eyes while speaking. I got the impression that they had lost some of their former ferocity. The government had mostly neutralized al-Ouda. He was forbidden from writing for newspapers and seldom appeared on television. He was banned from leaving the country.

Sheikh al-Ouda is an excellent example of how, in Saudi Arabia, clerics don't necessarily disappear into jail because of theological differences. Often, they just don't show enough loyalty to the monarchy, or they overstep a specific boundary by, for example, questioning the symbiotic relationship between religion and the regime.

Following his release from prison in 1999, al-Ouda initially refrained from provocation. "I don't want to return to jail," he told me.

Al-Ouda cooperated. He publicly denounced Osama bin Laden and his terror campaign against the monarchy and the US. In 2007, he even wrote an open letter to his "Brother Osama," in which he told him that he too will have to answer for his bloodthirsty actions in the afterlife. When al-Ouda's own son joined the jihad in Iraq in 2003—doing what his father had encouraged other young men to do—al-Ouda promptly notified the Ministry of the Interior. The young man was picked up at the border and brought back to his family by helicopter.

But then al-Ouda changed course once again. When the Arab Spring threatened the autocrats of the Middle East in 2011, he supported the uprising. Al-Ouda was convinced that the revolutionary wave would sweep through the kingdom and topple the absolute monarchy. In 2012, he published *Questions of Revolution*, a book in which, to everyone's surprise, he proclaimed that democracy was the only legitimate form of government, since Islam rejects theocracy—and that separation of state and religion was urgently needed. He referred to Islamic scripture to support his argument. In the book, al-Ouda also discussed Western thinkers like Machiavelli and Rousseau.

Questions of Revolution was banned immediately, but it can still be found online.

Al-Ouda attributed his change of heart, somewhat mundanely, to his advanced age. He now saw things more clearly than in his youth, he told the *New York Times* in April 2014. He believed that the time had come for an Islamic model of democracy, such as the one propagated by the Muslim Brotherhood. "More than any other time in my life, this is a time of surprises," he explained in the interview. "You can expect almost anything in the coming years."

"MAY GOD ALLOW THEIR HEARTS TO FIND HARMONY"

Associates who have known al-Ouda for a long time harbored doubts that the radical cleric had really become a liberal. It was more likely that he was using wolf-in-sheep's-clothing tactics to maintain contacts on all sides in case the revolution really did come.

In the end, al-Ouda misjudged the situation in his country. Saudi Arabia survived the revolutionary storm sweeping across the region. King Abdullah's government prohibited him from appearing on the one TV show in which he was still allowed to participate. Subsequently, he was limited to writing books and corresponding with his supporters.

But then an event took place, the consequences of which al-Ouda completely underestimated. After a row with the emirate of Qatar, young Crown Prince Mohammed bin Salman cut off all relations with Doha. Sheikh Salman al-Ouda and other clerics were expected to praise the monarchy's decision on Twitter. Instead, al-Ouda called upon the leaders to take a reconciliatory approach: "May God allow their hearts to find harmony."

His disobedience was interpreted as an expression of sympathy for the Qatari-supported Muslim Brotherhood. It was his very last political tweet and cost the preacher his freedom once more. It might even cost him his life.

سلمان العودة
Salman Al Odah

Follow

سلمان العودة ✔

@salman_alodah

لا تتبعني.. قد أتعثر، ولكن شاركني.. للتواصل : /goo.gl
6Cqkf8

◎ Saudi Arabia   𝒮 youtube.com/watch?v=qJYvh1...

🗓 Joined September 2009

229 Following   **13.3M** Followers

Not followed by anyone you're following

Tweets   **Tweets & replies**   Media   Likes

AL-OUDA'S TWITTER ACCOUNT WITH MORE THAN THIRTEEN MILLION FOLLOWERS:
UNTIL HIS DETENTION IN 2017, HE WAS PERHAPS THE MOST INFLUENTIAL ADVISOR ON
HOW TO LIVE ACCORDING TO SHARIA LAW.

Al-Ouda has been in prison since September 2017. The
prosecutor accused him of thirty-seven crimes, and is
demanding the death penalty. In Riyadh, it is rumored that
Prince Mohammed bin Salman wants the religious scholar
dead. They say only the international outcry over the murder
of Jamal Khashoggi has delayed the verdict and Salman al-
Ouda's execution.

LIBERATED ART

FOR DECADES, A PAINTER CHALLENGED THE RELIGIOUS PROHIBITION ON ART AND BECAME AN ACCIDENTAL CHRONICLER OF HIS NATION. NOW, FOR THE FIRST TIME IN SAUDI HISTORY, A YOUNG AVANT-GARDE ART SCENE IS EMERGING.

Entering Dia Aziz Dia's spacious attic studio feels like going back in time. The journey begins at the far end of the loft amid deep shelves where the painter's earlier works are stored. I pull out a dust-covered canvas. The oil painting is a life-sized depiction of a naked woman, her long, blonde hair cascading over her breasts and body. "I wanted to paint like Rubens, oil on canvas," Dia Aziz Dia grins.

The work was created fifty-six years ago when Dia was sixteen. Already then, the arts were considered the Devil's work in *Wahhabi* Saudi Arabia, even if the ultra-conservative Islamic scholars had yet to regulate every aspect of people's lives. Dia's work doesn't have much in common with Rubens's masterpieces, but it is extraordinary for the young artist's having come of age in a cultural desert in which any kind of figurative depiction was considered sinful. Despite the atmosphere of hostility, his parents supported their son's passion and gave him books about art.

Dia won a scholarship to study at the University of Fine Arts in Rome. He was eager to paint like Rembrandt, van Gogh, and Caravaggio. He was enchanted by the lifestyle of the Romans, who he felt inhabited a city that was itself a singular work of art. Dia often visited the Uffizi Gallery in Florence, the Sistine Chapel, and the Pantheon in Rome. He still draws on that wealth of experience today.

DIA AZIZ DIA'S OIL PAINTINGS OF RUBENESQUE WOMEN: "ART IS FREEDOM."

A TABOO IMAGE OF REBELLION

In the 1970s, Dia returned to Jeddah—the shining city by the sea with its turquoise and bottle-green balconies. The country was shaken by a cataclysmic event, the violent occupation of the Grand Mosque of Mecca by religious fanatics. The crisis threw Saudi Arabia back into darker times.

The catastrophe inspired Dia to paint a one-of-a-kind picture, perhaps the most controversial painting of his career. The image depicts the Kaaba within the Grand Mosque. In front of it is a sea of blood and a cut-off snake's head resembling the face of the leader of the attackers, Juhayman al-Otaybi.

Nowadays, the oil painting is lodged, unnoticed, behind Dia's desk. Furniture has to be moved to reach it. In the last forty years, no one has taken any interest in the painting titled *Juhayman*. But the work surely belongs in a museum, simply for its originality.

Saudi Arabia is a country with virtually no fine arts education. Figurative painting is completely taboo, *haram*. Even displaying pictures of one's own children or wife is frowned upon in most families. Regardless, Dia paints his wife and children regularly. The paintings hang all over his studio. "If visitors tell me it's a disgrace, I say: It's not a disgrace, it's art," he laughs. Dia is tall and thin. His pointy goatee turned gray long ago, but his oval eyes are alert. A century ago, Dia's grandfather came from Kazakhstan to study religion in Saudi Arabia. From him, the artist inherited his Asian features.

Dia's technique is proficient and conservative, and his imagery occasionally veers into kitschy territory. However, the artist has documented the transformation of the erstwhile Bedouin state into a high-tech nation unlike anyone else. Therein lies the true value of his work.

One picture depicts his father, a writer, reading in the light of a gas lantern under a village canopy. In another image, his father plays with his children. They are bathed in light shining through the window blinds typical of the balconied houses of Jeddah. In another work, Dia wards off the invading Iraqis. He has painted raped women and Palestinian mothers who lost their sons to the Intifada in the 1990s. Policy toward Israel is a recurring point of contention between the US and its Saudi allies.

He has painted a village choir, Bedouin children playing hopscotch, and the tearooms of the oases. He paints what moves him, but seldom earns any money for it.

THE DRAMATIC PAINTING TITLED *JUHAYMAN*: DOCUMENT OF ONE OF THE COUNTRY'S MOST SIGNIFICANT HISTORICAL TURNING POINTS.

When Osama bin Laden's terrorists piloted airliners into the World Trade Center on 9/11, Dia drew the earth opening up in rage—and bodies tumbling into the inferno of hell. He painted the leader of the Islamic State, Abu Bakr al-Baghdadi, as a terrifying, grimacing head engulfed by flames.

REMIXING SAUDI SYMBOLS

Dia earns his keep with jobs from wealthy Saudis, often members of the royal family, who are happy to have him paint their portraits. It is not unironic that his best clients are those who have suppressed art through their alliance with the radical Islamists.

The artist has painted the still-revered former king Faisal and the daughter of the governor of Mecca, Princess Al-Jawhara. For Princess Adila, the daughter of the deceased King Abdullah, he just completed a picture of the Italian opera singer, Andrea Bocelli. The painting was her gift to him. She asked Dia to create an especially rough surface so that the blind singer could sense the motif through his fingertips.

For years, Dia's attic in Jeddah was one of the few professional studios in the country. But times are changing. As religious rules have become more relaxed, a sizeable art scene has sprung up in Saudi Arabia. One of the big themes is the upheaval the country is going through, with all of its contradictions.

Until five years ago, Sultan bin Mutrad had never met anyone who expressed himself creatively. His life changed forever when he accompanied a friend to an opening at the L'Art Pur Gallery on Takhassusi Branch Street in central Riyadh, one of the country's very first art spaces. Mutrad was twenty.

For the first time in his life, he saw portraits that had been painted with unusual proportions. He saw works that played with symbols of Saudi identity: horse heads, sabers, carved wooden chests like those that brides bring to their husband's house as a dowry. There were large black-and-white photographs that showed only certain parts of the human body, such as the darkened half of a face.

For Mutrad, it felt as if an inner mechanism previously unknown to him had been set into motion. He has since seen the world with different eyes. Other things became important to him: "Beauty, logic, reflection."

When Mutrad spoke to the artists at the gallery that night, he realized he had never experienced such good conversation with complete strangers. He went online and discovered Andy Warhol and Banksy and began to educate himself and experiment with his own artwork. He combined patterns found in mosques with garish colors. He painted on wooden beams that looked like fence posts. "I tried to keep the old and transform it into something new," he explains.

Only time will tell if Mutrad's work has any lasting impact. At any rate, the burgeoning art scene is the only public arena where the issues facing this society are being addressed openly. Only very recently have the dark powers that punished anything and everything connected to the body, individuality, or personal expression begun to fade. People have started to communicate freely in parks, galleries, and malls. Music lessons now take place—with mixed groups. Westerners cannot fathom what an adventure it is for strangers of both sexes to meet in a room to play music together. To be able to do so here is nothing short of a sensation.

It takes Mutrad some time to figure out that he wants to devote his life to art.

We meet at his studio on Abdullah Abdulaziz Road. It is housed in a concrete building, a cube on stilts. The room is thirty feet by thirty feet, with a large industrial window overlooking the road. "Light, space, a view to the west, where the sun goes down, that's what we looked for," Mutrad says. He has rented the space with a friend. His concerned parents tell him he should go to college, but there are no art schools that accept men. "I'm the black sheep of the family now," Mutrad says. He swipes his brown locks out of his face, but they fall right back. On his nose rests a pair of large, brown aviator glasses.

Mutrad is the youngest of nine siblings. His brothers work as Arabic teachers, like his father. His sisters are housewives, like his mother. Naturally, Mutrad was also supposed to become a teacher.

THE UPSIDE OF BEING MISUNDERSTOOD

Mutrad has already taken part in several exhibitions. In one of his installations, he painted on an abacus, an old counting machine with rods and sliding colored beads. In the intense

Bedouin colors of red and blue, the beads form surprising images: a woman in a burka, a heart, a bat.

Another work is sprayed onto an uneven wooden panel covered in red and blue Islamic patterns. In the foreground, a graffiti artist with a Palestinian scarf thrown over his head is spray-painting the religious motifs onto the wood. Once again, East and West flow together. The religion that has molded Mutrad's life is put into a new context. A revolt against tradition. "I look for challenges, emotional confrontation, and I ask myself how I can lead a meaningful existence. How can I develop?"

Apart from a sofa and a TV, the nine-hundred-square-foot space is virtually empty. A light bulb hangs from the ceiling. There's a rug on the floor. This would be normal in New York or Berlin, but this is Riyadh. He pays 20,000 riyals rent per year, around $6,000. He splits the cost with his friend. Mutrad has a part-time job at a gallery and works on his art the rest of the time. The space provides him with serenity and strength, he emphasizes.

Around 150 artists are working in Riyadh, Mutrad estimates. They work in visual art, painting, photography, sculpture. The scene is small. Some 500 artists live in Jeddah, where conceptual art is most dominant.

BATTLEFIELD AS CHESSBOARD

A big opportunity for art lies, perhaps, in the fact that even critical content doesn't get taken too seriously. In all likelihood, it is simply not understood. This creates free spaces and allows exhilarating artistic impulses to flourish.

In 2018, the Saudi Art Council in Jeddah exhibited the work of eight Saudi artists. The show's title was promising: "Refusing to Be Still." The exhibition was curated by Vassilis Oikonomopoulos, a curator who works for institutions like the Tate Gallery in London.

ARTISTS LIKE ALAMOUDI IN SAUDI ARABIA ARE EXPERIENCING A REVOLUTION IN
COLOR AND ASK: "HOW CAN I LEAD A MEANINGFUL EXISTENCE?"

Several of the installations were profoundly moving. One of the
artists had written out the Qur'an in calligraphy on two huge
paper banners—one white, one black—hanging twenty feet from
the ceiling. In another installation, an ex-soldier arranged found
objects from the desert on sand—leftover materials of war, bullet
cartridges, discarded army ration packs—between two steel
plates, as if the battlefield were a giant chessboard.

The twenty-seven-year-old artist Ahaad Alamoudi printed
falcon feathers on the costumes of young men performing
the sufi-inspired dance of the *khabeti*, a tradition that has
almost disappeared entirely. She filmed the dancers leaping
and twirling—and then slowed down the footage to convey
the paradoxical dynamic of the times. Alamoudi's video loop
ran in front of a massive pile of desert sand that represented
the kingdom. The work was titled "Those who do not know of
falcons grill them"—a variation on an Arabic saying. For her, the
words capture the contrast between how the outside world sees

Saudi Arabia and how the people here see themselves. Loosely interpreted, the title implies that, in this time of upheaval, the ignorant—whether in the West or in Saudi Arabia—could make every kind of mistake and drive the country to ruin.

THE BEAUTY OF AL-AHSA
THROUGH THE EYES
OF ABDULLAH

AN ARCHITECT HAD A DREAM: TO TELL THE WORLD ABOUT THE
HISTORICAL SIGNIFICANCE OF HIS HOMELAND. TODAY, AL-AHSA'S
VAST PALM FOREST—AND ITS ARCHEOLOGICAL TREASURES—IS A
UNESCO WORLD HERITAGE SITE.

Driving through the desert on a four-lane asphalt highway, I
don't feel as if I am approaching the largest oasis in the world.
The buildings are composed of earth tones: sand, ochre, and
brown. Glass facades conceal shops selling high-end carpets
and inexpensive household goods. In between are swaths of
wasteland. In Hofuf—the administrative center of the Eastern
Province—alone, I count four KFC restaurants. A few new hotels
have been built. There are some older ones in the second-largest
city of the governorate, Al-Mubarraz. These informal settlements
are linked up by junctions and traffic circles.

At twenty-five thousand acres, Al-Ahsa oasis is a vast landscape
with palms everywhere you look. All in all, it feels a little like a
Middle Eastern version of a desolate small town in America.

But this first impression is deceptive. When I meet Abdullah,
everything looks different. Surrounded by palm trees, his office
is on Prince Sultan Road in Hofuf—which everyone here calls
Share Al Hyyat or "Serpent Street" because it winds through the
villages of the oasis. The building stands out from the rest: it's
higher than it is wide; the wooden window frames have a pointy,
oriental form and contain blue, yellow, and red glass elements.

I climb the stairs to the second floor. Abdullah greets me warmly.
"Ahlan wa-sahlan!" In his early sixties, he has a salt-and-pepper
beard, friendly brown eyes, and large hands. He is stirring a cup
of instant coffee.

Abdullah's surname is ash-Shayeb. Since we were introduced by a mutual friend, he asks me to address him by his first name.

PHILOSOPHY LESSON

"Why is your building so much nicer than the others here?" I ask. Abdullah is an architect. Before his retirement, he worked as a city planner for many years. In the old days, nearly everyone built like this, Abdullah replies. But with the discovery of oil, traditional craftsmanship was abandoned. People wanted to forget how life once was, Abdullah says. They moved to cities to live in modern concrete buildings made by machines. Villages were neglected.

I am here to find out more about Al-Ahsa, the oasis, and the Shi'ites, who have always had a difficult relationship with the Saudi state. I was told that no one has done as much for Al-Ahsa as Abdullah. And that nobody knows more about the region and its people. But from the first moment, Abdullah steers me away from such subjects. Instead, our conversation becomes a philosophy lesson on how meaningful and triumphant life can be—even in adversity—if you approach it with wisdom.

THE LARGEST OASIS IN THE WORLD: "ONE OF THE OLDEST HUMAN SETTLEMENTS—
IF NOT THE OLDEST."

Al-Ahsa lies in Saudi Arabia's Eastern Province, around forty miles from the Persian Gulf. The old crossroads between Bahrain, Qatar, and the United Arab Emirates is a long-overlooked spot on the map. That could soon change—thanks to Abdullah.

Some 2.5 million palm trees grow here. If that wasn't astonishing enough in the middle of a sea of sand, my host now says, "Did you know that Al-Ahsa is one of the oldest human settlements, if not the oldest?"

I sip my instant coffee. I was aware that the Saudi Shi'ites—about 900,000 in number—lived in Al-Ahsa and that the oasis was a trading post long before Christ. Merchants would transport precious spices and incense between Persia and the southern Arabian Peninsula via Al-Ahsa. I also knew that there are more than sixty hot and cold springs here, and that the early settlers had highly developed agriculture thanks to a sophisticated irrigation system. "But aren't the cities in Palmyra and Mesopotamia older?" I ask.

Abdullah smiles. Throughout his life, he has looked into a lot of incredulous faces. "Come with me." He opens the door and points the way outside.

We drive to the covered market in the city center, the Qaisariya Souk. We walk through the old stone gate, past a street full of spice merchants, into the alley of metalsmiths. Here the traders still make knives by hand in an open forge. For about eight bucks, I purchase a medium-length knife—the kind usually used to slaughter sheep—from one of the metalsmiths, a sturdy man with callused hands. The knife will come in handy in my kitchen.

HASAWI LEMON TREES AND HASAWI DONKEYS

Behind the wooden sheds of the souk's narrow passageways, traders sell fabric, natural cosmetics, prayer beads, abayas, and bishts. The tailors here specialize in making the elegant linen cloaks with gold trim that are usually worn by dignitaries.

I begin to see Al-Ahsa in a different light. It's as if Abdullah has brought the city to life. He is greeted joyfully everywhere we go in the labyrinthine market. Someone offers tea. Someone else slaps him on the shoulder. At the end of the souk, we reach the market's only teahouse, Al Sayyed.

THE AL SAYYED TEA HOUSE IN THE ANCIENT QAISARIYA SOUK. ABDULLAH ASH-SHAYEB (RIGHT): "HE OPENED ME TO THE ABUNDANCE OF MY CULTURAL HERITAGE."

The owner runs to Abdullah and insists that he sit down in one of the comfy armchairs. We are served coffee and sweets, followed by thick sour beans and chickpeas. The owner phones his brother to tell him to hurry over. Only now do I understand the magnitude of what Abdullah has done for this place. For forty years, he collected everything that distinguishes Al-Ahsa from every other desert town: writings by poets and urban chroniclers, the lyrics of popular songs. His private archive contains photos of early expeditions across the Arabian Peninsula, rare sketches of historical buildings that have long since disappeared, such as old family homes and mosques. Wealthy individuals are now reconstructing the ancient buildings.

SOUR BEANS AND CHICKPEAS: "THERE ARE TWO SCHOOLS OF THOUGHT ON HOW TO ACHIEVE THINGS."

Abdullah can tell stories of heroes who protected the palm forest from invaders hundreds of years ago. He knows the biographies of exceptional tribal leaders. He proved that the famous Hasawi lemon tree originated from Al-Ahsa, as did the Hasawi date and the Hasawi donkey. Abdullah's research on archeological sites such as Ain Qannas, in fact, produced evidence that the oasis was settled six thousand years ago.

TWO SCHOOLS OF THOUGHT

"He opened me to the abundance of my cultural heritage," says Khalil al-Muwayl, a musician from Al-Ahsa. Abdullah hired the *oud* player to research regional variations of Al-Ardha, the sword dance that ritualizes the story of the country's violent reunification and the oath of loyalty to the king. Al-Muwayl tells me that Abdullah has ensured that Al-Ahsa took its rightful place in world history. It was Abdullah who prodded the authorities to apply for UNESCO World Heritage status. The process took years, but finally the oasis was nominated for the list following a review of existing documents. Abdullah received dozens of researchers, historians, and experts. On behalf of the United Nations, they compiled the forgotten history of Al-Ahsa, and on June 29, 2018, the committee decided to accept the oasis city into the list of UNESCO World Heritage sites.

Anyone who wants to get something done in Saudi Arabia needs useful contacts in the (Sunni) royal family. For Shi'ites, that's not always a straightforward process. While they form the majority in Al-Ahsa, in the state administration they are nearly always monitored by Sunni superiors. The state does not trust the minority—and vice versa.

"Here in the Eastern Provinces, there are two schools of thought when it comes to achieving what you want," Abdullah explains. "The way of the Qatifis and the way of the Hasawis."

Shi'ites from Al-Qatif, the coastal city one hundred miles north of Al-Ahsa, have a proud history of revolt against the Riyadh regime—and for their suffering under the government. Rebellious groups are subjected to state oppression regularly, which in turn ignites more protests. Dissidents are routinely arrested and imprisoned, some even sentenced to death by the sword.

Many in Al-Qatif view the people of Al-Ahsa with contempt because they have never risen up against the state, although they have also suffered from humiliation and discrimination. "The Qatifis consider us cowards," says Abdullah. And, in fact, the Hasawis do cooperate with the monarch. "We are a part of this country. We belong here." The people of Al-Ahsa feel that fighting the state is the wrong strategy.

"HAPPINESS COMES TO THOSE WHO CAN WAIT"

"What have the so-called rebels of Al-Qatif achieved?" asks Abdullah laconically as he steers his car into a parking lot a few miles north of Hofuf. Instead of pointlessly agitating, people need a positive goal which they can pursue with conviction in good times and bad, he says. A door always opens at some point. You must take advantage of opportunities when they arise. "Happiness comes to those who wait."

Abdullah's big chance came in the form of the Saudi Commission for Tourism and National Heritage; in other words, the recognition that tourism could be a source of income. To prevent the Saudis from spending their money abroad, the renovation of archeological treasures was made a top priority, with the aim of encouraging Saudis to discover their own country.

Suddenly, everything Abdullah had been fighting for made sense: the preservation of old buildings such as Qaisariya Souk, which other urban planners in the city administration wanted to tear down, or the renovation of Al-Ahsa's first school which would have otherwise fallen into ruin. Today, the school, with its painstakingly carved wooden facade, is one of the region's architectural attractions.

ADAM AND EVE IN AL-AHSA

And of course, Abdullah is proud of the restoration of the remains of the Jawatha Mosque, which played a crucial role in the UNESCO nomination. The work was completed in 2015. The mosque is thought to be the second oldest Muslim place of worship in the world. Historians date the simple adobe building back to the year 636, the fourteenth year after the departure of the Prophet Mohammed from Mecca. Meanwhile, research has confirmed that the Al-Ahsa civilization was already flourishing in the fifth century BC.

ENTRANCE TO THE HISTORIC CENTER OF AL-AHSA'S TRADITIONAL MARKETPLACE:
"HAPPINESS COMES TO THOSE WHO WAIT."

When Al-Ahsa was finally officially recognized as a UNESCO
World Heritage site, and dignitaries from the city, the
district, and the Eastern Province convened to celebrate the
accomplishment with speeches and a visit from the royal family,
one person was missing from the guest list: Abdullah. The career
bureaucrats—mostly Sunnis—wanted to take all the credit for
the triumph.

When we visit the mosque, the sun has set, and worshippers
have gathered for the evening prayer. The ancient structure is
located next to an amusement park. Abdullah made sure that—
alongside waterslides and carnival rides—local craftsmen and
a small museum with a tearoom could have a place in the park.
Abdullah could have ended up a bitter man. The history books
will credit others for putting Al-Ahsa back on the map. He gulps.

To cheer him up, I attempt a joke and suggest that with his persistent ingenuity, he will finally prove that Adam and Eve themselves lived here. Abdullah's eyes light up once more. Naturally, the paradise that Adam and Eve were expelled from is located in the palm groves of Al-Ahsa, he enthusiastically asserts. "Or has someone else already claimed the geographic coordinates of paradise for themselves?"

SAUDI WOMAN AT THE NEW ARTS AND CRAFTS MARKET OF AL-AHSA: THE NEW SOCIAL REFORMS ALLOW FEMALE ARTISTS TO PARTICIPATE ACTIVELY IN THE NEWLY EMERGING ECONOMIES OF TRADITIONAL HANDICRAFTS AND TOURISM.

THE REVOLUTION COMES TOO LATE FOR PIOUS JAMILA

A PRETTY, FINANCIALLY-INDEPENDENT TWENTY-NINE-YEAR-OLD BANKER IS LOOKING FOR A HUSBAND SHE CAN HAVE A CONVERSATION WITH. BUT BECAUSE SHE LIVES IN THE ULTRA-CONSERVATIVE CITY OF BURAYDAH—SAUDI ARABIA'S VERSION OF THE BUCKLE OF THE BIBLE BELT—THE COUNTRY'S REVOLUTION IS RAPIDLY PASSING HER BY.

Taking the train to Buraydah is a little like checking into the starship *Enterprise* to travel at the speed of light back to the Middle Ages. The capital of Al-Qassim Province is considered the cradle of Wahhabism. Many influential sheikhs hail from the region and various battles were fought here during the unification of the Desert Kingdom. Nowhere else are religious laws taken more seriously than in Buraydah in the heart of central Arabia.

The new Riyadh train terminal looks like a futuristic airport departure lounge: luggage is checked in at the counter; passengers receive an electronic boarding pass and walk through an ultra-modern version of a TSA security checkpoint. Business-class travelers wait in an elegant lounge. Inside the trains, the plush, gray seats still smell of chemicals. Everything is brand new.

"Allahu akbar" ("God is great") booms from the loudspeakers three times, followed by the Prophet's prayer for safe travel. We roll out of the city and through the endless desert, past Bedouin tents, black camels, and palm groves. Travelers are served dates and Arabic coffee from golden vessels by elegantly clothed attendants. Breakfast arrives on plastic trays, like on a plane: an omelet, croissants, fresh fruit.

On a screen in the compartment flickers black-and-white footage of the construction of the first Saudi railroad in the 1940s.

Laborers conquer the desert with shovels and wheelbarrows. The film conveys optimism about the country's future. Aramco, the Arabian-American Oil Company, lays the first tracks. Saudis and Americans work hand in hand. The company needs to transport its oil extraction equipment from the Persian Gulf to the interior of the country. New scene: King Abdulaziz officially opens the first Saudi rail line between Riyadh and Dammam in a ceremony on October 20, 1951.

In fact, a previous line through the Arabian Desert had already been built. During the early twentieth century, the Hejaz Railway ran between Damascus and Medina and transported pilgrims to the holy sites. The railroad was built by the Ottoman Empire with the technical expertise of German engineers. The line was completed in 1908 but was abandoned in 1920.

WHERE THE PEOPLE ARE THE POLICE

I am in Buraydah to visit Jamila, a banker I met a few months ago at the wedding of her cousin Nazish at the Riyadh Holiday Inn. Weddings and funerals are among the few occasions when Jamila can leave her native city.

Jamila is curious, energetic, thoughtful, yet so conservative that even after a dozen trips to Saudi Arabia I have trouble understanding the contradictions of her life.

When the religious police, the mutawwa, were stripped of power in early 2015, a joke went around Riyadh: In Al-Qassim, it won't make any difference because the people there *are* the religious police. There is some truth to that. While the new, more liberal spirit has reached most of the larger provincial cities, here nothing much seems to have changed.

THREE GENERATIONS OF WOMEN IN BURAYDAH (AND THE AUTHOR, RIGHT):
THE ULTRA-CONSERVATISM OF ITS INHABITANTS MAKES THE RELIGIOUS
POLICE REDUNDANT.

Outdoors, most women wear the *niqab*. Many also wear black gloves. Men and women are strictly segregated—on the street, in parks, in restaurants. Only men shop at the vegetable market because women hardly ever leave the home. Even without the presence of the censorious guardians of virtue, people here continue to monitor each other, motivated by their own religious fervor.

Naturally, Jamila wears a face veil at her workplace. She is twenty-nine and majored in English literature. Now she works as the chief controller at the bank—and remains unmarried. She says she is looking for a man with whom she can have a conversation. This has earned her the reputation of a being a "difficult" woman. She has already turned down a number of marriage proposals.

Jamila has broad cheekbones. Her jet-black hair falls loosely over her shoulders. Her brown eyes are accented by long, striking eyebrows. Her lips are full, and there is something challenging yet melancholic about her gaze.

We agree to meet at her family's weekend house. She calls it a "chalet," as if we were meeting in the Swiss Alps, presumably a synonym for every Saudi's dream weekend getaway.

Jamila sends me the GPS coordinates. The taxi driver takes me through central Buraydah, which looks pretty much like every other Saudi city: lots of SUVs, modern malls, excellent infrastructure, but with very few people. We turn onto the freeway, then exit again after twenty minutes. We drive through empty lanes, past sand-colored villas. We enter the desert, and the houses become less frequent and have longer walls. There's not a person in sight. The driver stops the car abruptly: "This is it."

For a moment I feel as if I've gotten out at the wrong end of the desert, and picture myself stranded here without a soul around and without phone reception. The weather-beaten gates are the same sand color as the walls. In front of me I see two steps. I knock on a metal door. A servant opens the gate, revealing a lush garden: a green lawn, a swimming pool surrounded by light granite, a large terrace in front of a white bungalow with a huge glass facade. A hidden gem.

Jamila arrives at about the same time, having come directly from the bank. She takes me to a room with an elegant king-size bed, a view of the garden, and heavy brocade drapes. For the first time in the kingdom, I see actual golden faucets, in line with the common cliché of rich Saudis. Even the washbasin is gilded. Jamila belongs to the well-off middle class and earns about as much as a mid-level bank manager in the West. She tells me she's throwing a garden party tonight. Attending are her mother, her two cousins and their daughters, her brother's wife, and a friend from the bank—an all-women's event, naturally.

Until the guests arrive, we relax at the chalet. Jamila makes coffee and I tell her about Tarek, an electrician who works in a hospital in Riyadh. He's tall, thirty-eight years old, a helpful man with a high forehead, maybe a few too many pounds around his waist. But he has friends around the world, I tell her. He's a rarity in the kingdom: he's outspoken. He always says what he thinks. Like Jamila, Tarek is looking for a true life partner. Both of them are very conservative.

Tarek has never kissed a woman. He has asked four women for their hand in marriage; four times he was rejected. I think Jamila and Tarek would be perfect together.

"You want to send me a photo?" said Tarek, aghast, when I told him about Jamila. Simply sending a picture of a woman violates her dignity, Tarek explained.

REPUTATION ON THE LINE

Even in her own house, Jamila covers her face behind her *niqab* as long as the male Pakistani servant is present. The only men permitted to see her face are those who can't be considered a potential husband due to their already close familial relationship: father, sons, brothers. However, cousins, brothers-in-law, and uncles exist outside of Jamila's reality.

The only man we encounter together this weekend is Jamila's brother Ahmad. He also works in the financial sector. Ahmad is Jamila's ally in negotiations with the outside world and with their father. Her father has prohibited her from accepting a lucrative job offer from a bank in Dubai—though it would be a huge opportunity for his daughter. Her father says her reputation in Buraydah would be ruined forever if she went to live in the United Arab Emirates, where there is no segregation of the sexes at the workplace.

Later, sitting in the garden with her mother, we discuss whether Jamila will attend an Arab-European business conference in Munich in the summer. Her mother grimaces at the idea. She says she heard about a terrorist attack in Berlin: "It's not safe there."

That evening, two dozen women gather in the chalet. They
bring delicacies: lamb skewers, chicken, sauces, salad, desserts
made of dates and rice milk. They wear brightly colored dresses,
golden bracelets, glittering necklaces. Their faces are made
up beautifully; their hair and robes smell of the exclusive Oud
fragrance which is kept smoldering on hot coals. Throughout
the evening, the smoking chalice is passed around from woman
to woman.

BARS IN BURAYDAH?

Among the guests is Jamila's aunt, a striking woman in her
fifties. Her youngest son died two months ago, and she has
been suffering from depression. She asked her eldest son, who
lives in New York, to return home. In this difficult time, she
wants to have her children close to her. Rida, twenty-eight, has
been studying economics and international law for five years
in New York. He was close to finishing his master's in business
administration, yet he returned home immediately. Family
comes first.

It's rare that Western visitors travel to Buraydah. Jamila tells me
that Rida drove his mother here and would like to meet me. If
it's okay with me, she'll phone him. He is waiting at a friend's
nearby. A short time later, Rida is led through a second entrance
to another part of the house. Naturally, he's forbidden from
seeing the women in the garden.

Rida kisses his mother's head, then her hand. He's tall, thin,
and has a neatly trimmed full beard—like men in London or
New York—and wears a long *thawb*. "If you refuse the wishes
of your parents in Buraydah when they need you, you can no
longer show your face here," Rida says. In Buraydah, people
are proud of living in accordance with "pure, true Islam." It's
hard to say how much of that is rooted in Wahhabism and how
much comes from the traditions of the region. Rida estimates
that, in Buraydah, about 20 percent of the population is ultra-

conservative, 70 percent "relatively moderate," and 10 percent "liberal." Translated into Western terms, 90 percent of the people here are arch-conservative and maybe 10 percent of the men would shake a woman's hand or hire her in their company.

"What do you mean by liberal, exactly?" I ask, and find out that political rebels and reformers often originate from the conservative Al-Qassim region.

Extremes often bring forth exactly the opposite, says Rida. I am reminded of when I was growing up in Bavaria in Germany in the 1970s. I remember how powerful the grip of the church was on people, especially in the country and in the villages.

It turns out that Jamila's cousin's religious-political worldview is pretty flexible. Rida was born in 1991. He grew up in a conservative place but has seen the world and seems to fit in wherever he is—he can do ultra-conservative and he can do party boy. As a man, that's totally possible.

We sit on a thick velour rug in a small room at the far end of the garden, reclining on white foam cushions. "The religious establishment is broken," Rida says. "We laugh about the clerics who used to terrify us. Now, under Crown Prince Mohammed bin Salman, they are saying something completely different than before." He's right. Even the preachers have adapted their agenda in reaction to the changing political reality—showing that, for them, a hassle-free life is more important than their supposed convictions.

Rida believes change is coming very fast to Saudi Arabia. He tells me things he would be thrown into jail for saying if he posted them on social media or expressed them in public. "One day, we'll have a proper parliament, a constitutional monarchy, when we have solved our problems in Yemen, with Qatar, and in Lebanon," he says. According to Rida, this is the "talk of the town" in Buraydah.

THE FUTURISTIC CITY NEOM WILL BE BUILT IN THE MIDDLE OF THE DESERT:
"ONE DAY SOON WE WILL HAVE A REAL PARLIAMENT, A CONSTITUTIONAL MONARCHY,
AND ALCOHOL WILL BE LEGAL."

Rida enthusiastically explains how he imagines his future life, split between East and West. "Someday, bars will open here," he says. "It's coming!" I counter that the crown prince has repeatedly ruled that out. Rida insists that when the Neom Project becomes reality, at the latest, alcohol will become legally available in Saudi Arabia.

Neom is a futuristic project being planned by Crown Prince Mohammed bin Salman, a modern technology park and a new city that is supposed to rise up within a few years along the Red Sea Coast. The name combines the Greek word for new, *neo*, and an "m" for *mustabqbal*, Arabic for future. How will they attract people to the beaches of Neom, Rida asks, if they won't be able to sip a margarita at sunset?

DESTROYED CHILDHOOD PHOTOS

The all-female party winds down. It's a little past ten o'clock.
Before I go to bed, I take a snapshot of the golden faucets in the
bathroom to send to my friends—a funny example of how there's
always some truth to stereotypes, even if reality ends up being
very different.

GOLDEN FAUCETS AT THE SO-CALLED CHALET: A CONFIRMATION OF
PRECONCEIVED NOTIONS.

The day after our evening in the garden, Jamila and I have
lunch at an elegant restaurant with a roof terrace in downtown
Buraydah. We can see the entire city, including the bulbous
water tower, the trademark of this provincial metropolis. Tents

have been set up on the roof. Before the waiters approach, they warn us verbally so that Jamila can quickly pull her *niqab* over her face.

On the menu there's avocado toast, sushi, Caesar salad—not unlike a bistro in London or New York, although there we would probably order a glass of wine with our food, at least at night.

Jamila's phone lies in front of her, the latest Samsung. Once in a while, she looks for an English word on Google Translate or searches for an image of a place, a person, or an object to show to me. On her phone, Jamila sees everything I see, and has access to everything I know. The device is Jamila's window to the globalized, modern world. But the window isn't fully opening up for her.

Jamila wants to belong to the righteous. She is deeply pious. She wants to do everything right. For a long time, Jamila believed the preachers who said that women shouldn't drive because it damaged their ovaries. She doesn't celebrate birthdays, because it's *haram* to do so, and she covers not only her face, but also her hair and feet, and often wears dark gloves to conceal her hands. When she was younger, Jamila destroyed all childhood photographs of herself after clerics claimed it was un-Islamic to hold on to such memories of the body.

Right now, she is finding out that most of the rules she has lived under since her youth were indeed written by people and not by God. And now that the rules no longer match their goals, those people are rewriting the rules.

Torn by doubt, Jamila recently called Fatwa TV, one of the many channels on which a well-known imam shares his religious perspective on daily ritual practice. Jamila asked whether it was really necessary to cover her face. She asked for clarification why there were suddenly different points of view on the matter.

In their reply, Fatwa TV pointed to the Hadiths, the oral teachings of the Prophet that have been passed down in the

Islamic tradition. Once again, she was told that she should definitely wear the *niqab*, otherwise her face would burn in hell.

ROOFTOP RESTAURANT WITH A VIEW OF THE CITY OF BURAYDAH: FOR WOMEN IN THEIR LATE TWENTIES, THE REVOLUTION COMES TOO LATE.

Jamila feels betrayed. She wishes she was ten, twenty years younger so she could enjoy the transformation of Saudi society. Not being able to show her face for so many years made her feel she was just one woman out of many. She was never recognized as an individual. "It's a trap that is snapping shut a second time now that everything is changing," she says. It is no longer possible for her to remove her *niqab*: her father would be disappointed, her mother sad, and her reputation in Buraydah destroyed.

I ask Jamila if she would perhaps like to meet Tarek for a coffee during her next business trip to Riyadh. "Of course not," Jamila answers, indignant. "What would he think of me?"

For some Saudis, the social revolution is simply coming too late, even though it's happening at breakneck speed. This is the case for Tarek and Jamila: Both of them are the product of a religious fanaticism that dominated the country for decades and that robbed them of their lives.

Once more, the tent flap is lifted. Jamila covers her face and asks for the check. She pays with her credit card, with money she earned herself as a highly qualified banker.

We take the elevator downstairs. Jamila's driver waits on the street to take me to the train station. She remains here. She waves goodbye, and I catch the train back to the future.

Epilogue

Whoever governs Saudi Arabia over the next few decades will require a healthy dose of wisdom and a generous serving of luck. It is no exaggeration to call the current transformation of the country drastic; it is historic. Far more is at stake than the fate of individual Saudi rulers or the future of the world's wealthiest and perhaps most powerful family.

The Saudis will experience radical change in the coming years, not unlike Eastern Europeans after the fall of the Berlin Wall, or the inhabitants of Hong Kong following the withdrawal of the British in 1997. Crown Prince Mohammed bin Salman is attempting to transform the kingdom into an open society with a flourishing private sector by 2030. The success or failure of this ambitious undertaking will have grave repercussions around the world.

Those hoping that the project fails or that the House of Saud is overthrown in the name of democracy would be foolish to expect that either scenario would lead to improved human rights and better conditions for women. Failure would result in rising unemployment among young Saudis, lead to increasing poverty, and eventually trigger an uprising. Radical forces would rapidly gain the upper hand. Billions in petrodollars would land in the hands of extremists, possibly sparking worldwide market turmoil and new streams of refugees.

The Saudis would surely appreciate the benefits of a democratic system, yet a revolution ushering in sweeping democratic reforms seems highly unlikely here.

The Saud family has shown remarkable perseverance over the past two and a half centuries. After every defeat, they have always been able to rise again to reconquer their kingdom. They have held on to power uninterrupted for more than one hundred years. The House of Saud will likely reign for many years to come.

The success of the transformation will depend largely on the political situation in the immediate vicinity of the kingdom. The undeclared war between Iran and Saudi Arabia must urgently be contained. Currently, the only countries that enjoy any influence over political developments in Riyadh are the US and China. The Europeans could act as mediators to ease tensions in the region.

The growing hostility between Tehran and Riyadh, the two regional powers, is adding gasoline to the fire in one of the world's most volatile regions. The proxy wars and growing number of secondary battlefields—in Libya, Syria, Iraq, Yemen—are fueled by the same sources of rivalry and hate. The precarious international situation also puts the Saudi leadership under intense pressure domestically.

At the end of the day, it's all about power, of course. And more precisely, the pressing question of which kind of political system will prevail in a region in the grip of tumultuous change—an absolute monarchy or a democratic, republican model?

One thing is for sure: what began with the Arab Spring is far from over. People's rage against autocratic governments that neither serve their needs nor provide them with adequate employment, education, or healthcare continues to simmer. The situation could boil over at any moment.

The Saudis are attempting to counteract the ongoing disintegration by propping up reactionary regimes in countries like Egypt and Algeria. The current Saudi leadership has chosen to take a hard line, a policy of self-assertion through strength. The latest examples are the war in Yemen in the south of the Arabian Peninsula, and the abrupt suspension of diplomatic relations with Qatar.

By contrast, the previous king, Abdullah, would regularly meet with one of Iran's most influential religious leaders, former president Akbar Hashemi Rafsanjani. Such discreet discussions helped keep tensions between the two countries in check. Since the deaths of both men, such channels of communication have been abandoned.

The fragile situation calls for forces that work against further division in the region, as well as courageous individual actors willing to make conciliatory gestures. The fact that the exact opposite seems to be happening doesn't make it any less urgent.

And perhaps, readers, you should indulge your curiosity. For most travelers, Saudi Arabia was a "black box" for forty years, even more isolated than North Korea. But an enormous change has come: since September 2019, tourists from dozens of countries can apply for a visa online or purchase one directly upon entering the kingdom.

Saudi Arabia is the homeland of Osama bin Laden. But it is also the country of Eman, Fahd, Tarek, Nora, and Abdullah, and all the other warm, cordial people you have gotten to know in this book.

Have a nice trip—the time to visit is now.

Acknowledgments

This book was only possible thanks to the help of many facilitators, supporters, expert advisors, and publishing professionals. Karen Guddas of DVA showed great interest in the subject of Saudi Arabia, which seemed as secretive as a black box. She pushed tirelessly for the publication of this book. My gracious editor Christiane Naumann elegantly redacted the manuscript and always had encouraging words at hand after sleepless nights of writing. The literary scholars Lene Glinsky and Theresa Rüger facilitated the writing process with their intelligent comments and suggestions. Yannic Osterburg helped with corrections.

Our translator, US-German journalist Maurice Frank, did everything he could to ensure that wit and readability were expressed in equal measure, despite the complexity of the subject. Hal Wyner was always ready to offer comprehensive insights and intellectual guidance. Mango editor Yaddyra Peralta immediately became passionate about the topic, always asked the right questions, and put the finishing touches to the manuscript. I am extremely grateful for her professional support. My literature agent Christina Bracken never had the slightest doubt that this book would appeal to a broad readership in the USA, Europe, and the Gulf. With her enthusiasm, she inspired Mitchell Kaplan and the wonderful team at Mango Publishing. Together they had the good instinct and the courage to make this project a reality. I am extremely grateful for our collaboration, also because I had a chance to discover a new, radiant side of my sister Christina, who immigrated to Miami many years ago. None of it would have been possible without the guidance and support from inspiring friends and the generous connections they offered her. Her special thanks are addressed to Armando Chapelli, Jane Torres, Neal Goodman, John Pratt, and Jean Abi Nader.

Kathy Lubbers deserves a special mention as she is always a generous mentor, an adviser and most importantly, a precious friend.

From the moment I started to travel to Saudi Arabia, Karen Elliott House has been an inspiration and an invaluable source of insight. It is an honor and a real joy for me that her foreword highlights the significance of this new chapter in the kingdom.

On my various trips through the kingdom and while I was living in Riyadh, I always tried to stick to the advice of the long-time Saudi ambassador to Berlin, Osama Shobokshi: "Just write the truth." I also owe my heartfelt thanks to his successors, who always supported the project: Dr. Awwad al-Awwad, who later became the Saudi information minister, Prince Khaled bin Bandar Al Saud, and Rida Said, as well as former ambassador Prince Faisal bin Farhan Al Saud, who now serves as foreign minister.

I greatly benefited from the knowledge and insight of recently retired scholar Dr. Samir N. Anabtawi who served more than two decades as academic advisor to Prince Alwaleed Bin Talal and his foundation, Alwaleed Philanthropies. Thanks as well to my interpreter Nimer Hudaib who safely guided me on my first trips around the country. I was lucky to receive the advice of the Arabist Ingo Schendel, who is extremely knowledgeable about Saudi Arabia, as well as the former German ambassador in Riyadh, Volkmar Wenzel. I owe Dr. Gabriela Guellil a very special thank you. She generously offered support while juggling her strenuous schedule as the German ambassador in Nouakchott, Mauretania. Her knowledge of the Middle East, the Arabic language and culture has been invaluable. *SPIEGEL* foreign-desk heads Britta Sandberg, Mattieu von Rohr, und Juliane von Mittelstaedt showed much patience and good will. Editor in chief, Steffen Klusmann, believes in the success of our project. Thank you all! The documentarian Thorsten Oltmer checked statistics, dates, and events and created a fascinating chronology of the kingdom's history.

The writing process was made more palatable by the encouraging crew of the Sharks Bay Umbi Diving Village, a modest, most charming Egyptian resort in Sharm El Sheikh (www.sharksbay.com). Several chapters of this book were written in their Bedouin tents. Furthermore, I bow before my family and friends for the stoicism they showed over the past six months, during which I talked to them about nothing else but Saudi Arabia, especially Christina Bracken, Stefan Berchtold, Anne-Franziska Gleinig, my parents Herlinde Koelbl and Robert Kölbl, Jutta Pfaffenberger, Rupp Doinet, and Jacqueline Stäuble, as well as Martin and Regina Koelbl, Matthias Ohnsmann, Moritz and Luis and Christine Thalmann.

Finally, I would like to thank the extraordinary people of Saudi Arabia, who offered me their kind hospitality and their time, showed me their country, and welcomed me into their lives. That was the greatest gift.

Timeline of Saudi History

by Thorsten Oltmer

1744 In Diriyah, near present-day Riyadh, Mohammed bin Saud of the Saud dynasty forges an alliance with the radical Sunni reformer Mohammed bin Abd al-Wahhab. Wahhabism, named after the religious zealot, becomes Saudi Arabia's official religion. Little by little, the first Saudi state grows out of this alliance.

1765 Ibn Saud dies. His successors continue his strategy of expansion, and conquer Riyadh in 1773. In the decades to follow, military victories result in the growth of Saudi territory.

1802–1803 Saudi troops conquer Karbala and destroy Shi'a shrines, an event that poisons the relationship between Sunnis and Shi'ites to this day. In the following year, they take the Hejaz, including Mecca and Medina—a direct threat to the Ottoman Empire. The sultan in Constantinople orders his viceroy in Cairo to raise an army to march on the Sauds.

1816 After years of fighting, the sultan's troops gain the upper hand and decisively defeat the Sauds.

1818–1819 The Egyptian troops take Diriyah, the *Wahhabis'* last bastion. Numerous clerics and Saudi leaders are executed.

1824 Saudi soldiers quickly reconquer large areas. The second Saudi state is founded. Low-level warfare continues for decades. King Faisal, who, with interruptions, rules between 1834 and 1865, manages to partially reinstate Saudi rule over the Arabian Peninsula.

1865 After Faisal's death, civil war breaks out: rival families battle over land and power. The rise of the dynasty begins. Mohammed bin Rashid, a shrewd political realist, enters an alliance guaranteeing the protection of the Ottoman Empire, initially helping the ascent of the Rashids.

1884 The Saudi rulers lose control of the Najd in central Arabia.

1891 The Rashids subjugate the Sauds, putting an end to the second state. In 1918, after the end of the First World War, the Ottoman Empire collapses, resulting in the downfall of the Rashids. They submit to Saudi rule once and for all.

1902 Abdulaziz (Ibn Saud), the founder of modern Saudi Arabia, captures Riyadh with a surprise attack. In the official version of history, the event is elevated to the status of a founding myth. From now on, Ibn Saud wages war against the ruler of the Hejaz.

1924–1925 The Saudis conquer the Hejaz, including the holy sites in Mecca and Medina. Ibn Saud regains control of the Najd region from the Rashid family.

1926 Ibn Saud names himself king of both regions.

1927–1931 Domestic unrest and the effects of the worldwide economic decline trigger a severe crisis. With more territorial gains and suppression of local rebellions, Ibn Saud consolidates his reign over large parts of the Arabian Peninsula.

1932 On September 18, Ibn Saud declares the Kingdom of Saudi Arabia and proclaims himself king.

1933 The first oil concession is signed between the kingdom and the American Standard Oil Company. Significant oil reserves are soon discovered. Large-scale oil production begins in 1938, forming the foundation of the country's prosperity.

1944 Aramco (Arabian-American Oil Company) is founded. In the coming decades, the kingdom gradually buys up the corporation's shares. By 1980, it is entirely in state hands. In 1988 the company is renamed Saudi Aramco.

1953 The monarch dies in November, marking the end of an era. Ibn Saud's son Saud assumes the throne. His younger half-brother Faisal becomes prime minister. They have serious differences over how to lead the country.

From 1960 on, groups of reactionary professors and university students begin to form under the name "Sahwa" ("Awakening"), combining elements of Salafism and the ideas of the Muslim

Brotherhood. The Sahwa movement becomes increasingly politically active and fundamentally opposes the monarchy.

1962 Following decades of intervention by Western countries, Saudi Arabia officially outlaws slavery.

1964 In November, Faisal achieves his goal: he deposes his brother following a drawn-out struggle for the throne and becomes king. Saud goes into exile in Geneva, Switzerland.

1966 Beginning of the oil boom. The country produces 2.6 million barrels per day, twice as much as in 1960. Daily production will reach ten million barrels by the 1980s, making Saudi Arabia the biggest producer in the world, ahead of the United States.

1973 The oil crisis in the fall and winter damages economies around the world. As a measure protesting Western support of Israel during the Yom Kippur War, seven OPEC states, including Saudi Arabia and the United Arab Emirates, throttle oil production, causing shortages in the West.

1975 King Faisal is murdered by one of his nephews. Faisal ruled the country for more than ten years. His successor, Khaled—a sick man—dies of a heart attack in 1982 after just a few years in power.

1979 In Iran, the shah is toppled as a consequence of the Islamic Revolution. Shi'ite fundamentalists led by Ayatollah Ruhollah Khomeini assume power. The Islamic Republic of Iran becomes Saudi Arabia's archenemy and its main rival in the struggle for regional dominance.

1979 The occupation of the Grand Mosque of Mecca by Muslim fundamentalists on the first day of the Islamic year 1400 comes as a shock, introducing the country—which had previously promoted "true" Islam as a radical ideology—to Islamic terrorism. Armed men storm the building and take thousands of worshippers as hostages. Hundreds die. when the mosque is stormed by French anti-terrorist commandos. In the wake of the tragedy, the country undergoes a phase of radical Islamization.

1982 In June, Fahd is appointed king. Already under Khaled, he was the country's de facto leader. As the fifth king, he reigns until 2005, when he dies of lung disease.

1986 One of the greatest challenges for Fahd is the extreme drop in oil prices that year. Saudi Arabia and other OPEC states attempt to win global market share by drastically increasing their output—a tactic that fails.

1990–1991 In August, the Iraqi dictator Saddam Hussein invades Saudi Arabia's neighbor, Kuwait. A thirty-four-nation military coalition led by the US deploys forces to Saudi Arabia. The troops enter Kuwait in January 1991. After fighting ends, nearly 80,000 US troops remain in Saudi Arabia, enraging the Islamic fundamentalists of the Sahwa movement.

1991 Subsequent years see moderate efforts to liberalize the country through the creation of democratic institutions. At the same time, the government implements stringent measures against forces who openly or covertly contest the *Wahhabi* state religion. Upon his return from Afghanistan, Osama bin Laden is celebrated as a hero but then placed under house arrest in 1991. He opposes the stationing of US troops in the kingdom. Bin Laden had offered the Saudi government his *mujahideen* to deploy against the Iraqi invaders. Bin Laden leaves the country in 1991 to settle in Sudan. In 1994 he is stripped of his Saudi citizenship.

1996 In June a truck loaded with explosives drives into the Khobar Towers, a compound housing US troops in the eastern city of Khobar. Nineteen soldiers die. After years of investigation, it remains unclear who carried out the attack. Evidence suggests the involvement of Iran and the Hezbollah militia.

2001 After the 9/11 attacks, it emerges that fifteen of the nineteen terrorists are Saudi citizens. The monarchy comes under intense international pressure to explain how that could be possible.

2003 In May and November, attacks are carried out against compounds housing foreigners in and around Riyadh. A total of fifty-six residents die in the shootings and bombings. Hundreds are wounded. Blame for the attacks is placed on al-Qaeda, which strives to combat the "modernization and westernization" of the country.

2005 On August 1, King Abdullah ascends to the throne at the age of eighty-one. He had already run the country for ten years, since his half-brother King Fahd was partially paralyzed by a stroke and was unable to attend to government affairs. Abdullah reigns for ten years.

2011 Thanks to the Arab Spring, Islamic groups gain influence in many Muslim states. The Muslim Brotherhood, in particular, profits from the disintegration of existing structures. Their objective is an Islamic democracy based on Sharia law. In Egypt, Mohammed Mursi, a member of the Muslim Brotherhood, is elected president. However, by 2013, he is already toppled by the military. For Saudi Arabia, the Muslim Brotherhood and similar Islamic organizations promising democratic participation and justice are a severe threat. The leadership in Riyadh fears the long-term erosion of their power and influence in the region.

2015 King Salman becomes king, the sixth son of the nation's founder Ibn Saud to do so. He has to wait until the age of seventy-nine before he can take the throne.

In March, Saudi Arabia, as part of a military alliance with other Gulf states, intervenes in neighboring Yemen. In a brutal civil war, the Shi'ite Houthi rebels have driven out the Saudi-supported president and taken control of most of the country. A ceasefire negotiated in May holds for only a few days.

2017 In a cunning move, King Salman names his son Mohammed bin Salman crown prince and successor to the throne. Up until Salman's assumption of power, the thirty-year-old MBS (as he is nicknamed) served as defense minister.

Immediately after his promotion, MBS carries out "cleansings," targeting allegedly corrupt officials and businessmen. It soon becomes clear that the action serves to marginalize critics of the regime and the crown prince's competitors.

2018 The fighting in Yemen continues unabated. The Saudi-led military coalition continues to bomb the country. The US and Britain provide intelligence and logistical support. The situation in Yemen is chaotic. Al-Qaeda and Islamic State control large areas of the country. Cholera breaks out. Tens of thousands of people die, including many children. By early 2019, around 50,000 people have died of starvation, according to UN estimates. In December, another ceasefire goes into effect but does not last.

2019 In March, following the US House of Representatives, the Senate passes a resolution ending American support for the Saudi military campaign in Yemen, going against the will of President Trump, who stands by his Saudi allies and justifies his position with trade interests—arms exports and oil.

On September 14, drones and missiles attack refineries belonging to state-owned oil corporation Aramco, east of the capital. Although the Yemeni Houthi rebels claim responsibility for the nineteen strikes, Saudi officials see Iran behind the attack. The US, Britain, and France support this view, as satellite images show that the drones were launched from an Iranian airfield. Saudi oil exports are initially cut by about 50 percent but reach their former level by the end of the month.

In early December, Aramco, one of the most valuable and definitely the most profitable company in the world, goes public. Crown Prince Mohammed bin Salman draws up plans to offer up to 5 percent of the state-owned company's shares. The initial public offering at Tadawul, the Saudi stock exchange, raises more than twenty-five billion dollars. Ibn Salman plans to invest the money into the restructuring of the economy with the aim of making the country less dependent upon its dwindling oil revenues.

GLOSSARY

Abaya Traditional Islamic garment worn by women over their clothing. Long-sleeved, between ankle- and floor-length. Styles vary according to region, societal norms, and the wearer's taste.

Al Jazeera Arabic-language TV news channel based in Doha, Qatar.

Allah Arabic for "God."

Allahu akbar "God is great," used in the daily prayer and in life as an expression of surprise or enthusiasm. Also used in combat.

Ancestors Described as *as-salaf al-saleh* in Muslim scripture. The first three generations of Muslims who lived with and directly after the Prophet Mohammed, who called them "the best people."

Arabian Peninsula/Arabia Geographic region on the Persian Gulf, encompassing the states of Saudi Arabia, Yemen, Oman, Bahrain, Qatar, Kuwait, and the United Arab Emirates, as well as parts of Iraq and Jordan.

Arab Spring/Arabellion Terms used primarily in the West to describe the protests, uprisings, and revolutions in Maghreb, Egypt, Syria, Lybia, the Arabian Peninsula, and neighboring countries beginning in 2011. The populations of these countries rose up against their autocratic leaders and demanded more democracy. The movements were triggered by Tunisian vegetable seller Mohamed Bouazizi, who set himself on fire in December 2010, to protest against police mistreatment and humiliation.

Ashura Islamic holiday with special significance for the Shi'ites. Commemorates the killing of Imam Husayn in the battle of Karbala.

Bakhur Traditional Arab incense, usually in the form of chips, made mostly out of oud.

Bedouins Nomads living in the deserts of the Arabian Peninsula.

Bisht Festive cloak with gold trim, usually black and made of camel hair or wool.

Da'wah Call or invitation. Used to describe the "call to Islam," i.e. Islamic missionary work.

Diplomatic Quarter Riyadh neighborhood populated primarily by foreign diplomats and their families.

Eid al-Adha Islamic holiday: "Feast of the Sacrifice" after the month of pilgrimage.

Eid al-Fitr Islamic holiday: "Day of Breaking the Fast" after Ramadan.

Emir Title, ruler, prince, or governor.

Emirate An emir's territory.

Fatwa Legal opinion on all kinds of religious matters, issued by a mufti. It can also contain a death warrant issued by a Muslim authority due to a religious offense on the basis of sharia.

Gata Colorful swaths of fabric used by the Bedouin nomads to separate areas of their tents.

Ghutra Traditional headdress worn by men. In Saudi Arabia, it is usually either white or with a checked pattern and bound to the head with a cord. Originates from the Bedouins and serves as sun protection throughout the Gulf states. Styles vary according to tastes and region and can also signify the wearer's social status.

Gulf States Countries on the Persian Gulf: Iran, Iraq, Kuwait, Saudi Arabia, Bahrain, Qatar, United Arab Emirates, Oman. With the exception of Iran and Iraq, all of the above belong to the Gulf Cooperation Council.

Grand Mufti/Mufti Islamic legal scholar issuing binding legal opinions within his constituency.

Hadith Record of the words, actions, and silent approval of the Prophet Mohammed.

Hajj Pilgrimage to Mecca, one of the Five Pillars of Islam.

Hamas Palestinian political party of Sunni-Islamist Palestinians in Gaza, belongs to the Muslim Brotherhood. Parts of the international community, especially in the West, classify Hamas and especially its military arm as a terrorist organization.

Haram (adjective) Prohibited, impure according to the laws of Islam (Sharia).

Henna Plant-based powder mixed with water, used to adorn the body.

Hezbollah "The Party of God," Shi'ite political party in Lebanon. Founded in the 1980s in resistance to the Israeli invasion of Lebanon. Some members of the international community classify their military wing, the Hezbollah militia, as a terrorist organization.

Hijab Traditional Islamic voluminous scarf worn by women to cover the head and hair.

Hindu Kush Mountain range in Central Asia, mostly in Afghanistan.

Houthi Rebels Political and military movement representing the Zaydi population in northern Yemen. Named after their founder Hussein Badreddin al-Houthi.

Ikhwan Arabic for "the Brethren"; an early movement of Bedouin fighters who were deployed by King Abdulaziz.

Incense Route Trade route used primarily for the transportation of incense linking the southern Arabian Peninsula and the Mediterranean.

Intifada Palestinian uprisings (first and second intifada) against Israel.

Isha Night prayer

Istiraha A weekend house.

al-Janadriyah Annual culture festival in Saudi Arabia.

Jabal Shammar Shammar Mountain, former territory of the emir of Ha'il.

Jihadism From jihad, meaning a struggle or fight on the path of God. In Western discourse, Jihadism is a catch-all term used to describe diverse Islamic and militant groups. Sometimes used as a synonym for Islamic terrorism.

Kaaba "The house of God": A cuboid construction in the courtyard of the Grand Mosque of Mecca.

Kafala A system legally binding a migrant worker's immigration status to an individual employer or sponsor (*kafeel*) for their contract period.

Karak Black, sweet tea with spices and condensed milk.

Khabeti Traditional sufi-inspired dance.

Khoya A type of soft cheese made of thickened milk.

Kingdom Tower/Jeddah Tower Construction project in Jeddah. Slated for completion in 2020–21, the skyscraper is under construction to become the world's tallest building.

al-Mujahid A military unit made up of *mujahideen* formed during the Bosnian War.

Madrasa School for Islamic legal studies; the Qur'anic school of a mosque.

Mahdi According to Islamic religious writings, a redeemer sent by God who appears before the Day of Judgment.

Mahram A relative with whom marriage and sexual intercourse are considered *haram*, i.e. brothers, fathers—and before whom a Muslim woman is not required to wear a hijab.

MBS Abbreviation for Mohammed bin Salman; crown prince, defense minister, and deputy prime minister of Saudi Arabia.

Misyar A secret second marriage permitted under *Wahhabi* Islam.

Mujahideen Those engaged in jihad. Members of Islamic guerilla groups. The term was popularized by Western media when referring to the Afghan guerillas resisting the Soviet occupation of Afghanistan.

Muezzin Calls for Muslims to pray at mosque five times per day.

Muslim World League International Salafi NGO, financed primarily by Saudi Arabia, that propagates Muslim religion and culture around the world.

Muslim Brotherhood/Muslim Brothers Sunni movement, founded in Egypt in the 1920s, classified as a terrorist organization by several countries.

Mutawwa (pl. mutawween) Religious overseers, often working for the Committee for the Promotion of Virtue and the Prevention of Vice, a.k.a. religious police.

Neom Crown Prince MBS's futuristic construction project—the world's most advanced technology park with its own city.

Niqab Traditional Muslim face veil worn in combination with the hijab over the nose and mouth.

OPEC Organization of the Petroleum Exporting Countries: international organization of fourteen states, including some of the world's biggest oil producers.

Oud Fragrance derived from the sap of the agarwood tree.

Oud Musical instrument; traditional lute with four to seven strings.

Petrodollars US dollars earned through the export of petroleum.

al-Qaeda Arabic for "the base" or "the foundation." A terrorist network.

Qahwah Light coffee made with unroasted beans.

Qur'an Islam's holy book.

Rabiah Older woman who educates young brides about the wedding night, lovemaking, and how to deal with their husbands.

Rak'ah Ritual movements performed during prayer.

Riyal (SAR) Saudi Arabia's currency.

Sahwa Group of Islamic clerics. During the second Gulf War, they opposed the stationing of US troops in Saudi Arabia. A hybrid movement linking Wahhabism and the Muslim Brotherhood.

Salafis/Salafists Fundamentalists within conservative Sunni Islam advocating the return to the traditions of the "ancestors."

Sambusa Baked dumplings.

Saudi Aramco Formerly the Arabian-American Oil Company (abbreviation: Aramco); the world's largest oil company.

Shah Title, Persian for ruler.

Sharia The entirety of all norms and laws arising from the Islamic tradition.

Sheba Bedouin mud hut or tent.

Sheikh Arab honorary title, "spiritual leader."

Shi'ites Followers of the second-largest confession in Islam They consider Mohammed's son-in-law Ali to be the Prophet's legitimate successor and their first imam. About 15 percent of Muslims worldwide are Shi'ites.

Shura In Saudi Arabia, a consultative council of 150 members appointed by the king that can propose and interpret laws.

Souk Bazaar, Arab market quarter.

South Pars Gas Field The largest gas field ever discovered, claimed by Qatar and Iran.

Sufism Collective term for various branches of Islamic mysticism organized in different orders.

Sunni Follower of the largest denomination in Islam that draws upon the *sunnah*. Around 85 percent of all Muslims are Sunnis. The Sunni Islam practiced in Saudi Arabia is known as Salafism.

Surah Chapter of the Qur'an; there are 114 altogether.

Tajine Clay pot for stewing vegetables or meat, usually with a pointy or rounded top; the term also describes the dishes cooked in such pots.

Taliban Radical Islamic militia that has dominated large regions of Afghanistan and Pakistan since the early 1990s.

Thawb Traditional ankle-length robe worn by men in the nations of the Arabian Peninsula and neighboring desert regions. Usually made of white cotton. Styles can vary.

Vision 2030 Economic transformation project of the Saudi leadership designed to make the country less dependent on oil revenue. Includes large investments in solar power. Women are encouraged to enter the workforce.

Wahhabism Ultra-conservative movement within Sunni Islam, based on the teachings of Abd al-Wahhab (Wahhabiya). So-called Wahhabism stands for a strict literal interpretation of the Qur'an as well as the political legitimation of the ruling House of Saud. It is the state doctrine.

Wali Male guardian of a woman in Saudi Arabia and the Muslim world.

Wasta Nepotism, "who you know." Refers to using one's connections and influence.

Zaydi Follower of a Shi'ite religious school who are also known as Fivers because they believe that the chain of legitimate successors of the Prophet Mohammed ends with the fifth imam (Zayd).

Selected Bibliography

al Ajroush, Madeha, *reSURFACE. Images of Women in the Rock Art of Saudi Arabia* (2016).

Al-Naimi, Ali, *Out of the Desert: My Journey from the Nomadic Desert to the Heart of Global Oil* (Penguin UK, 2016)

al Sanea, Rajaa, *The Girls of Riyadh* (Fig Tree, 2005, translated by Marilyn Booth).

Feuer, Sarah, *Course Correction: The Muslim World League, Saudi Arabia's Export of Islam, and Opportunities for Washington* (Washington Institute for Near East Policy, 2019).

Hubbard, Ben, *MBS: The Rise to Power of Mohammed Bin Salman* (Tim Duggan Books, 2020)

Keating, Aileen, *Power, Politics and the Hidden History of Arabian Oil* (Saqi Books, 2006).

Ghattas, Kim, *Black Wave: Saudi Arabia, Iran, and the Forty-Year Rivalry That Unraveled Culture, Religion, and Collective Memory in the Middle East* (Henry Holt, 2020).

Lacey, Robert, *Inside the Kingdom: Kings, Clerics, Modernists, Terrorists and the Struggle for Saudi Arabia* (Corner Stone Digital, 2011)

Lacroix, Stéphane, *Awakening Islam. The Politics of Religious Dissent in Contemporary Saudi Arabia* (Harvard University Press, 2011).

Ménoret, Pascal, *Joyriding in Riyadh: Oil, Urbanism, and Road Revolt* (Cambridge University Press, 2014).

Oikonomopoulos, Vassilis, *Refusing to be Still* (Saudi Art Council, 2018).

Simpson, William, *The Prince: The Secret Story of the World's Most Intriguing Royal, Prince Bandar Bin Sultan* (William Morrow, 2006).

Sons, Sebastian *Auf Sand gebaut. Saudi-Arabien—Ein problematischer Verbündeter* (Propyläen Verlag, 2016).

Steinberg, Guido, *Saudi-Arabien. Politik Geschichte Religion* (C.H. Beck, 2014).

Wald, Ellen R., *Saudi Inc.: The Arabian Kingdom's Pursuit of Profit and Power* (Pegasus Books, 2018).

About the Author

Susanne Koelbl is an award winning journalist and a military and foreign correspondent for the German news magazine *DER SPIEGEL*. Her stories highlight the intricate dynamics in conflict areas and wars around the world, including the Balkans, Central Asia, the Middle East, and Africa.

Koelbl is known for her probing reports from Syria, Afghanistan, and North Korea. Her book *Zwoelf Wochen in Riad: Saudi-Arabien zwischen Diktatur und Aufbruch* was published in Germany in 2019 by Random House. *Behind the Kingdom's Veil: Inside the New Saudi Arabia under Crown Prince Mohammed bin Salman* is the English-language version. Her highly acclaimed book *Dark Beloved Country: People and Power in Afghanistan* was published in 2009 by Siedler-Verlag/Random House.

Koelbl documents history through her interviews with many influencers, specifically in conflict zones. Among these are: Afghani presidents Hamid Karzai and Ashraf Ghani; Madam Fu Ying, former vice-foreign minister of China; Pakistan's President Pervez Musharraf; current prime minister Imran Khan; General Stanley McChrystal; and former president Joseph Kabila from the Democratic Republic of Congo, to name a few.

In her exceptional dialogs with state leaders, intelligence chiefs, and Islamic extremists, Koelbl repeatedly challenges the powerful, such as Syrian president Bashar al-Assad, the former Sudanese president Omar al-Bashir, who is wanted for genocide with an international arrest warrant, or the underground Hamas leader Khaled Mashal. Koelbl has excellent contacts in all political camps in the Middle East.

For her in-depth and thorough reporting she received several industry awards, including the Liberty Award and the Henry Nannen Award together with colleagues from SPIEGEL. In January, she received the ITB Book Award of the year for this book, in the category "Cultures." She is also a fellow of the

Bertelsmann Foundation's German-Israeli Young Leaders Program. As a Knight Wallace Fellow at the University of Michigan, Koelbl gave guest lectures in 2012 on the war in Syria and the forty-year Afghanistan crisis. Koelbl is a much sought-after participant in international conferences and TV talk shows. The author has been traveling extensively to Saudi Arabia since 2011. Most recently she lived in Riyadh during 2018/19.

SusanneKoelbl.com

Twitter: SusanneKoelbl

Facebook: SusanneKoelbl2020

Instagram: Susanne.Koelbl

www.susannekoelbl.com

Mango Publishing, established in 2014, publishes an eclectic list of books by diverse authors—both new and established voices—on topics ranging from business, personal growth, women's empowerment, LGBTQ studies, health, and spirituality to history, popular culture, time management, decluttering, lifestyle, mental wellness, aging, and sustainable living. We were recently named 2019's #1 fastest growing independent publisher by *Publishers Weekly*. Our success is driven by our main goal, which is to publish high quality books that will entertain readers as well as make a positive difference in their lives.

Our readers are our most important resource; we value your input, suggestions, and ideas. We'd love to hear from you—after all, we are publishing books for you!

Please stay in touch with us and follow us at:

Facebook: Mango Publishing

Twitter: @MangoPublishing

Instagram: @MangoPublishing

LinkedIn: Mango Publishing

Pinterest: Mango Publishing

Sign up for our newsletter at www.mangopublishinggroup. com and receive a free book!

Join us on Mango's journey to reinvent publishing, one book at a time.